FAMILY BY THE BOOK

HOW TO BUILD THE FAMILY GOD INTENDED

MARK HOBAFCOVICH

NERA HOUSE
PUBLISHING

Family by the Book: How to Build the Family God Intended

With Mark Hobafcovich

© 2025 Mark Hobafcovich

Published by Nera House Publishing, Athens, Georgia, USA

Printed in the United States of America

ISBN: (paperback) 978-1-968541-24-8

ISBN: (hardcover) 978-1-968541-25-5

ISBN: (ebook) 978-1-968541-26-2

Library of Congress Control Number: 2025925498

Dedication

Every construction project requires skilled craftsmen, faithful laborers, and wise mentors who understand both the blueprint and the building process. As I reflect on the journey that led to this book about building families according to God's design, I am deeply grateful for the master builders who have shaped not only my understanding of biblical family construction, but who have also demonstrated through their own lives what it truly means to follow the Master Architect's plans.

This book is dedicated to those faithful builders who have been my greatest teachers in the art of constructing a family that honors God.

To Christine, my wife and faithful companion for over four decades in the journey of building the family God intended. Your unwavering commitment to our marriage and family has been the cornerstone that has held our construction project together through every season. You have been my co-builder, my encourager, and my greatest earthly blessing as we have learned together what it means to follow God's blueprint for family life.

To my daughters, Hadassah and Elizabeth, who inspired the writing of this book during their teenage years and who continue to be living testimonies of God's faithfulness in building the family He intended. Watching you grow into godly women and now seeing you construct your own families according to biblical principles has been one of my greatest joys. You have taught me as much about family building as I have ever taught you.

To my parents, Vichentie and Elena Hobafcovici, who modeled what it means to build together a family that God intended through their faithful parenting and their marriage of over six decades. Your example of love, commitment, and biblical faithfulness laid the foundation upon which my own understanding of family construction was built. The legacy you created continues to influence generations.

To the many families whom I have had the privilege to serve over the years in my pastoral role, who have modeled excellence in building families that honor God. You have been my teachers, showing me through your lives what biblical family construction looks like in practice. Your faithfulness, your struggles, your victories, and your perseverance have enriched my understanding and deepened my appreciation for the beautiful work of family building according to God's design.

Together, you have all contributed to the construction of this book and to my understanding that building a family by the Book is both the most challenging and the most rewarding construction project any of us will ever undertake.

Acknowledgments

First and foremost, I give thanks to God, who designed marriage as a reflection of Christ's relationship with His church and who continues to teach me daily about covenant love, grace, and faithfulness.

I am deeply grateful to Christine, my wife, whose support made my ministry possible. Your willingness to walk this journey with me has been invaluable. Many of the principles in these pages were born in our lives as we journeyed together for over four decades.

I am grateful to the many authors and teachers whose works have influenced my understanding of biblical marriage. I stand on the shoulders of these and many other faithful servants who have gone before us.

I am deeply grateful to my editorial and publishing team for their dedication and support in bringing this book to completion. Their efforts have transformed my vision into the finished work you hold today.

Special thanks to John William Halladay for his specialized editorial work, meticulous attention to detail, and ability to strengthen every aspect of this manuscript. I am equally grateful to Lucas Herrington for his editorial expertise and professionalism, which have greatly contributed to the quality and clarity of this project.

I am also deeply thankful to Marcus Lewis for his publishing expertise, strategic guidance, and commitment to excellence that has ensured this project reached its full potential. His professional expertise and support have been instrumental in this book's success.

Your combined professionalism and dedication have made this work possible.

Contents

Background of the Book

At the age of 42, I found myself facing one of parenthood's most challenging seasons. Our two daughters were 15 and 12 years old, navigating the turbulent waters of their teenage years. As a father, and together with my wife as parents, we were confronted daily with situations that tested our wisdom, patience, and faith. It was during this time of intense family dynamics that I felt compelled to return to Scripture for guidance on how to build a Christian family according to God's design.

The result was a six-point article titled *"The Christian Family and Its Responsibilities: Relationships in the Christian Family."* This work emerged from a deep personal need to understand God's blueprint for family life and to find practical guidance for the challenges we were facing as Christian parents.

The original article was organized around six fundamental building blocks that I believed encompassed the full scope of Christian family construction:

1. Biblical Perspective of Family
2. Relationship between husband and wife
3. Relationship between children and parents
4. Relationship between family members and Lord Jesus Christ
5. Relationship between family members and the world
6. Conclusions

As I reflected on these six areas, a central theme emerged that would become the foundation of this expanded work: when families follow God's blueprint found in Scripture, the result is a beautiful structure of relationships that reflects His design and brings glory to His name. Like any successful construction project, building a godly family requires the right foundation, quality materials, skilled craftsmanship, and careful attention to the Master Builder's plans.

The key insight that shaped my understanding was this: when families build according to God's specifications found in His Word, we see that wives support their husbands "as to the Lord," while husbands love their wives "as Christ loved the church." Children obey their parents "in the Lord," while parents raise their children "in the training and instruction of the Lord." Even in broader relationships, all family members relate to others with Christ-like character, "knowing that their Master and yours is in heaven."

All of this construction is made possible through the Spirit of God who dwells in believers. As Romans 5:5 reminds us, *"God's love has been poured out into our hearts through the Holy Spirit, who has been given to us."* What seemed impossible through human effort becomes reality through dependence on God's power, enabling us to say with Paul, "I can do all things through Christ who strengthens me."

Now, writing this book more than two decades later, I find myself reflecting on how those original blueprints have been tested, refined, and proven through years of pastoral ministry, continued study of Scripture, and ongoing experience in family life. Our daughters, who were teenagers when I first penned those thoughts, are now adults building families of their own. I have had the privilege of watching them apply these biblical principles in their own marriages and parenting, seeing firsthand how God's design for the family transcends generations.

Through years of pastoral counseling, I have walked alongside countless families in their building process, facing the same challenges we encountered in 2002, and many others besides. I have seen marriages rebuilt through the application of biblical love and respect. I have witnessed children flourish as parents learned to balance love and discipline according to Scripture. I have observed families find their identity and purpose as they construct their relationships according to Christ's blueprints.

This expanded work represents not merely an academic exercise but the fruit of decades of practical construction, pastoral observation, and continued biblical study. The principles that seemed so crucial during our daughters' teenage years have proven themselves as solid building materials through every season of family life—from the early foundation-laying years of marriage through the active construction phase of child-rearing, from launching young adults to the legacy-building years of grandparenthood, from seasons of blessing to times when the structure was tested by storms.

The church's need for biblical family construction guidance has only intensified in the years since 2002. Cultural pressures that were emerging then have now become wrecking balls aimed at the family structure. The very definition of family itself is under attack, and Christian families find themselves building against increasingly strong opposition. Yet this makes the timeless blueprints of Scripture even more precious and necessary.

It is my prayer that these biblical building principles, now expanded and deepened through more than two decades of ministry and life experience, will provide clear guidance and encouragement to Christian families seeking to construct homes that honor God and demonstrate His love to the world around them. Whether you are newlyweds just breaking ground on your family foundation, parents in the midst of active construction, or mature believers seeking to strengthen and maintain existing family structures, these blueprints from God's Word remain as relevant and reliable today as they were when first revealed in Scripture.

The central theme remains unchanged: families built according to God's specifications create beautiful structures that bring glory to Him and blessing to others. But the application of this truth has been enriched through years of seeing God's faithfulness to families who dare to build according to His design, even when the world around them chooses different blueprints.

Preface

When I first sat down to write about Christian family life more than two decades ago, I never imagined that those initial thoughts would eventually grow into the book you now hold in your hands. What began as a father's search for biblical wisdom during the challenging teenage years of our two daughters has evolved into a comprehensive exploration of God's design for the family—a design that requires both divine blueprints and human labor to become reality.

The journey from that original six-point article to this expanded work has been one of continuous learning, pastoral observation, and deepening appreciation for the timeless wisdom found in Scripture. Along the way, I have been profoundly shaped not only by my own family experiences but by the many families I have had the privilege to counsel, encourage, and learn from during my years in pastoral ministry. What I have discovered through this journey is that building a family according to God's design is indeed hard work—work that exposes our human limitations and drives us to depend completely on God's grace and mercy.

Throughout this book, we will be using building language that will guide us in our journey together. This is not merely a literary device, but a reflection of the biblical truth that families, like buildings, require intentional construction. However, building implies labor, and that labor reveals an important reality: to have the family God intended, you and your spouse will have to work hard in building and maintaining what He has designed. This work is necessary not because God's design is flawed, but because we who are called to do the building are flawed.

Why must we work so hard? The answer lies in the fundamental truth of human nature. Husbands and wives, being human and therefore tainted by sin, are imperfect builders working with imperfect materials—themselves.

We bring to the construction site our selfishness, our pride, our fears, and our failures. We misread the blueprints, use inferior materials, and sometimes abandon the project altogether when the work becomes difficult. Left to our own strength and wisdom, we would construct families that reflect our fallen nature rather than God's perfect design.

This is precisely why building a family God intended requires us to rely on God's grace and mercy. Grace provides the power we lack to love sacrificially, to forgive repeatedly, and to serve willingly. Mercy covers our construction mistakes, repairs our faulty workmanship, and gives us the courage to continue building even when we feel like failures. Only through this divine assistance can the hard work of family building result in the beautiful structure God intended.

As I reflect on this process, I am struck by how much this book represents not just my own insights but the accumulated wisdom of generations of faithful believers who have wrestled with the same construction challenges that face Christian families today. Every principle explored in these pages, every practical application suggested, and every biblical truth examined has been tested and refined by countless mothers and fathers, husbands and wives, who have discovered that building families by the Book requires both human effort and divine enablement.

It is with a deep sense of humility and reliance on those who have gone before that I offer these reflections on building families by the Book. I can hardly claim originality in this work, since, like many, I am standing on the shoulders of giants of the faith who endured, learned, wrote, and experienced so we can have their example as we follow Christ in our generation. There is nothing new under the sun, as the wise man observed, and I acknowledge that truth as we embark on this construction journey together. I don't have the courage to call myself the 'Author', but humbly note that this book's title page lists my contribution 'With' others, acknowledging the extensive reliance on the work that so many others have done before us, as evidenced by the notes that follow.

The great commentators, theologians, and pastoral writers whose works fill our bibliography have provided the theological foundation upon which this building project rests. These are the master builders whose insights into Scripture continue to illuminate our understanding centuries later. Contemporary voices whose practical wisdom has helped millions of couples learn to construct marriages that honor God. Each of these contributors, and dozens of others, has laid stones in the foundation that supports the structure of this book.

But beyond the scholarly resources, I am equally indebted to the ordinary families who have allowed me to witness their construction projects firsthand. The young couple learned to navigate their first major structural crisis using biblical principles. The parents who watched their prodigal child return home after years of prayer and faithful building. The grandparents who modeled Christ-like marriage for fifty-plus years, showing their children and grandchildren what it looks like to build a family by the Book, one day at a time, through seasons of joy and sorrow, success and failure.

These real-life examples have taught me that while the blueprints of Scripture are unchanging, their application must be both practical and grace-filled. Families are not construction projects to be completed and then forgotten, but living structures that require constant maintenance, occasional renovation, and continuous dependence on the Master Builder's guidance. The building metaphor that runs throughout this book should be understood as recognizing that families require the same careful attention to foundation, structure, and ongoing maintenance that any worthwhile construction project demands, with the added complexity that we are both the builders and the building materials.

The hard work of family building becomes a means of grace in our lives. As we struggle to love when we don't feel like it, to forgive when we've been hurt, to serve when we're tired, and to persevere when we want to quit, we discover our desperate need for God's strength. This dependence is not a weakness to be overcome but a design feature to be embraced. God intends for the labor of family building to drive us to Him, to teach us about His character, and to transform us into the image of His Son.

My prayer is that this book will serve as both a blueprint and encouragement for families at every stage of their building process. Whether you are newlyweds just breaking ground on your family foundation, parents in the midst of the active construction phase with children at home, or mature believers seeking to strengthen and maintain the family structure you have built over many years, my hope is that you will find both biblical wisdom and practical guidance in these pages. More importantly, I pray you will discover afresh your need for God's grace in the daily work of family building.

The title *"Family by the Book"* reflects my conviction that Scripture provides not just general principles for family life, but specific, practical blueprints for building relationships that honor God and bless others. When we build our families according to God's specifications, using the materials He provides and following the construction methods He has given us in His Word, the result is a structure that can weather any storm and stand as a testimony to His goodness for generations to come. But this building process requires our labor—hard, daily, grace-dependent labor.

As you read, please remember that the goal is not perfection but faithfulness in the building process. None of us constructs a perfect family, just as no construction project proceeds without setbacks. Our sin nature guarantees that we will make errors, use poor judgment, and sometimes damage what we're trying to build. But when we commit ourselves to building by the Book, depending on the Master Builder's guidance and grace, acknowledging our need for His mercy when we fail, we can trust that He will bless our efforts and use our families for His glory.

The hard work is worth it. When husbands and wives, despite their imperfections, choose to love each other as Christ loved the church, something beautiful emerges. When parents, despite their failures, consistently point their children to God's truth and grace, transformation happens. When families, despite their struggles, commit to building according to God's design, they become living testimonies to the power of the Gospel.

May God use these pages to strengthen your commitment to His design for family life, to encourage you in the hard work of daily construction, and to remind you of your constant need for His grace and mercy. May your family become a beautiful testimony to the watching world of what happens when ordinary, imperfect people choose to build their lives according to the extraordinary wisdom found in God's Word, depending not on their own strength but on His enabling grace.

With gratitude for the privilege of serving families in Christ's name, and with deep appreciation for God's grace that makes family building possible,

Mark Hobafcovich

Long Island, New York

June 15, 2025

Introduction

The family stands as God's foundational institution in human society, established before government, before the church, and before any other social structure. From the very beginning, when God declared, "It is not good for man to be alone," He set in motion His perfect blueprint for human relationships that would reflect His own character and bring glory to His name.

In our contemporary world, the family faces unprecedented challenges. Cultural shifts, technological advances, economic pressures, and changing social norms have created a landscape that often seems hostile to biblical family construction. Yet it is precisely in such times that the church must return to Scripture to rediscover God's timeless blueprints for family building.

This book is written for Christian families who desire to build according to God's design—families who want their relationships to reflect the character of Christ and serve as a testimony to the watching world. Whether you are just beginning to lay the foundation of your family or seeking to renovate and strengthen existing structures, the principles contained in these pages are drawn from the unchanging Word of God.

The central thesis of this work is that healthy Christian families are built upon God's original blueprint, enabled by Christ as the cornerstone, and constructed through mutual love and respect "in the Lord." This is not the world's understanding of family construction, which often lacks both a solid foundation and quality building materials. Rather, this is God's design for willing service motivated by love for Christ and empowered by the Holy Spirit. When each family member understands their God-given role in the construction process, and when all relationships are built according to divine specifications, the result is a strong, beautiful structure that can weather any storm.

Throughout these pages, we will explore how God's building principles apply to every family relationship: between husband and wife, between parents and children, and between the family unit and the broader community. We will see how God's original design provides the perfect blueprint, how Christ's relationship with His church serves as the enabling cornerstone for marriage construction, and how the family's relationship with God shapes its interaction with the world.

This is not merely an academic study of family relationships, but a practical construction manual for Christian living. Each chapter includes biblical blueprints, real-life building techniques, and encouragement for those who desire to construct families that honor God and reflect His love to a watching world.

Like any good construction project, building a godly family requires patience, skill, the right tools, and careful attention to both the Master Architect's blueprints and the Cornerstone's enabling power. But the result— a family structure that glorifies God and blesses others—is worth every effort invested in the building process.

IMPORTANT NOTE: This book addresses general biblical principles for family building. Specific situations involving divorce, remarriage, separation, and family crisis require individual pastoral guidance and professional counseling, with careful consideration of unique circumstances. Readers facing such situations are encouraged to seek wise pastoral counsel from their local church leadership and appropriate professional help when needed.

Chapter 1
God's Blueprint

In the Beginning: His Design for Family

Every master builder knows that successful construction begins long before the first nail is hammered or the first brick is laid. It starts with a vision, develops into detailed plans, and requires careful selection of materials and methods. When we open the pages of Scripture to discover how to build strong families, we find that God Himself serves as the Master Architect who has provided us with the perfect blueprint for family construction.

The very first pages of the Bible reveal God's heart for family relationships [1]. Before governments were established, before religious institutions were formed, before any human culture developed its own traditions, God created the family. This makes family the oldest and most fundamental institution in human history, designed by divine wisdom to serve eternal purposes.

As we begin our journey through Family by the Book: How to Build the Family God Intended, we discover that building a godly family requires more than good intentions or cultural wisdom [2]. It demands that we understand and follow the Master Architect's original design. Just as no wise contractor would attempt to build a house without consulting the blueprints, no family can truly flourish without understanding God's plan for relationships, roles, and responsibilities within the home.

The Foundation: God's Original Intent

"Therefore a man shall leave his father and mother and hold fast to his wife, and they shall become one flesh" (Genesis 2:24). These words, spoken in the perfect environment of Eden before sin corrupted human relationships, establish the

foundational principles for all family construction. They represent God's original blueprint, untainted by human failure or cultural confusion.

The Creation Blueprint for Marriage

When God surveyed His creation during those first six days, He repeatedly declared His work to be "good." The sun, moon, and stars were good [3]. The plants and animals were good. Even man himself was pronounced good. But then came an unexpected declaration: *"It is not good that the man should be alone; I will make him a helper fit for him"* (Genesis 2:18).

This statement reveals something profound about God's design for human relationships [4]. Loneliness was not part of God's perfect plan for humanity. The solution He provided shows us His blueprint for marriage and family life. Rather than creating another man or simply providing Adam with animal companionship, God fashioned woman from Adam's own rib, creating a being who was both like him and different from him.

Adam's response to seeing Eve for the first time demonstrates the joy and completion that God intended marriage to provide [5]. "This at last is bone of my bones and flesh of my flesh!" he exclaimed. The Hebrew text suggests Adam was practically singing with delight. Here was someone who shared his nature, understood his heart, and completed what was missing in his solitary existence.

This divine act of creation establishes marriage as more than a social contract or romantic partnership [6]. It represents a sacred joining of two complementary beings into one unified whole. When families are built according to this blueprint, they reflect God's intention that marriage should provide companionship, completion, and cooperation in fulfilling His purposes on earth.

The permanence implied in God's design becomes clear in His instruction that a man should "leave" his parents and "hold fast" to his wife

[7]. This leaving and cleaving establishes a new family unit that takes priority over all other human relationships. It creates a bond that is intended to last for life, providing the stability and security that children need and that society requires for healthy function.

Family as God's Foundational Institution

Before any human government was established, before religious institutions were formed, before educational systems were developed, God created the family [8]. This chronological priority reveals the fundamental importance that God places on family relationships. The family serves as the basic building block from which all other social institutions derive their strength and purpose.

Within the family structure, children receive their first lessons about authority, responsibility, and relationships [9]. They learn to obey before they learn to lead. They discover what it means to love and be loved, to serve and be served, to give and receive. These early experiences within the family context shape their understanding of how to function in every other area of life.

The family also serves as God's primary method for transmitting truth from one generation to the next [10]. Moses instructed the Israelites to teach God's commandments diligently to their children, talking about them throughout the day in every context of life (Deuteronomy 6:6-7). This makes the family God's original educational institution, responsible for passing on not just practical knowledge but spiritual wisdom and moral values.

When we examine Family by the Book: How to Build the Family God Intended, we see that God designed the family to be self-perpetuating [11]. God's design is for families to produce children who grow up to establish their own families, creating a positive cycle that strengthens society and advances God's kingdom purposes. This generational impact makes family construction a matter of eternal significance, affecting not just immediate family members but countless future generations.

The Divine Purpose Behind Human Relationships

God did not create family relationships merely for human happiness or social convenience, though these are wonderful benefits [12]. His ultimate purpose reaches far beyond our immediate comfort or personal fulfillment. Family relationships exist to reflect God's own character and to demonstrate His love to a watching world.

Every aspect of family life provides opportunities to display divine attributes [13]. When husbands love their wives sacrificially, they demonstrate Christ's love for the church. When wives respond to their husbands with respect and support, they illustrate how God's people should relate to their heavenly Father. When children honor their parents, they model the reverence and obedience that all people owe to God.

This divine purpose elevates family life far above mere human relationships [14]. Every interaction between family members becomes an opportunity to proclaim God's character. Every act of love, forgiveness, service, or sacrifice becomes a living sermon that declares God's goodness to those who observe our family life.

The witness potential of godly families becomes especially powerful in a culture where family breakdown is common [15]. When people observe marriages that last, children who honor their parents, and families that genuinely love and support each other, they are drawn to discover the source of such stability and joy. This creates natural opportunities for sharing the gospel and explaining the difference that faith makes in family relationships.

Building Materials: What Makes a Biblical Family

"Unless the Lord builds the house, those who build it labor in vain" (Psalm 127:1). This ancient wisdom reminds us that successful family construction requires more than human effort and good intentions. Just as a physical building requires quality materials - strong foundation stones, sturdy lumber, reliable mortar - a biblical family requires specific spiritual building materials that only God can provide.

Old Testament Construction Principles

The Old Testament provides us with detailed construction principles for family building that remain relevant today [16]. These are not merely ancient customs or cultural preferences, but timeless truths that reflect God's unchanging character and design. When we study the families described in Scripture, we discover both positive examples to follow and negative examples to avoid.

Abraham's family demonstrates the importance of faith as a fundamental building material [17]. When God called Abraham to leave his homeland and follow divine direction, Abraham's obedience affected not only his own life but the lives of his wife and descendants for generations. His willingness to trust God's promises, even when they seemed impossible, created a legacy of faith that continues to influence families today. Abraham understood something profound about construction that goes beyond earthly building projects. The writer of Hebrews tells us that 'he was looking forward to the city that has foundations, whose designer and builder is God' (Hebrews 11:10). This eternal perspective shaped how Abraham approached his own family construction, recognizing that God serves as both the designer who creates the blueprint and the builder who provides the power to complete the project.

The relationship between Isaac and Rebekah shows us how God's providence works in family formation [18]. Abraham's servant prayed specifically for God's guidance in finding a wife for Isaac, and God answered by directing him to Rebekah. Their courtship and marriage demonstrate that God cares about the details of family construction and desires to be involved in every aspect of our relationships.

Even the struggles within Jacob's family provide important construction lessons [19]. The favoritism, deception, and conflict that marked Jacob's household show us what happens when families are built on human wisdom rather than divine principles. These negative examples serve as warning signs, helping us avoid the same construction mistakes that have plagued families throughout history.

The stories of families like David's household reveal both the blessings that come from following God's blueprint and the consequences that result from ignoring His design [20]. David's success as a king was often undermined by failures in his family relationships, demonstrating that public success cannot compensate for private family dysfunction.

The Covenant as Binding Agent

In construction, mortar serves as the binding agent that holds individual stones together to create a strong, unified wall [21]. In family construction, God's covenant serves as the binding agent that transforms separate individuals into a unified family unit. Understanding the covenant nature of family relationships is essential for anyone who wants to build according to biblical principles.

A covenant differs fundamentally from a contract or agreement [22]. While contracts are based on performance and can be broken when one party fails to meet their obligations, covenants are based on commitment and endure even through difficulties and failures. When a man and woman enter into marriage, they are not simply agreeing to a set of terms and conditions but entering into a sacred covenant that reflects God's own covenant relationship with His people.

This covenant understanding explains why God expresses such strong feelings about divorce [23]. It is not that God wants people to be miserable or trapped in destructive relationships. Rather, divorce represents the breaking of a sacred covenant that was designed to reflect God's faithful love for His people. When marriages end in divorce, the world loses a powerful picture of God's unchanging commitment to those He loves.

The covenant nature of family relationships also explains why biblical family construction requires more than emotional feelings or romantic attraction [24]. Covenants are based on commitment, not emotion. They endure through seasons when feelings fluctuate and circumstances become difficult. This covenant foundation provides the stability and security that families need to weather the inevitable storms of life.

When families understand and embrace the covenant nature of their relationships, they develop a different approach to conflict resolution and problem-solving [25]. Instead of asking "How can I get out of this relationship?" covenant thinking asks "How can I faithfully fulfill my commitments regardless of circumstances?" This shift in perspective provides the foundation for building families that last.

God's Character Reflected in Family Structure

The family structure that God designed is not arbitrary or culturally determined [26]. Instead, it reflects fundamental aspects of God's own character and His relationship with humanity. When families function according to God's blueprint, they become living demonstrations of spiritual truths that might otherwise remain abstract or theoretical.

The husband's role as family leader reflects God's position as the ultimate authority over all creation [27]. Just as God exercises His authority with love, wisdom, and self-sacrifice, husbands are called to lead their families with the same character qualities. This leadership is not domination or control, but loving service that seeks the best interests of every family member.

The wife's role as helper and supporter reflects the Holy Spirit's ministry in the life of believers [28]. Just as the Holy Spirit comes alongside believers to encourage, strengthen, and enable them to fulfill God's purposes, wives come alongside their husbands to support and strengthen them in their God-given responsibilities. This helping role is not inferior or secondary, but essential and valuable.

The parent-child relationship reflects God's relationship with His people [29]. Parents exercise authority over their children not for their own benefit, but for the children's good. They provide guidance, correction, protection, and provision just as God does for His children. Children learn to trust, obey, and honor their parents as preparation for trusting, obeying, and honoring their heavenly Father.

When families embrace these role definitions and function according to God's design, they create a living picture of spiritual realities [30]. The watching world sees demonstrations of divine love, authority, submission, and care that help them understand what God is like and how He relates to His people.

The Architectural Plan: Reflecting Divine Design

"Then God said, 'Let us make man in our image, after our likeness'" (Genesis 1:26). These words reveal something profound about God's architectural plan for family life. The use of plural pronouns - "us" and "our" - points to

the Trinity, the perfect community of Father, Son, and Holy Spirit. Human family relationships are designed to reflect this divine community in miniature.

The Trinity as the Ultimate Construction Model

Within the Trinity, we observe perfect unity combined with distinct roles [31]. The Father, Son, and Holy Spirit are equal in essence and dignity, yet each has unique functions and responsibilities. The Father plans, the Son executes, and the Spirit applies. There is no competition, jealousy, or conflict within the Godhead, only perfect harmony and cooperation.

This Trinitarian model provides the blueprint for healthy family relationships [32]. Just as the members of the Trinity are equal in value while having different roles, family members are equal in dignity while having distinct responsibilities. The husband's leadership role does not make him more valuable than his wife, any more than the Father's role makes Him more valuable than the Son or Spirit.

The love that flows between the members of the Trinity also provides the model for family love [33]. This is not merely emotional affection or romantic attraction, but a self-sacrificing commitment that seeks the good of others above personal interests. When families operate with this kind of love, they create an environment where every member can flourish and grow.

The communication within the Trinity demonstrates perfect transparency and trust [34]. There are no hidden agendas, secret plans, or deceptive strategies. Everything is open, honest, and characterized by complete mutual understanding. Families that follow this model develop communication patterns based on truth, trust, and genuine care for one another.

The eternal nature of the Trinity also speaks to the permanence that God intends for family relationships [35]. Just as the Father, Son, and Spirit have existed in perfect relationship for all eternity, family relationships are designed to endure through time and even into eternity. This eternal perspective helps families invest in relationships that will last far beyond this present life.

Marriage as a Picture of Divine Relationship

The apostle Paul reveals that marriage serves as a living illustration of Christ's relationship with the church [36]. *"This mystery is profound, and I am saying that it refers to Christ and the church"* (Ephesians 5:32). This means that every Christian marriage has the potential to serve as a sermon about God's love for His people.

When a husband loves his wife as Christ loved the church, he demonstrates the sacrificial, unconditional love that God has for His people [37]. This love is not based on performance or merit, but flows from commitment and choice. It perseveres through difficulties, forgives failures, and seeks the beloved's highest good even at personal cost.

When a wife respects and supports her husband's leadership, she illustrates how God's people should respond to Christ's authority [38]. This response is not a grudging submission or fearful compliance, but joyful cooperation with someone who has proven trustworthy and loving. It demonstrates the beauty of willing partnership with divine leadership.

The intimacy and exclusivity of marriage also reflect spiritual truths [39]. Just as married couples forsake all others to commit themselves exclusively to each other, God's people are called to forsake all other gods and commit themselves exclusively to the Lord. The jealousy that God expresses when His people turn to idols reflects the same kind of exclusive love that should characterize marriage relationships.

The permanence of marriage reflects God's unchanging commitment to His people [40]. Just as God promises never to leave or forsake those who belong to Him, married couples promise to remain faithful to each other through all circumstances. This permanence provides security and stability that enables both partners to grow and flourish.

Parental Authority Reflecting God's Fatherhood

The Bible frequently uses the parent-child relationship to help us understand God's relationship with His people [41]. God is called our heavenly Father, and we are described as His children. This means that human parenting provides a powerful opportunity to demonstrate God's character to the next generation.

Like God, parents exercise authority for the benefit of those under their care [42]. Divine authority is never arbitrary, selfish, or capricious, but always motivated by love and directed toward the good of God's children. Human parents are called to exercise their authority with the same character qualities, using their position to protect, guide, and nurture their children toward maturity.

The discipline that loving parents provide reflects God's own discipline of His children [43]. *"For the Lord disciplines the one he loves, and chastises every son whom he receives"* (Hebrews 12:6). This discipline is not punishment for its own sake, but corrective training designed to develop character and wisdom. When parents discipline their children with love and consistency, they help their children understand how God works in their own lives.

The provision and protection that parents offer their children also reflect God's care for His people [44]. Just as earthly parents work to meet their children's needs and shield them from harm, our heavenly Father provides for our needs and protects us from spiritual dangers. Children who experience faithful parental care develop a foundation of trust that helps them understand God's faithful care.

24

The gradual release of control that wise parents practice as their children mature reflects God's desire for His people to grow into spiritual maturity [45]. Just as parents eventually launch their children into independent adult life, God desires His children to grow from spiritual infancy into mature believers who can make wise decisions and serve Him effectively.

Family Roles Designed for Harmony

God's blueprint assigns specific roles to each family member, not to create hierarchy or inequality, but to promote harmony and effectiveness [46]. Just as an orchestra requires different instruments playing different parts to create beautiful music, a family requires different members fulfilling different roles to create a harmonious whole.

These roles are not based on superiority or inferiority, but on function and calling [47]. A violin is not superior to a cello simply because it plays the melody while the cello provides harmony. Both instruments are essential for the full musical experience. Similarly, the husband's leadership role and the wife's supporting role are both essential for healthy family function.

The beauty of God's design becomes apparent when each family member embraces their role with joy and excellence [48]. When husbands lead with love and wisdom, wives respond with respect and support, children obey with honor and cheerfulness, and parents guide with patience and consistency, the result is a family that reflects God's character and demonstrates His goodness to the world.

This harmony does not mean the absence of all conflict or difficulty [49]. Even the best families face challenges, disagreements, and seasons of struggle. However, when family members are committed to fulfilling their God-given roles, they have the tools and framework needed to work through difficulties and emerge stronger than before.

The roles that God has designed also provide security and identity for each family member [50]. When everyone knows their responsibilities and feels confident in their contributions to the family, there is less confusion, competition, and conflict. Each person can focus on excelling in their assigned role rather than competing with others or feeling uncertain about their place in the family structure.

The Purpose: Why Build a Christian Family

"Train up a child in the way he should go; even when he is old he will not depart from it" (Proverbs 22:6). This familiar verse points to one of the key purposes behind God's design for family life. Families exist not merely for the happiness and fulfillment of the adults involved, but to serve God's larger purposes in the world.

Companionship and Mutual Support

God's first stated purpose for creating woman was to provide companionship for man [51]. *"It is not good that the man should be alone; I will make him a helper fit for him"* (Genesis 2:18). This reveals that God designed family relationships to meet the deep human need for intimate connection and mutual support.

The companionship that God intended goes far beyond mere physical presence or shared activities [52]. It involves emotional intimacy, spiritual partnership, and mutual encouragement in the journey of life. When families function according to God's blueprint, they provide a safe haven where members can be known, loved, and supported through all of life's challenges.

This mutual support extends beyond the marriage relationship to include the entire family unit [53]. Parents support each other in the challenging task of raising children. Children support their parents through obedience and honor. Siblings support each other through friendship and loyalty. The family becomes a team where everyone contributes to the success and well-being of the whole.

The support that families provide becomes especially important during times of crisis or difficulty [54]. When illness strikes, when financial pressures mount, when emotional struggles arise, the family serves as God's primary means of providing comfort, encouragement, and practical help. This is why building strong family relationships before a crisis comes is so important for those who want to construct their families by the book.

The companionship aspect of family life also provides opportunities for spiritual growth and development [55]. Family members challenge each other, encourage each other, and help each other grow in faith and character. The daily interactions of family life become a laboratory where spiritual principles are tested and refined.

Procreation and Godly Child-Rearing

God's command to "be fruitful and multiply" reveals another key purpose for family life [56]. Children are not accidents or inconveniences, but gifts from God that fulfill His design for family construction. *"Behold, children are a heritage from the Lord, the fruit of the womb a reward"* (Psalm 127:3).

The process of raising children provides parents with opportunities to participate in God's creative work [57]. While God creates physical life, parents have the privilege and responsibility of shaping character, instilling values, and preparing children for their own future roles as adults. This is one of the most significant responsibilities that any human being can undertake.

Godly child-rearing involves more than providing food, shelter, and education [58]. It requires intentional character development, spiritual training, and preparation for adult responsibilities. Parents serve as God's representatives in their children's lives, demonstrating His character and teaching His ways through both instruction and example.

The goal of Christian parenting is not merely to raise successful or happy children, but to raise children who know and serve God [59]. This means that every aspect of family life - from daily routines to major decisions - should be evaluated in light of its impact on the children's spiritual development. When families embrace this purpose, they become instruments in God's hands for raising up the next generation of believers.

The responsibility of child-rearing also provides parents with opportunities for their own spiritual growth [60]. The challenges of parenting reveal character weaknesses, test patience and love, and drive parents to depend on God's wisdom and strength. In this way, children become God's tools for sanctifying their parents and helping them grow in spiritual maturity.

Spiritual Formation and Discipleship

The family serves as God's primary context for spiritual formation and discipleship [61]. Long before churches developed formal discipleship programs or Christian schools created spiritual curricula, God designed the family to be the place where faith is nurtured and spiritual growth occurs.

This spiritual formation happens through both formal instruction and informal modeling [62]. Parents teach their children about God through family devotions, Bible reading, and prayer. But they also teach through their daily responses to stress, their treatment of others, their handling of money, and their priorities in life. Children learn as much from what they observe as from what they are formally taught.

The family provides a laboratory where spiritual principles can be tested and applied [63]. Concepts like forgiveness, love, sacrifice, and service move from abstract ideas to concrete realities when they are practiced within family relationships. Children learn to forgive by watching their parents forgive each other. They learn to serve by participating in family service projects. They learn to love by experiencing unconditional love from their parents.

This spiritual formation process continues throughout life as family members grow and mature [64]. Adult children continue to learn from their parents' example. Parents learn from their children's fresh perspectives and honest questions. Grandparents pass on wisdom gained through years of experience. The family becomes a multi-generational community of faith where everyone contributes to everyone else's spiritual growth.

The effectiveness of family-based spiritual formation explains why God places such emphasis on parents teaching their children [65]. The intimate, long-term relationships within families provide ideal conditions for spiritual growth and development. When families embrace this responsibility and build according to biblical principles, they become powerful instruments for advancing God's kingdom purposes.

Witness to the Watching World

Perhaps the most significant purpose of Christian family life is to serve as a witness to the watching world [66]. When families function according to God's blueprint, they provide compelling evidence of God's goodness, wisdom, and love. They become living demonstrations of what life looks like when it is lived according to divine principles.

This witness happens naturally as families interact with neighbors, coworkers, classmates, and community members [67]. People observe how family members treat each other, how they handle conflicts, how they respond to crises, and how they celebrate joys. These observations often speak more powerfully than any sermon or evangelistic presentation.

The witness of a godly family becomes especially powerful in a culture where family breakdown is common [68]. When people see marriages that last, children who honor their parents, and families that genuinely love and support each other, they are drawn to discover the source of such stability and joy. This creates natural opportunities for sharing the gospel and explaining the difference that faith makes in family life.

However, this witness responsibility also creates accountability for Christian families [69]. When families claim to follow Christ but demonstrate the same dysfunction, selfishness, and conflict as non-Christian families, they damage the gospel's credibility. This is why building families according to biblical principles is not just a personal preference but a spiritual responsibility that affects the church's witness to the world.

The witness potential of Christian families extends beyond their immediate communities to influence future generations [70]. Children who grow up in godly homes often establish their own godly homes, creating a positive cycle that impacts society for generations. This generational influence makes family construction a matter of eternal significance that affects far more people than just the immediate family members.

As we conclude our examination of God's blueprint for family construction, we see that His design is both comprehensive and practical [71]. Every detail serves a purpose, and every instruction contributes to the overall strength and beauty of the finished structure. When families commit themselves to building according to this divine blueprint, they position themselves to experience the joy, stability, and purpose that God intended for family life.

The foundation has been carefully laid through our understanding of God's original intent for family relationships [72]. We have examined the building materials He has provided and the purposes He intends to accomplish through family life. We have seen how family structure reflects divine character and serves eternal purposes. Now we are ready to discover how Jesus Christ serves as the cornerstone that makes this blueprint achievable for imperfect people living in a fallen world.

In the next chapter, we will explore how Christ's life, death, and resurrection provide both the motivation and the power needed to build families according to God's design [73]. We will learn how the gospel transforms not only individual hearts but also family relationships, creating the possibility for ordinary people to achieve extraordinary family life when they build their families by the book.

The blueprint that God has provided for family construction is both comprehensive and practical. Every detail serves a purpose, every instruction contributes to the overall strength and beauty of the finished structure [74]. As we continue our journey through *Family by the Book: How to Build the Family God Intended*, we will see how each element of God's design works together to create families that honor Him and bless the world.

Understanding God's blueprint is only the beginning of our construction project [75]. In the chapters that follow, we will learn how Christ serves as the cornerstone that makes this blueprint achievable for imperfect people living in a fallen world. We will discover practical techniques for implementing these principles in our daily family life. We will explore how to handle the inevitable challenges and setbacks that come with any major construction project.

Most importantly, we will see how ordinary families can become extraordinary testimonies to God's goodness when they commit themselves to building according to His perfect design [76]. The Master Architect has provided everything we need for successful family construction. Our responsibility is to study His plans carefully, gather the right materials, and begin building with confidence in His wisdom and guidance.

The foundation has been laid through our understanding of God's original intent [77]. The blueprint has been examined and found to be perfect in every detail. Now the real work of construction begins. As we move forward, we do so with the assurance that families built according to God's design will stand strong against every storm and provide shelter, security, and joy for all who dwell within their walls.

This is the promise that motivates every family that chooses to build by the book [78]. This is the hope that sustains us through the challenges of construction. This is the vision that calls us to embrace God's blueprint and begin the rewarding work of building families that reflect His character and demonstrate His love to a world that desperately needs to see authentic examples of His goodness in action.

The journey of family construction according to God's blueprint requires patience, perseverance, and complete dependence on the Master Builder's guidance [79]. But for those who commit themselves to this process, the rewards are beyond measure. Strong marriages, thriving children, and homes filled with love, joy, and peace are not accidents or lucky breaks. They are the natural result of careful construction according to divine specifications.

As we conclude this foundational chapter and prepare to examine how Christ serves as our cornerstone, let us commit ourselves afresh to the task of building families that honor God and bless the world [80]. Let us embrace His blueprint with confidence, knowing that His design is perfect and His guidance is sure. Let us begin this construction project with excitement and anticipation, knowing that the finished product will exceed our highest expectations and bring glory to the Master Architect who designed it all.

Chapter 2

The Cornerstone

Building Everything Around Jesus

In any construction project, the cornerstone determines the alignment and stability of the entire structure. Ancient builders understood that if the cornerstone was properly positioned, every other stone would find its correct place. If the cornerstone was flawed or misaligned, the entire building would be compromised. As we continue our journey through *Family by the Book: How to Build the Family God Intended*, we discover that Jesus Christ serves as the cornerstone that makes God's blueprint for family life both achievable and sustainable.

The apostle Paul declares this foundational truth: *"And he is before all things, and in him all things hold together"* (Colossians 1:17). This cosmic reality applies directly to family construction [1]. When Christ is properly positioned as the cornerstone of family life, every relationship finds its proper alignment. When He is ignored or displaced, even families that appear successful on the surface will eventually show signs of structural weakness.

Many families attempt to build using other cornerstones - financial security, educational achievement, social status, or even religious activity [2]. While these may provide temporary stability, they lack the strength to support a family through the inevitable storms of life. Only Christ possesses the character, authority, and power necessary to serve as the cornerstone for lasting family construction.

Understanding Christ's role as the cornerstone transforms our approach to every aspect of family life [3]. It affects how husbands lead, how wives respond, how children obey, and how parents guide. It influences our priorities, our decision-making processes, and our responses to both blessings and challenges. When families truly embrace Christ as their cornerstone, they discover that building according to God's blueprint becomes not only possible but joyful.

Christ's Lordship in Family Life

"But as for me and my house, we will serve the Lord" (Joshua 24:15). Joshua's declaration represents more than a personal commitment; it establishes a family constitution that places Christ's authority at the center of all family decisions and relationships. This is where successful family construction must begin - with a clear recognition that Jesus Christ is Lord over every aspect of family life.

Making Jesus the Center of Family Building

Establishing Christ as the cornerstone of family construction requires intentional decisions and daily practices [4]. It begins with the recognition that marriage and family are not merely human institutions designed for personal happiness, but divine gifts intended to reflect God's character and advance His kingdom purposes. When couples understand this truth, they approach their relationship with reverence and purpose that transcends personal preferences and cultural expectations.

The centrality of Christ in family building affects every major decision that families face [5]. Career choices are evaluated not only for financial benefits but for their impact on family spiritual health and ministry opportunities. Housing decisions consider not just comfort and convenience but the neighborhood's influence on children and opportunities for Christian witness. Educational choices weigh academic excellence alongside spiritual formation and biblical worldview development.

This Christ-centered approach also transforms daily family interactions [6]. Conflicts are resolved using biblical principles rather than worldly wisdom. Discipline is administered with love and grace that reflects God's character. Celebrations acknowledge God's goodness and provision. Even routine activities like meals, bedtime, and transportation become opportunities to demonstrate Christ's lordship and teach spiritual truths.

When Christ truly occupies the central position in family construction, family members develop a shared sense of purpose that unifies their efforts [7]. Instead of competing for personal interests or struggling with conflicting priorities, they work together toward common goals that honor God and serve others. This unity provides strength and stability that enables families to weather difficulties and celebrate blessings with equal grace.

The process of making Christ central requires ongoing commitment and regular evaluation [8]. Families must regularly examine their priorities, schedules, and decisions to ensure that Christ's lordship remains practical rather than merely theoretical. This involves honest conversations about where time and energy are invested, what values are actually being demonstrated, and whether family life is reflecting Christ's character to those who observe it.

Family Worship as Daily Construction Practice

One of the most practical ways to establish and maintain Christ's centrality in family life is through regular family worship [9]. This practice acknowledges God's authority, expresses gratitude for His blessings, seeks His guidance for daily decisions, and teaches children that spiritual matters take priority over all other concerns. Family worship becomes the daily cornerstone-laying ceremony that keeps Christ in His proper position.

Effective family worship does not require elaborate programs or lengthy time commitments [10]. Simple practices like reading Scripture together, sharing prayer requests, singing hymns or worship songs, and discussing how biblical principles apply to current family situations can transform the spiritual atmosphere of any home. The key is consistency rather than complexity, making worship a natural part of family rhythm rather than an additional burden.

The content of family worship should reflect the spiritual needs and maturity levels of all family members [11]. Young children benefit from simple Bible stories, short prayers, and songs with memorable melodies. Teenagers appreciate discussions about how biblical principles apply to their current challenges and opportunities. Adults need opportunities to share deeper spiritual insights and pray for complex family and ministry concerns.

Family worship also provides opportunities for parents to model spiritual leadership and teach children how to interact with God [12]. When children observe their parents reading Scripture with reverence, praying with sincerity, and applying biblical principles to real-life situations, they learn that faith is practical and relevant rather than merely theoretical. These observations often prove more influential than formal religious instruction.

The timing and format of family worship should fit the unique rhythms and needs of each family [13]. Some families find that morning devotions help them start each day with proper spiritual focus. Others prefer evening worship that allows them to reflect on the day's events and seek God's guidance for tomorrow. The important thing is establishing a consistent pattern that demonstrates the priority of spiritual matters in family life.

Creating a Home That Welcomes Christ

The physical environment of the home can either support or hinder Christ's centrality in family life [14]. This does not mean that Christian homes must look like churches or display religious symbols in every room. Rather, it means creating an atmosphere where spiritual conversations feel natural, biblical values are reinforced through daily routines, and family members feel encouraged to grow in their relationship with God.

A Christ-welcoming home prioritizes relationships over possessions and people over programs [15]. The family schedule allows time for meaningful conversations, unhurried meals, and spontaneous expressions of love and affection. Entertainment choices reflect biblical values and provide opportunities for spiritual discussion. The home becomes a place where family members want to spend time together rather than a launching pad for individual pursuits.

The hospitality that Christian families extend to others also reflects Christ's centrality in their lives [16]. When families regularly welcome guests, serve those in need, and open their homes for ministry purposes, they demonstrate that their resources belong to God and exist to serve His purposes. Children who grow up in hospitable homes learn that their family exists not just for their own benefit but to bless others.

Creating a Christ-welcoming home also involves establishing boundaries that protect the family's spiritual health [17]. This might mean limiting exposure to entertainment that contradicts biblical values, choosing friends who support rather than undermine spiritual growth, or saying no to activities that would compromise the family's ability to worship and serve together. These boundaries are not legalistic restrictions but loving protections that preserve the family's spiritual focus.

The goal of creating a Christ-welcoming home is to establish an environment where every family member can flourish spiritually [18]. This requires ongoing attention to the spiritual climate of the home, regular evaluation of how family practices support or hinder spiritual growth, and willingness to make adjustments when necessary. When families succeed in creating this kind of environment, they discover that their home becomes a place of refuge, renewal, and spiritual strength.

Submitting Family Plans to Divine Authority

One of the most practical expressions of Christ's lordship in family life involves submitting major decisions to His authority through prayer, Scripture study, and wise counsel [19]. This means that families do not make important choices based solely on personal preferences, financial considerations, or cultural expectations, but seek to understand and follow God's will for their specific situation.

The process of submitting family plans to divine authority begins with prayer [20]. Families that recognize Christ as their cornerstone regularly bring their decisions, concerns, and opportunities before God in prayer. They ask for wisdom to understand His will, courage to follow His leading, and faith to trust His provision. This prayer is not merely a formality but a genuine seeking of divine guidance for family direction.

Scripture study also plays a crucial role in submitting family plans to Christ's authority [21]. Families committed to building according to God's blueprint regularly examine biblical principles that apply to their current decisions and circumstances. They seek to understand not just what the Bible says about specific issues, but how biblical principles should shape their approach to decision-making and priority-setting.

Seeking wise counsel from mature believers provides another important element in submitting family plans to divine authority [22]. Families that recognize their need for outside perspective regularly consult with pastors, mentors, and other godly families who can provide biblical insight and practical wisdom. This counsel helps families avoid blind spots and consider factors they might otherwise overlook.

The willingness to change direction when God's leading becomes clear demonstrates genuine submission to Christ's authority [23]. Families that truly recognize Christ as their cornerstone are prepared to adjust their plans, sacrifice personal preferences, and embrace unexpected opportunities when they become convinced that God is leading in a different direction. This flexibility requires faith and humility but results in greater spiritual growth and family unity.

The Holy Spirit's Role in Building

"But the Helper, the Holy Spirit, whom the Father will send in my name, he will teach you all things" (John 14:26). The construction of godly families requires more than human effort, good intentions, and biblical knowledge. It demands supernatural enablement that only the Holy Spirit can provide. Understanding and depending on the Spirit's ministry in family life is essential for anyone who wants to build according to God's blueprint.

Depending on Divine Power for Human Building

The Holy Spirit provides the power necessary to live according to biblical principles in family relationships [24]. Without this divine enablement, even families that understand God's blueprint will struggle to implement it consistently. The Spirit transforms hearts, changes attitudes, and provides strength to love sacrificially, forgive completely, and serve joyfully even when natural inclinations point in different directions.

This dependence on divine power begins with the recognition that successful family building is ultimately a spiritual endeavor [25]. While practical skills, communication techniques, and conflict resolution strategies all have their place, they cannot address the heart issues that lie at the root of most family problems. Only the Holy Spirit can change selfish hearts, heal wounded emotions, and create the love and unity that characterize truly godly families.

The Spirit's power becomes especially evident during times of conflict and crisis [26]. When family members are hurt, angry, or disappointed, natural

40

human responses often involve retaliation, withdrawal, or manipulation. The Holy Spirit enables supernatural responses of forgiveness, grace, and reconciliation that demonstrate God's character and restore family harmony. These Spirit-enabled responses often surprise both family members and outside observers.

Depending on the Spirit's power also involves recognizing the limitations of human effort in family construction [27]. Families that try to build godly relationships through willpower, determination, and behavioral modification alone will eventually become exhausted and discouraged. Those who learn to depend on the Spirit's enablement discover that obedience to biblical principles becomes increasingly natural and joyful rather than burdensome and forced.

The practical expression of dependence on divine power includes regular prayer for the Spirit's work in family relationships [28]. Family members pray for each other's spiritual growth, ask for wisdom in handling specific challenges, and seek the Spirit's guidance in making decisions that affect the entire family. This prayer acknowledges that successful family building requires divine intervention and assistance.

The Spirit's Fruit in Family Construction

The apostle Paul describes the fruit of the Spirit as *"love, joy, peace, patience, kindness, goodness, faithfulness, gentleness, self-control"* (Galatians 5:22-23). These character qualities provide the essential building materials for godly family relationships [29]. When the Holy Spirit is actively working in family members' lives, these qualities become increasingly evident in their interactions with each other.

Love serves as the foundational building material that holds all other elements together [30]. Spirit-produced love is not merely emotional affection or romantic attraction, but self-sacrificing commitment that seeks the good of others above personal interests. When this love characterizes family relationships, it creates an environment where every member feels valued, secure, and encouraged to grow.

Joy provides the emotional climate that makes family life attractive and fulfilling [31]. Spirit-produced joy is not dependent on circumstances but flows from the confidence that God is working all things together for good. Families characterized by this joy are able to celebrate blessings with gratitude and face challenges with hope, creating positive memories and strong emotional bonds.

Peace establishes the relational harmony that enables families to function effectively [32]. Spirit-produced peace is not merely the absence of conflict but the presence of unity and understanding. When peace characterizes family relationships, members feel safe to be vulnerable, honest, and authentic with each other, creating the intimacy that God intended for family life.

Patience provides the emotional stability necessary for long-term relationship building [33]. Spirit-produced patience enables family members to work through difficulties without giving up, to forgive repeated failures without becoming bitter, and to invest in each other's growth without demanding immediate results. This patience is especially important in parenting and marriage relationships.

The remaining fruit of the Spirit - kindness, goodness, faithfulness, gentleness, and self-control - each contributes essential elements to healthy family construction [34]. When these qualities characterize family interactions, they create an environment that reflects God's character and demonstrates His love to both family members and outside observers.

Praying Together as a Building Family

Prayer serves as both a means of grace and a family-building activity that strengthens relationships while seeking God's blessing and guidance [35]. When families pray together regularly, they acknowledge their dependence on God, share their deepest concerns with each other, and invite divine intervention in their circumstances. This shared spiritual activity creates bonds that transcend natural family ties.

Effective family prayer involves more than reciting formal prayers or asking God to bless family activities [36]. It includes honest sharing of struggles and concerns, grateful acknowledgment of God's blessings and provision, and earnest seeking of wisdom for current decisions and challenges. When family members pray authentically together, they learn to know and care for each other at deeper levels.

The practice of praying together also teaches children how to communicate with God and demonstrates the reality of His presence in family life [37]. When children hear their parents pray with sincerity and see their prayers answered, they develop confidence in God's love and power. When parents pray for their children in their presence, children feel valued and secure in their parents' love and God's care.

Family prayer should include intercession for others as well as requests for family needs [38]. When families regularly pray for missionaries, church leaders, community needs, and world events, they develop a perspective that extends beyond their own concerns. This broader focus helps family members understand their role in God's larger purposes and develop compassion for others.

The timing and format of family prayer should accommodate the needs and schedules of all family members [39]. Some families find that brief prayers before meals and bedtime work best for their situation. Others prefer longer prayer times during family devotions or special occasions. The important thing is establishing consistent patterns that make prayer a natural part of family life rather than an unusual or burdensome activity.

Supernatural Enablement for Natural Relationships

The Holy Spirit's ministry in family life demonstrates that God intends to be actively involved in the most intimate and practical aspects of human relationships [40]. This divine involvement does not eliminate the need for human effort, wisdom, and skill, but it provides the supernatural enablement necessary to live according to biblical principles consistently and joyfully.

This supernatural enablement becomes evident in the transformation of natural human responses to family challenges [41]. Instead of responding to conflict with anger and retaliation, Spirit-filled family members learn to respond with patience and grace. Instead of withdrawing during difficult times, they learn to draw closer together and seek solutions cooperatively. Instead of competing for personal advantage, they learn to serve each other's interests.

The Spirit's enablement also provides wisdom for handling complex family situations that have no simple solutions [42]. When families face decisions about education, career changes, financial pressures, or relationship difficulties, the Holy Spirit provides insight that goes beyond human understanding. This divine wisdom often leads to creative solutions that address multiple concerns and serve everyone's best interests.

Supernatural enablement does not mean that Christian families avoid all difficulties or conflicts [43]. Rather, it means that they have access to divine resources for handling these challenges in ways that strengthen rather than weaken family relationships. The Spirit's power enables families to grow through difficulties rather than being destroyed by them.

The evidence of supernatural enablement in family life often becomes most apparent to outside observers [44]. When non-Christian friends and neighbors observe how Christian families handle stress, resolve conflicts, and support each other through difficulties, they often comment on the unusual love, peace, and unity they witness. This supernatural quality of family relationships becomes a powerful testimony to God's reality and goodness.

Hospitality as Christian Witness

"Do not neglect to show hospitality to strangers, for thereby some have entertained angels unawares" (Hebrews 13:2). The practice of hospitality provides one of the most natural and effective ways for families to demonstrate Christ's love and share the gospel with others. When families open their homes and hearts to others, they create opportunities for ministry that extend far beyond formal church programs.

Opening Your Home to Fellow Believers

Christian hospitality begins with welcoming fellow believers into the family's life and home [45]. This practice strengthens the church community, provides encouragement for struggling believers, and teaches children the importance of Christian fellowship. When families regularly host other believers for meals, fellowship, and mutual encouragement, they participate in the biblical model of church life.

The practice of hosting fellow believers also provides opportunities for spiritual growth and learning [46]. When families with different backgrounds, experiences, and perspectives share meals and conversations, they learn from each other's insights and testimonies. Children benefit from hearing how God has worked in other families' lives and observing different approaches to Christian living.

Hospitality toward fellow believers should extend beyond social entertainment to include practical ministry [47]. This might involve providing meals for families with new babies, offering temporary housing for those in transition, or creating space for small group meetings and Bible studies. When families use their homes as ministry centers, they demonstrate that their resources belong to God and exist to serve His purposes.

The key to effective Christian hospitality is creating an atmosphere where guests feel genuinely welcomed and valued rather than impressed or entertained [48]. This means focusing on relationships rather than elaborate preparations, encouraging authentic conversation rather than superficial pleasantries, and demonstrating Christ's love through practical service rather than formal presentations.

Regular practice of hospitality toward fellow believers also strengthens the host family's own spiritual life [49]. When families open their homes to others, they are reminded of their blessings and motivated to gratitude. When they serve others, they experience the joy that comes from following Christ's example. When they share their faith with others, their own faith is strengthened and encouraged.

Serving Others as a Family Unit

Hospitality provides opportunities for entire families to serve together in ways that strengthen family bonds while blessing others [50]. When families work together to prepare meals, clean house, and care for guests, they learn cooperation, develop servant hearts, and create positive memories of serving others. These shared ministry experiences often become some of the most meaningful family memories.

Family service projects also teach children practical skills while developing their character [51]. When children help prepare food for guests, they learn cooking skills and the joy of serving others. When they help clean and organize for visitors, they learn responsibility and the importance of creating welcoming environments. When they participate in conversations with guests, they learn social skills and gain exposure to different perspectives.

The practice of serving others as a family unit also provides natural opportunities for parents to teach children about Christian values and priorities [52]. When families sacrifice personal comfort to serve others, children learn that following Christ involves putting others' needs before their own. When families give generously to meet others' needs, children learn that material possessions exist to be shared rather than hoarded.

Serving others together also strengthens family relationships by creating shared purposes and experiences [53]. When family members work together toward common goals of blessing others, they develop teamwork skills and mutual appreciation. When they see how their combined efforts can make a significant difference in others' lives, they gain confidence in their ability to serve God effectively.

The key to successful family service is choosing opportunities that match the family's abilities, resources, and schedule [54]. Young families with small children might focus on simple acts of hospitality like sharing meals or providing childcare. Families with teenagers might take on more complex service projects that require greater time and energy commitments. The important thing is finding ways for the entire family to participate meaningfully.

Your Home as a Ministry Center

When families embrace the concept of their home as a ministry center, they discover numerous opportunities to serve God and others without leaving their neighborhood [55]. This approach to ministry is especially valuable for families with young children or limited mobility, as it allows them to serve others while maintaining their primary responsibilities to family members.

Using the home as a ministry center might involve hosting Bible studies, prayer groups, or fellowship gatherings for neighbors and friends [56]. It could include providing space for church activities, community meetings, or support groups. Some families create informal counseling ministries by making themselves available to listen and pray with others who are facing difficulties.

The home can also serve as a ministry center through practical service to community members [57]. This might involve providing meals for sick neighbors, offering childcare for single parents, or creating space for community children to play safely. When families consistently demonstrate Christ's love through practical service, they earn the right to share the gospel with those they serve.

Technology also provides opportunities for families to use their homes as ministry centers [58]. Some families host online Bible studies, create Christian content for social media, or provide technical support for church and ministry activities. These technology-based ministries allow families to serve others regardless of geographical limitations or physical constraints.

The key to effective home-based ministry is maintaining a balance between service to others and care for family members [59]. Families must ensure that their ministry activities strengthen rather than weaken their own relationships and spiritual health. This requires wisdom in setting boundaries, saying no to some opportunities, and regularly evaluating the impact of ministry activities on family life.

Building Bridges Through Family Life

One of the most powerful aspects of family-based ministry is its ability to build bridges with people who might never enter a church building or attend a formal religious event [60]. When families demonstrate Christ's love through their daily interactions with neighbors, coworkers, and community members, they create natural opportunities for spiritual conversations and gospel witness.

These bridge-building opportunities often arise through children's activities and relationships [61]. When Christian families participate in community sports leagues, school events, and neighborhood activities, they meet other families who are facing similar challenges and opportunities. The relationships that develop through these shared experiences often provide openings for deeper spiritual conversations.

The witness of a godly family becomes especially powerful when it is demonstrated consistently over time [62]. When neighbors observe how Christian families handle stress, resolve conflicts, and support each other through difficulties, they often become curious about the source of such stability and love. This curiosity creates natural opportunities for sharing the gospel and explaining the difference that faith makes in family life.

Building bridges through family life also involves being genuinely interested in others' lives and concerns [63]. When Christian families take time to listen to their neighbors' struggles, celebrate their successes, and offer practical help during difficult times, they demonstrate Christ's love in tangible ways. These acts of love often speak more powerfully than any verbal presentation of the gospel.

The goal of bridge-building through family life is not to manipulate others into religious conversations but to demonstrate authentic Christian love that naturally leads to spiritual discussions [64]. When families consistently live according to biblical principles and show genuine care for others, they create environments where spiritual conversations feel natural and welcome rather than forced or uncomfortable.

Growing Together in Faith

"Iron sharpens iron, and one man sharpens another" (Proverbs 27:17). The family provides an ideal environment for spiritual growth and development because of the intimate, long-term relationships that exist between family members. When families commit themselves to growing together in faith, they create opportunities for mutual encouragement, accountability, and spiritual development that benefit every family member.

Supporting Each Other's Spiritual Growth

Effective spiritual growth within families requires intentional effort to encourage and support each other's relationship with God [65]. This involves more than simply attending church together or participating in family devotions. It includes taking genuine interest in each other's spiritual struggles and victories, offering encouragement during difficult times, and celebrating evidence of spiritual growth and maturity.

Parents play a crucial role in supporting their children's spiritual development by creating environments where spiritual questions are welcomed and spiritual conversations feel natural [66]. This means being available to discuss spiritual matters when children are ready to talk, providing age-appropriate answers to difficult questions, and demonstrating through their own lives that faith is practical and relevant to daily living.

Spouses support each other's spiritual growth by encouraging personal devotional time, sharing spiritual insights and struggles, and working together to apply biblical principles to family decisions and challenges [67]. When husbands and wives view themselves as spiritual partners rather than competitors, they create an environment where both can flourish in their relationship with God.

Children can support their parents' spiritual growth by asking thoughtful questions, sharing their own spiritual insights, and demonstrating obedience and respect that encourages their parents' faith [68]. When children take their own spiritual development seriously, they often motivate their parents to greater spiritual maturity and commitment.

The key to supporting each other's spiritual growth is creating an atmosphere of grace and acceptance where family members feel safe to share their struggles and failures without fear of judgment or condemnation [69]. When families demonstrate the same grace that God shows to His children, they create environments where spiritual growth can flourish naturally and joyfully.

Celebrating God's Faithfulness Together

Regular celebration of God's faithfulness provides opportunities for families to acknowledge His goodness, strengthen their faith, and create positive memories that sustain them through difficult times [70]. These celebrations might involve formal thanksgiving services, informal sharing times, or creative expressions of gratitude that reflect the family's unique personality and interests.

Celebrating God's faithfulness should include both major milestones and daily blessings [71]. While families naturally celebrate obvious answers to prayer, significant achievements, and special occasions, they should also develop habits of recognizing and acknowledging God's daily provision, protection, and guidance. This regular acknowledgment of God's goodness helps family members develop grateful hearts and confident faith.

The practice of keeping family records of God's faithfulness provides valuable resources for future encouragement [72]. Some families maintain prayer journals that record both requests and answers. Others create photo albums or scrapbooks that document God's blessings and provision. Still others establish family traditions that commemorate significant spiritual milestones and answered prayers.

Celebrating God's faithfulness also involves sharing testimonies of His goodness with others [73]. When families regularly tell others about how God has blessed and provided for them, they strengthen their own faith while encouraging others to trust God more completely. These testimonies become powerful tools for evangelism and discipleship.

The goal of celebrating God's faithfulness is not to boast about personal blessings but to acknowledge God's character and encourage continued trust in His goodness [74]. When families develop habits of recognizing and celebrating God's faithfulness, they build spiritual momentum that carries them through seasons when His blessings are less obvious or His purposes are unclear.

Facing Trials with United Faith

Every family will face trials and difficulties that test their faith and challenge their unity [75]. When families have established Christ as their cornerstone and committed themselves to growing together spiritually, they are better equipped to handle these challenges in ways that strengthen rather than weaken their relationships and faith.

United faith during trials begins with a shared understanding that God is sovereign over all circumstances and that He works all things together for good for those who love Him [76]. When families embrace this truth together, they are able to face difficulties with hope and confidence rather than fear and despair. This shared perspective provides stability and strength during uncertain times.

The practice of praying together during trials provides both spiritual strength and relational unity [77]. When family members bring their concerns, fears, and requests to God together, they acknowledge their dependence on

Him while supporting each other emotionally and spiritually. These shared prayer times often become some of the most meaningful and bonding experiences in family life.

Facing trials with united faith also involves supporting each other practically during difficult times [78]. This might mean adjusting family schedules to accommodate someone's special needs, sharing financial resources to meet unexpected expenses, or providing emotional support during times of grief or disappointment. When families demonstrate practical love during trials, they strengthen their bonds and demonstrate God's love to each other.

The key to maintaining united faith during trials is remembering that difficulties are temporary while God's love and purposes are eternal [79]. When families keep this eternal perspective, they are able to endure present hardships with patience and hope. They are also able to learn from their trials and use their experiences to help other families facing similar challenges.

Building a Spiritual Legacy for Future Generations

One of the most significant aspects of growing together in faith involves building a spiritual legacy that will influence future generations [80]. When families commit themselves to following Christ faithfully, they create patterns and traditions that often continue for generations. This generational impact makes family spiritual development a matter of eternal significance.

Building a spiritual legacy begins with establishing family traditions and practices that reinforce biblical values and spiritual priorities [81]. These might include regular family devotions, annual spiritual retreats, service projects, or celebration traditions that help family members remember God's faithfulness and their commitment to following Him. When these traditions are meaningful and enjoyable, they often continue into the next generation.

The stories and testimonies that families share also contribute to their spiritual legacy [82]. When parents regularly tell their children about how God has worked in their lives, when grandparents share stories of God's faithfulness through difficult times, and when family members celebrate answered prayers together, they create a family narrative that demonstrates God's reality and goodness.

Building a spiritual legacy also involves teaching children and grandchildren practical skills for following Christ [83]. This includes instruction in Bible study, prayer, Christian service, and biblical decision-making. When older family members invest time and energy in training younger members, they multiply their spiritual influence and ensure that their faith will continue beyond their own lifetime.

The ultimate goal of building a spiritual legacy is not family pride or personal recognition but the advancement of God's kingdom through successive generations [84]. When families successfully pass on their faith to their children and grandchildren, they participate in God's plan for reaching the world with the gospel and building His church. This eternal perspective motivates families to invest in spiritual development even when the immediate benefits are not apparent.

As we conclude our examination of Christ's role as the cornerstone of family construction, we see that His presence transforms every aspect of family life [85]. When families truly embrace Jesus as their cornerstone, they discover that building according to God's blueprint becomes not only possible but joyful. The supernatural enablement that Christ provides through His Spirit makes it possible for ordinary families to achieve extraordinary unity, love, and purpose.

The cornerstone has been properly positioned through our understanding of Christ's lordship in family life [86]. We have seen how the

Holy Spirit provides the power necessary for biblical family construction and how hospitality creates opportunities for ministry and witness. We have discovered how families can grow together in faith and build a spiritual legacy for future generations.

In the next chapter, we will examine how husbands can fulfill their role as foundation layers in family construction [87]. We will learn how Christ's example of sacrificial love provides the model for husband leadership and how this leadership creates security and stability that enables the entire family to flourish. The cornerstone is in place; now we are ready to begin laying the foundation that will support the entire family structure.

Chapter 3
The Husband's Foundation

Leading Through Love

With the cornerstone of Christ properly positioned in our family construction project, we are ready to begin laying the foundation that will support the entire family structure. In any building project, the foundation determines the stability and strength of everything that follows. A weak or poorly constructed foundation will eventually cause the entire structure to fail, regardless of how beautiful or well-designed the upper levels might be. As we continue our journey through Family by the Book: How to Build the Family God Intended, we discover that God has assigned husbands the crucial role of foundation layers in family construction.

The apostle Paul provides the blueprint for this foundational work: *"Husbands, love your wives, as Christ loved the church and gave himself up for her"* (Ephesians 5:25). This single verse contains the complete architectural plan for husband leadership in Christian families [1]. It establishes love as the primary building material, Christ as the model, and sacrificial service as the construction method. When husbands understand and embrace this divine design, they create foundations strong enough to support flourishing families for generations.

Many men struggle with the concept of foundation laying because they misunderstand what biblical leadership actually involves [2]. Cultural definitions of leadership often emphasize authority, control, and personal advantage. Biblical leadership, however, focuses on responsibility, service, and sacrificial love. The husband who leads according to God's blueprint discovers that true strength comes through serving others rather than demanding service from them.

The foundation that husbands lay through loving leadership affects every aspect of family life [3]. When wives feel genuinely loved and cherished, they find it natural to respond with respect and support. When children observe their father treating their mother with consistent love and honor, they learn what healthy relationships look like and develop security in their family's stability. When extended family and community members witness this kind of leadership, they see a picture of Christ's love for His church.

Understanding the husband's role as a foundation layer also helps men approach marriage and family with the proper perspective [4]. Marriage is not primarily about personal happiness or fulfillment, though these often result from biblical marriage. Rather, marriage provides an opportunity for men to demonstrate Christ's character and advance God's kingdom purposes through sacrificial love and servant leadership.

The foundation laying process requires patience, skill, and careful attention to detail [5]. Just as construction workers must prepare the ground, mix the concrete properly, and allow adequate time for curing, husbands must develop the character qualities, communication skills, and spiritual maturity necessary for effective family leadership. This process takes time and often involves learning from mistakes, but the results justify the investment.

Laying Love's Foundation

"We love because he first loved us" (1 John 4:19). The foundation of Christian marriage must be built with love, but not just any kind of love. The love that provides adequate support for lifelong marriage is agape love - the same unconditional, sacrificial love that God demonstrates toward His people. This love serves as the concrete that binds all other elements of marriage together and provides the strength necessary to withstand the pressures that every marriage faces.

Understanding Agape as Building Material

Agape love differs fundamentally from the romantic feelings and emotional attraction that often characterize the early stages of relationships [6]. While these emotions play important roles in marriage, they are not strong enough to serve as foundational building materials. Emotions change with circumstances, health, stress levels, and countless other factors. Agape love, however, remains constant because it is based on choice and commitment rather than feelings and circumstances.

The agape love that husbands are called to demonstrate involves a deliberate decision to seek their wives' highest good regardless of personal cost or convenience [7]. This love does not depend on the wife's behavior, appearance, or response. It flows from the husband's commitment to obey God and reflect Christ's character rather than from his wife's ability to earn or deserve such treatment. This unconditional quality makes agape love suitable as a foundational building material.

Agape love also involves understanding and accepting responsibility for the wife's well-being and spiritual growth [8]. Just as Christ takes responsibility for the church's development and sanctification, husbands are called to invest in their wives' flourishing as individuals and as believers. This responsibility extends beyond providing financial support to include emotional encouragement, spiritual leadership, and practical assistance in pursuing God-given dreams and callings.

The practical expression of agape love requires husbands to study their wives carefully and learn what makes them feel genuinely loved and valued [9]. This might involve learning their love languages, understanding their emotional needs, recognizing their unique gifts and abilities, and discovering their hopes and dreams. When husbands invest this kind of attention in understanding their wives, they demonstrate the same kind of intimate knowledge that Christ has of His church.

Agape love also involves protecting the wife from harm and creating an environment where she can flourish [10]. This protection includes physical safety, emotional security, and spiritual encouragement. Husbands who love with agape love work to eliminate sources of stress and anxiety from their wives' lives while creating opportunities for growth, rest, and joy. This protective aspect of love reflects Christ's commitment to guard and care for His church.

The development of agape love requires spiritual maturity and ongoing dependence on God's grace [11]. Men cannot generate this kind of love through willpower or determination alone. It must flow from their own relationship with Christ and their understanding of how much they have been loved and forgiven. As husbands grow in their appreciation for God's love toward them, they become increasingly able to love their wives with the same unconditional commitment.

Christ's Example of Foundation Leadership

Jesus Christ provides the perfect model for husband leadership because He demonstrates how to exercise authority through service and how to lead through love [12]. When husbands study Christ's relationship with the church, they discover principles and practices that transform their approach to marriage and family leadership. Christ's example shows that true leadership involves taking responsibility for others' welfare rather than demanding service for personal benefit.

Christ's leadership of the church demonstrates the importance of vision and purpose in family leadership [13]. Jesus has a clear understanding of what He wants to accomplish in and through the church, and He works consistently toward those goals. Similarly, husbands need to develop a clear vision for their families and work intentionally to help their families achieve God's purposes. This vision provides direction and motivation that unifies family efforts and creates a sense of shared mission.

The way Christ communicates with the church also provides a model for husband-wife communication [14]. Jesus speaks truth in love, provides clear guidance and instruction, listens to the concerns and requests of His people, and responds with patience and grace even when they fail to understand or obey. Husbands who follow this example learn to communicate with their wives in ways that build trust, encourage growth, and strengthen their relationship.

Christ's willingness to sacrifice for the church demonstrates the cost that effective leadership often requires [15]. Jesus gave up the privileges of heaven, endured the hardships of earthly life, and ultimately died on the cross to secure the church's salvation and sanctification. While husbands are not called to die physically for their wives, they are called to sacrifice their own interests, preferences, and convenience for their wives' benefit. This sacrificial attitude transforms marriage from a competitive relationship into a partnership focused on mutual service.

The patience that Christ demonstrates with the church provides another crucial element for husband leadership [16]. Jesus continues to love, forgive, and work with His people despite their repeated failures, misunderstandings, and acts of disobedience. Husbands who follow this example learn to extend grace to their wives during difficult seasons, to forgive quickly and completely when conflicts arise, and to maintain hope for growth and change even when progress seems slow.

Christ's commitment to the church's sanctification also guides husbands in their role as spiritual leaders [17]. Jesus works consistently to help the church become more holy, mature, and effective in ministry. Similarly, husbands should invest in their wives' spiritual growth, encourage their development of spiritual gifts, and create opportunities for them to serve God and others. This sanctifying love helps wives become everything that God intends them to be.

Moving Beyond Cultural Construction Methods

Many men approach marriage with construction methods learned from cultural observation rather than biblical instruction [18]. These cultural methods often emphasize male dominance, emotional distance, and competitive relationships that undermine rather than strengthen marriage foundations. Men who want to build according to God's blueprint must be willing to abandon these ineffective methods and learn biblical approaches to marriage and family leadership.

Cultural definitions of masculinity often discourage the emotional vulnerability and intimate communication that strong marriages require [19]. Many men have been taught that showing emotion or admitting weakness demonstrates a lack of strength or leadership ability. Biblical masculinity, however, recognizes that true strength includes the ability to be vulnerable with one's wife, to admit mistakes and seek forgiveness, and to express emotions appropriately and honestly.

The competitive mindset that characterizes many cultural approaches to relationships also undermines marriage foundations [20]. When husbands view their wives as competitors for control, recognition, or resources, they create adversarial relationships that weaken rather than strengthen their families. Biblical marriage, however, is based on partnership and mutual service rather than competition and control. Husbands who embrace this partnership approach discover that their wives become allies rather than opponents.

Cultural emphasis on personal rights and individual fulfillment also conflicts with biblical marriage principles [21]. Many men approach marriage expecting their wives to meet their needs, support their goals, and adapt to their preferences without requiring similar sacrifice in return. Biblical marriage, however, calls both partners to sacrificial love and mutual service. Husbands who focus on serving their wives rather than being served discover that their own needs are met more completely than they ever imagined.

Love as Choice and Commitment

One of the most important truths that husbands must understand about foundational love is that it operates primarily as a choice and commitment rather than an emotion or feeling [22]. While emotions play important roles in marriage relationships, they are not reliable enough to serve as the foundation for lifelong commitment. Emotions change with circumstances, health, stress levels, and countless other factors. Choice and commitment, however, can remain constant regardless of external circumstances.

The choice to love involves a deliberate decision to seek the wife's highest good even when personal feelings suggest different courses of action [23]. This might mean choosing to serve when feeling tired, choosing to listen when feeling impatient, choosing to forgive when feeling hurt, or choosing to encourage when feeling discouraged. These choices demonstrate the reality of agape love and create emotional connections that strengthen the marriage relationship.

Commitment provides the stability and security that enables marriages to weather the inevitable storms that every couple faces [24]. When wives know that their husbands are committed to the marriage regardless of circumstances, they feel safe to be vulnerable, honest, and authentic in their relationships. This security creates an environment where both partners can grow, change, and develop without fear of abandonment or rejection.

The choice to love also involves ongoing decisions to invest time, energy, and resources in the marriage relationship [25]. This might mean choosing to spend time together rather than pursuing individual interests, choosing to communicate about important issues rather than avoiding difficult conversations, or choosing to work on marriage problems rather than ignoring them and hoping they will resolve themselves.

Understanding love as choice and commitment also helps husbands maintain their love during seasons when emotional feelings are weak or absent [26]. Every marriage experiences periods when romantic feelings diminish due to stress, illness, conflict, or simple familiarity. Husbands who understand that love is primarily a choice can continue to demonstrate love through actions and service even when they do not feel particularly loving emotions.

Three Walls of Christlike Love

"Greater love has no one than this, that someone lay down his life for his friends" (John 15:13). The foundation of marriage requires three distinct but interconnected types of love that work together to create the stability and strength necessary for lifelong partnership. These three types of love - sacrificial, sanctifying, and satisfying - correspond to different aspects of Christ's love for the church and provide the framework for husband leadership in marriage.

Sacrificial Love: Giving for Wife's Good

Sacrificial love involves the willingness to give up personal interests, preferences, and convenience for the wife's benefit [27]. This type of love reflects Christ's ultimate sacrifice on the cross and demonstrates the husband's commitment to his wife's welfare above his own. Sacrificial love provides the strength and stability that enables marriages to survive difficult seasons and challenging circumstances.

The practice of sacrificial love begins with small, daily choices that demonstrate the husband's commitment to his wife's well-being [28]. This might involve giving up personal leisure time to help with household responsibilities, choosing restaurants and entertainment that the wife enjoys rather than personal preferences, or adjusting work schedules to accommodate family needs and priorities. These small sacrifices create a pattern of selfless love that strengthens the marriage foundation.

Sacrificial love also involves making major life decisions based on what is best for the family rather than what is most advantageous for the husband personally [29]. This might mean turning down job promotions that would require excessive travel or relocation, choosing housing based on family needs rather than personal preferences, or adjusting career goals to accommodate the wife's calling and ministry opportunities. These major sacrifices demonstrate the depth of the husband's commitment to his family's welfare.

The willingness to sacrifice also extends to emotional and relational areas of marriage [30]. Husbands who love sacrificially are willing to admit when they are wrong, to apologize sincerely when they have hurt their wives, and to change behaviors that cause problems in the relationship. This emotional vulnerability requires a significant sacrifice of pride and self-protection, but it creates intimacy and trust that strengthen the marriage bond.

Sanctifying Love: Helping Wife Grow in Holiness

Sanctifying love involves the husband's commitment to his wife's spiritual growth and development [31]. Just as Christ works to sanctify the church and help believers become more like Him, husbands are called to encourage and support their wives' spiritual maturity. This type of love recognizes that marriage serves God's purposes of spiritual formation and character development.

The practice of sanctifying love begins with the husband's own spiritual growth and maturity [32]. Men cannot lead their wives spiritually if they are not growing in their own relationship with God. This means that husbands must prioritize their personal devotional lives, participate actively in church fellowship, and seek opportunities for spiritual learning and development. Their own spiritual vitality provides the foundation for effective spiritual leadership in marriage.

Sanctifying love also involves creating an environment in the home that encourages spiritual growth for all family members [33]. This might include establishing regular family devotions, encouraging participation in church activities, providing resources for spiritual learning, and modeling Christian character in daily interactions. When husbands create spiritually nurturing environments, they help their wives and children develop stronger relationships with God.

The husband's role in sanctifying love includes gentle correction and encouragement when the wife struggles with sin or spiritual immaturity [34]. This correction must be offered with humility, grace, and love rather than condemnation or superiority. The goal is restoration and growth rather than punishment or control. When husbands approach correction with the right heart and methods, it strengthens rather than weakens the marriage relationship.

Satisfying Love: Meeting Wife's Deepest Needs

Satisfying love involves the husband's commitment to understanding and meeting his wife's deepest emotional, physical, and spiritual needs [35]. This type of love recognizes that God has created women with specific needs and desires that can be met most completely within the context of marriage.

When husbands learn to provide this kind of satisfying love, they create marriages that are fulfilling and joyful for both partners.

Understanding the wife's deepest needs requires careful observation, thoughtful communication, and ongoing attention to her changing circumstances and development [36]. Different women have different primary needs, and these needs may change over time due to life circumstances, personal growth, and seasonal challenges. Husbands who want to provide satisfying love must become students of their wives and learn what makes them feel most loved and valued.

Many women have deep needs for emotional connection and intimate communication that can only be met through quality time and focused attention from their husbands [37]. This might involve regular date nights, daily conversation times, or simply being fully present and engaged during routine interactions. When husbands provide this kind of emotional connection, they meet needs that no other relationship can satisfy.

Physical affection and intimacy also represent important needs that husbands are uniquely positioned to meet [38]. This includes not only sexual intimacy but also non-sexual physical affection like holding hands, hugging, and cuddling. When husbands provide appropriate physical affection consistently, they help their wives feel loved, valued, and secure in the relationship.

Building Techniques for Leadership

"Whoever would be great among you must be your servant" (Matthew 20:26). Effective family leadership requires specific skills and techniques that enable husbands to guide their families with wisdom, grace, and strength. These leadership techniques are based on biblical principles rather than worldly

66

management strategies, and they focus on serving others rather than advancing personal interests.

Creating Security and Stability

One of the most important leadership techniques that husbands can develop is the ability to create security and stability for their families [39]. This security includes financial provision, emotional consistency, and spiritual leadership that enables family members to feel safe and confident about the future. When husbands provide this kind of security, they create environments where wives and children can flourish and develop their God-given potential.

Financial security involves more than simply earning an adequate income, though provision is certainly an important aspect of a husband's responsibility [40]. It also includes wise money management, careful budgeting, appropriate insurance coverage, and long-term financial planning that prepares for future needs and unexpected circumstances. When husbands handle financial responsibilities with wisdom and integrity, they provide peace of mind that enables their families to focus on other important priorities.

Emotional security requires consistency in mood, behavior, and responses that enables family members to predict how the husband will react in various situations [41]. This does not mean that husbands should never express emotions or always respond in identical ways, but it does mean that their responses should be appropriate, controlled, and consistent with their character and values. When family members know what to expect from their husbands, they feel safe to be vulnerable and authentic in their relationships.

Spiritual security involves consistent spiritual leadership that demonstrates the husband's commitment to God and his family's spiritual welfare [42]. This includes regular participation in church activities, consistent personal devotional practices, and ongoing efforts to grow in spiritual maturity and biblical knowledge. When wives and children observe this kind of spiritual consistency, they develop confidence in their husband and father's spiritual leadership.

Leading in Prayer and Scripture Study

Spiritual leadership represents one of the most important aspects of the husband's role in family construction [43]. This leadership involves more than simply attending church or saying grace before meals; it requires active engagement in prayer, Scripture study, and spiritual development that models authentic faith and encourages family members' spiritual growth.

Leading family prayer involves more than reciting formal prayers or asking God to bless family activities [44]. Effective prayer leadership includes teaching family members how to pray, creating opportunities for everyone to participate in prayer, and demonstrating through personal example that prayer is a vital part of daily life. When husbands lead prayer with sincerity and authenticity, they help their families develop meaningful relationships with God.

Scripture study leadership involves more than reading Bible verses during family devotions [45]. It includes helping family members understand how biblical principles apply to their daily lives, answering questions about faith and spiritual matters, and creating an environment where spiritual discussions feel natural and welcome. When husbands lead Scripture study effectively, they help their families develop biblical worldviews and spiritual maturity.

The husband's spiritual leadership also involves recognizing and encouraging the spiritual gifts and callings of other family members [46]. This might mean supporting the wife's ministry activities, encouraging children's spiritual development, or creating opportunities for family members to use their gifts in service to others. When husbands lead with this kind of encouragement and support, they help their families flourish spiritually.

Providing and Protecting with Purpose

The husband's role as provider and protector extends beyond meeting basic physical needs to include creating an environment where family members can pursue their God-given callings and develop their full potential [47]. This comprehensive approach to provision and protection requires wisdom, planning, and ongoing attention to each family member's changing needs and circumstances.

Financial provision involves more than earning an adequate income to meet current expenses [48]. It includes planning for future needs, preparing for unexpected circumstances, and making wise decisions about spending, saving, and investing that reflect biblical principles and family priorities. When husbands approach financial provision with wisdom and integrity, they create stability that enables their families to focus on spiritual and relational priorities.

Educational provision involves ensuring that children receive appropriate education that prepares them for their future callings while developing their character and spiritual maturity [49]. This might involve choosing schools that support family values, supplementing formal education with additional learning opportunities, or providing resources for developing special talents and interests. When husbands take active roles in their children's education, they demonstrate their commitment to their development and success.

Emotional provision involves creating an atmosphere in the home where family members feel loved, valued, and encouraged to pursue their dreams and callings [50]. This includes offering support during difficult times, celebrating achievements and milestones, and providing guidance and wisdom when family members face important decisions. When husbands provide this kind of emotional support, they help their families develop confidence and resilience.

Common Building Challenges

"Be kind to one another, tenderhearted, forgiving one another, as God in Christ forgave you" (Ephesians 4:32). Every husband who attempts to build according to God's blueprint will face challenges and difficulties that test his commitment, character, and leadership skills. Understanding these common challenges and learning biblical approaches to handling them is essential for successful family construction.

Balancing Authority with Humility

One of the most difficult challenges that husbands face involves learning to exercise appropriate authority while maintaining humility and servant-heartedness [51]. Many men struggle with either being too passive and failing to provide necessary leadership or being too controlling and dominating their families in unhealthy ways. Biblical leadership requires finding the balance between these extremes.

The authority that God gives to husbands is not absolute or arbitrary but is delegated authority that must be exercised according to biblical principles and for biblical purposes [52]. This authority exists to serve the family's welfare rather than the husband's personal interests. When husbands understand this principle, they approach leadership with humility and responsibility rather than pride and selfishness.

Exercising authority with humility requires the willingness to admit mistakes, seek forgiveness when necessary, and change course when better approaches become apparent [53]. This vulnerability does not undermine the husband's authority but actually strengthens it by demonstrating integrity and genuine concern for the family's welfare. When husbands lead with this kind of humility, they earn respect and cooperation rather than demanding it.

The balance between authority and humility also requires wisdom in knowing when to make unilateral decisions and when to seek input and consensus from family members [54]. Some decisions require immediate action and clear leadership, while others benefit from discussion and collaborative decision-making. Husbands who develop this wisdom create families that function effectively while maintaining healthy relationships.

Leading When You Don't Feel Ready

Many husbands struggle with feelings of inadequacy and uncertainty about their ability to provide effective family leadership [55]. These feelings are normal and often indicate a healthy recognition of the responsibility and importance of family leadership. The key is learning to lead faithfully despite these feelings rather than waiting until confidence and competence are fully developed.

Leading when feeling unprepared requires dependence on God's wisdom and strength rather than personal abilities and experience [56]. This dependence involves regular prayer for guidance, consistent study of biblical principles, and willingness to seek counsel from mature believers who can provide insight and encouragement. When husbands acknowledge their need for divine assistance, they often discover that God provides the wisdom and strength necessary for effective leadership.

The process of learning to lead also requires patience with the learning curve and willingness to make mistakes while growing in competence [57]. No husband begins marriage with all the skills and knowledge necessary for effective family leadership. These abilities develop over time through experience, study, and spiritual growth. Husbands who embrace this learning process rather than being paralyzed by their limitations often become effective leaders more quickly than those who wait for perfect preparation.

Seeking mentorship from older, more experienced men provides valuable resources for husbands who feel unprepared for leadership responsibilities [58]. These mentoring relationships can provide practical advice, emotional encouragement, and accountability that accelerate the leadership development process. When younger husbands humble themselves to learn from others, they often avoid common mistakes and develop more effective leadership skills.

Growing in Love When Feelings Change

Every marriage experiences seasons when romantic feelings diminish or disappear due to stress, conflict, illness, or simple familiarity [59]. During these seasons, husbands must learn to demonstrate love through actions and choices rather than depending on emotional feelings to motivate their behavior. This ability to love despite changing feelings is essential for building marriages that last throughout life's various seasons.

Understanding that love is primarily a choice and commitment rather than an emotion helps husbands maintain their loving behavior even when feelings are weak [60]. The commitment to love involves deliberate decisions to serve, encourage, and care for the wife regardless of her current emotional state. These choices often result in renewed emotional feelings, but they are valuable even when emotions remain unchanged.

Growing in love during difficult seasons often requires focusing on the wife's positive qualities and contributions rather than dwelling on sources of frustration or disappointment [61]. This might involve keeping a gratitude journal, regularly expressing appreciation for the wife's efforts, or simply choosing to notice and acknowledge her positive actions and attitudes. When husbands focus on their wives' strengths, they often rediscover reasons for emotional connection.

The practice of serving the wife during seasons of weak emotional feelings often helps restore and strengthen the emotional bond [62]. Acts of service demonstrate love in tangible ways that often touch the wife's heart and create positive responses that encourage renewed emotional connection. When husbands serve consistently despite their feelings, they often discover that their emotions follow their actions.

Overcoming Selfishness in Marriage

Selfishness represents one of the greatest threats to successful marriage construction because it undermines the sacrificial love that serves as the foundation for biblical marriage [63]. Every husband struggles with selfish tendencies that must be recognized, confessed, and overcome through spiritual growth and deliberate effort. Learning to overcome selfishness is essential for building marriages that reflect Christ's love for the church.

Recognizing selfishness requires honest self-examination and willingness to acknowledge when personal interests are taking priority over the wife's welfare [64]. This might involve examining motivations for decisions, evaluating how time and energy are invested, or simply asking whether current behaviors demonstrate love for the wife or focus on personal interests. When husbands develop this kind of self-awareness, they can address selfish patterns before they damage the marriage relationship.

Confessing selfishness to God and to the wife when appropriate helps break the power of selfish patterns and creates opportunities for growth and change [65]. This confession should be specific and sincere rather than general or superficial. When husbands acknowledge their selfishness honestly, they often experience God's grace and their wives' forgiveness in ways that motivate continued growth and change.

Developing habits of service and sacrifice helps overcome selfish tendencies by creating new patterns of behavior that focus on the wife's welfare [66]. These habits might include daily acts of service, regular expressions of appreciation, or simply choosing to put the wife's interests first in routine decisions. When these serving behaviors become habitual, they help transform the husband's heart and motivations.

Seeking accountability from other mature believers provides external support for overcoming selfish patterns [67]. This accountability might involve regular meetings with a mentor, participation in a men's group, or simply asking trusted friends to pray for and encourage growth in this area. When husbands humble themselves to seek help from others, they often experience breakthroughs in areas where they have struggled alone.

The ultimate motivation for overcoming selfishness comes from understanding how much Christ has sacrificed for the church and for individual believers [68]. When husbands regularly contemplate the cost of their salvation and the depth of God's love for them, they become increasingly motivated to demonstrate similar love toward their wives. This spiritual motivation provides the strength necessary to overcome selfish tendencies and build marriages that honor God.

As we conclude our examination of the husband's role as foundation layer in family construction, we see that this responsibility requires both character development and skill acquisition [69]. The foundation of sacrificial love that husbands are called to lay provides the stability and strength necessary for families to flourish according to God's design. When husbands embrace their calling to lead through love, they create environments where wives and children can develop their full potential while bringing glory to God.

The three walls of Christlike love - sacrificial, sanctifying, and satisfying - work together to create foundations strong enough to support families through all of life's seasons and challenges [70]. The building techniques of creating security, providing spiritual leadership, and representing the family with honor enable husbands to fulfill their calling effectively while growing in their own spiritual maturity and character development.

The common challenges that every husband faces - balancing authority with humility, leading when feeling unprepared, maintaining love when feelings change, and overcoming selfishness - provide opportunities for growth and development that strengthen both the husband's character and the marriage relationship [71]. When husbands approach these challenges with faith, humility, and dependence on God's grace, they often discover that their greatest struggles become their greatest strengths.

The foundation that husbands lay through loving leadership creates the stability necessary for entire families to flourish according to God's design [72]. When men understand their calling to lead through sacrificial love rather than demanding service, they discover that true strength comes through serving others rather than controlling them. This servant leadership reflects Christ's own example and creates families that demonstrate God's character to a watching world.

The journey of learning to love like Christ requires ongoing spiritual growth and dependence on God's grace [73]. No husband begins marriage with perfect love or complete understanding of how to lead effectively. These abilities develop over time through experience, study, prayer, and the sanctifying work of the Holy Spirit. Husbands who embrace this growth process with humility and determination often become the kind of leaders their families need.

As we move forward in our exploration of *Family by the Book: How to Build the Family God Intended*, we will discover how wives can fulfill their calling as support structures that enable the husband's foundation to support the entire family [74]. The foundation has been carefully laid with love, sacrifice, and servant leadership. Now we are ready to examine how the support structure of biblical wifely response creates the framework for family flourishing.

The construction project continues, and each element builds upon what has come before [75]. God's blueprint provides clear instructions for every aspect of family building, and when we follow His design with faith and obedience, we create families that bring glory to His name and blessing to future generations. The husband's foundation of love provides the strength; now we will see how the wife's support creates the structure that enables the family to rise according to divine design [76].

Chapter 4
The Wife's Support Structure

Responding with Respect

In any well-constructed building, the support structure works in harmony with the foundation to create stability and strength. While the foundation bears the primary load, the support beams, walls, and framework distribute that weight and provide the internal strength that enables the building to withstand external pressures. As we continue our exploration of Family by the Book: How to Build the Family God Intended, we discover that the wife's role as support structure is not secondary in importance but essential in function, creating the internal strength that enables the entire family to flourish according to God's design.

The apostle Paul provides the blueprint for this support structure when he writes, *"However, let each one of you love his wife as himself, and let the wife see that she respects her husband"* (Ephesians 5:33). This verse reveals that while the husband's primary building material is love, the wife's primary contribution is respect. These two elements work together to create the relational framework that supports all other aspects of family life [1]. When both are present and properly applied, they create a structure strong enough to support the weight of daily challenges while flexible enough to adapt to changing circumstances.

Understanding the wife's role as a support structure requires us to move beyond cultural stereotypes and examine God's original design for marriage and family. The Hebrew word *"ezer,"* translated as "helper" in Genesis 2:18, appears throughout Scripture to describe God Himself as our helper, particularly in times of trouble and need [2]. This reveals that the wife's supportive role is not one of inferiority but of essential partnership, providing strength and assistance that enables the entire family structure to function as God intended.

The beauty of God's design becomes evident when we observe how respect and love work together in marriage relationships. When a wife demonstrates genuine respect for her husband's leadership, she creates an environment where his love can flourish and grow [3]. When a husband responds to that respect with increased love and care, he creates conditions where respect feels natural and joyful rather than forced or artificial. This positive cycle strengthens the entire family structure and creates a model of healthy relationships for children to observe and emulate.

The wife's support structure role extends far beyond the marriage relationship to encompass every aspect of family life. Her influence shapes the emotional climate of the home, the spiritual atmosphere that pervades daily activities, and the relational patterns that children learn and carry into their own future families [4]. When she understands and embraces her role according to biblical principles, she becomes a powerful force for building a family that reflects God's character and advances His kingdom purposes.

Understanding Your Building Role

"The Lord God said, 'It is not good that the man should be alone; I will make him a helper fit for him'" (Genesis 2:18). This foundational verse reveals God's heart for marriage and family construction. The declaration that it was "not good" for man to be alone represents the only negative assessment in the creation account, highlighting the essential nature of the partnership that God intended to establish through marriage [5]. The wife's role as "helper" addresses this fundamental incompleteness, providing what is necessary to create a complete and functional family unit.

Partnership as Strength, Not Weakness

The modern world often misunderstands the concept of partnership in marriage, viewing the wife's supportive role as evidence of weakness or inferiority. However, biblical partnership represents a position of strength that requires wisdom, courage, and spiritual maturity [6]. The wife who understands her role as a support structure recognizes that she possesses unique gifts and perspectives that are essential for successful family construction. Her partnership is not passive compliance but active participation in building something beautiful and lasting.

This partnership strength becomes evident in the way godly wives contribute to family decision-making processes. Rather than simply agreeing with every suggestion or remaining silent during important discussions, the wise wife offers insights, raises important questions, and provides perspectives that her husband might otherwise miss [7]. Her input strengthens the final decisions because it represents additional wisdom and consideration that improves the overall quality of family choices.

The strength of biblical partnership also appears in the wife's ability to provide emotional and spiritual support during challenging times. When families face financial pressures, health crises, or relational difficulties, the wife's supportive presence often provides the stability and encouragement that enables everyone to persevere [8]. Her strength does not compete with her husband's leadership but complements it, creating a foundation of mutual support that can bear the weight of whatever challenges arise.

Understanding partnership as strength also means recognizing that the wife's contributions are valuable and necessary, rather than optional or supplementary. God designed marriage as a partnership because He knew that the challenges of family life would require the combined strengths, gifts, and perspectives of both husband and wife [9]. When wives embrace this understanding, they approach their role with confidence and purpose rather than reluctance or resentment.

The Voluntary Nature of Christian Building

One of the most important aspects of the wife's support structure role is its voluntary nature. Biblical submission is not forced compliance but willing cooperation based on trust in God's design and love for family members [10]. When wives choose to embrace their supportive role out of love for God and commitment to His blueprint for family life, their actions flow from internal motivation rather than external pressure.

This voluntary aspect transforms the entire dynamic of marriage relationships. Instead of viewing submission as something imposed upon her, the Christian wife sees it as a gift she chooses to give to her husband and family [11]. This perspective changes her attitude, her approach, and her experience of marriage in ways that benefit everyone involved. When submission is voluntary, it becomes an expression of love rather than evidence of oppression.

The voluntary nature of Christian building also means that wives retain their dignity, personality, and individual gifts while choosing to work within God's design for marriage [12]. Biblical submission does not require wives to become passive, silent, or invisible, but rather to channel their strengths and abilities in ways that support and strengthen the family structure. This approach allows for individual expression while maintaining relational harmony.

Understanding the voluntary nature of her role also helps the wife navigate situations where submission becomes difficult or challenging. When she remembers that her choice to support her husband's leadership flows from her commitment to God rather than from her husband's perfection, she can maintain her supportive stance even when disagreements arise [13].

This perspective provides stability and consistency that strengthens the entire family structure.

Building "As to the Lord" - The Spiritual Dimension

The apostle Paul's instruction for wives to submit to their husbands *"as to the Lord"* (Ephesians 5:22) reveals the spiritual dimension that elevates the wife's role from a mere human relationship to divine service [14]. When wives understand that their respect and support for their husbands represents an act of worship and obedience to God, their motivation transcends personal feelings and circumstances.

This spiritual dimension provides strength and purpose during difficult seasons of marriage. When husbands make poor decisions, demonstrate immaturity, or fail to lead effectively, wives who understand the spiritual nature of their role can continue to show respect and support because their ultimate allegiance is to God rather than to their husband's performance [15]. This perspective enables them to maintain their supportive stance while trusting God to work in their husband's heart and life.

The spiritual dimension also transforms daily interactions within the family. Simple acts of service, words of encouragement, and demonstrations of respect become offerings to God when they flow from a heart committed to building *Family by the Book: How to Build the Family God Intended* [16]. This understanding elevates routine activities and gives eternal significance to temporal actions.

Understanding the spiritual dimension of her role also helps the wife maintain a proper perspective during seasons of blessing and success. When families experience prosperity, achievement, or recognition, the wife who sees her role in spiritual terms can celebrate these blessings while maintaining humility and dependence on God [17]. She recognizes that her husband's success reflects God's blessing rather than merely human effort, and she continues to provide the support and encouragement that enabled that success.

Helper as Co-Builder and Partner

The Hebrew word *"ezer,"* translated as "helper" in Genesis 2:18, carries connotations of strength, support, and essential assistance that go far beyond our modern understanding of helping [18]. This same word describes God's relationship to His people throughout the Old Testament, revealing that the helper role involves providing what is necessary for success and survival. When applied to the wife's role in marriage, it suggests that she provides essential elements that enable the family to function and flourish.

This co-builder understanding transforms how wives view their daily contributions to family life. Instead of seeing household management, child care, and emotional support as mundane tasks, they recognize these activities as essential construction work that builds the family structure [19]. Every meal prepared with love, every conflict resolved with wisdom, and every child nurtured with care represent important building activity that strengthens the entire family foundation.

The co-builder role also encompasses the wife's participation in major family decisions and long-term planning. While the husband bears ultimate responsibility for family leadership, the wise husband actively seeks his wife's input and perspective before making important choices [20]. The wife who understands her co-builder role offers her insights freely while respecting her husband's authority to make final decisions.

Understanding herself as a co-builder also helps the wife maintain a proper perspective about her value and importance within the family structure. She recognizes that her contributions are essential rather than optional, valuable rather than merely helpful, and necessary rather than supplementary [21]. This understanding provides confidence and purpose that enables her to embrace her role with joy and enthusiasm rather than reluctance or resentment.

The Wife as Co-Builder

"An excellent wife is the crown of her husband, but she who brings shame is like rottenness in his bones" (Proverbs 12:4). This vivid imagery reveals the profound impact that wives have on their husbands and families. A crown represents honor, beauty, and dignity - qualities that an excellent wife brings to her marriage relationship [22]. When wives understand and embrace their role as co-builders, they become sources of strength and encouragement that enable their husbands to lead more effectively and their families to flourish more completely.

The Meaning of "Helper" in Construction

In construction terminology, helpers are not unskilled laborers who perform menial tasks, but trained workers who provide essential support that enables the primary craftsman to complete complex projects [23]. The construction helper anticipates needs, provides necessary tools and materials, and offers assistance that improves both the quality and efficiency of the work. This understanding provides a helpful framework for understanding the wife's role in family construction.

The wife, as a construction helper, brings unique skills and perspectives that complement her husband's abilities and compensate for his limitations. Where he might focus on long-term goals and overall direction, she might attend to immediate needs and relational dynamics [24]. Where he might approach problems with logic and analysis, she might offer intuitive insights and emotional wisdom. These differences are not weaknesses to be overcome but strengths to be celebrated and utilized.

The construction helper also serves as a quality control specialist, identifying potential problems before they become serious issues and suggesting improvements that enhance the final product [25]. In family construction, the wife often serves this function by recognizing relational tensions, identifying areas where children need additional attention, and suggesting adjustments to family routines and practices that improve overall family health.

Understanding the helper role in construction terms also reveals the importance of communication and coordination between the primary builder and the helper. Successful construction projects require constant communication about goals, methods, and progress [26]. Similarly, successful family construction requires ongoing communication between husband and wife about family direction, individual needs, and necessary adjustments to family practices and priorities.

Partnership: Complementarity, Not Competition

God designed marriage as a partnership of complementary strengths rather than competing interests. The wife's role as co-builder involves understanding how her unique gifts and abilities complement her husband's strengths and compensate for his weaknesses [27]. This complementarity creates a more complete and effective family leadership team than either spouse could provide individually.

Complementarity appears in numerous aspects of family life. In financial management, one spouse might excel at budgeting and saving while the other demonstrates strength in earning and investing [28]. In child-rearing, one parent might provide structure and discipline while the other offers nurture and emotional support. In social relationships, one spouse might excel at hospitality and relationship building while the other provides wisdom and discernment about appropriate boundaries.

85

The key to successful complementarity is recognizing and celebrating these differences rather than viewing them as sources of conflict or competition. When wives understand that their different approaches and perspectives strengthen rather than threaten the family structure, they can offer their contributions with confidence and receive their husbands' different contributions with appreciation [29]. This mutual appreciation creates an atmosphere of teamwork rather than competition.

Complementarity also requires ongoing communication and coordination to ensure that different approaches work together harmoniously rather than at cross purposes. Spouses must regularly discuss their different perspectives, negotiate their different preferences, and coordinate their different strengths to create a unified family direction [30]. This process requires humility, flexibility, and commitment to family unity above personal preferences.

Supporting Husband's God-Given Calling

Every husband has received unique gifts, abilities, and calling from God that shape his approach to family leadership and his contribution to God's kingdom [31]. The wife's role as co-builder includes understanding, supporting, and encouraging her husband's pursuit of his God-given calling, even when that calling requires sacrifice or adjustment from other family members.

Supporting her husband's calling might involve practical assistance such as managing household responsibilities that free him to pursue ministry opportunities, educational goals, or career advancement [32]. It might involve emotional support during challenging seasons when his calling requires perseverance through difficulties or disappointments. It might involve spiritual support through prayer, encouragement, and faith-building conversations that strengthen his confidence in God's leading.

Understanding her husband's calling also helps the wife maintain proper perspective during seasons when family resources must be directed toward supporting his goals and opportunities. When wives recognize that supporting their husband's calling serves God's purposes and benefits the entire family in the long term, they can embrace temporary sacrifices with grace and enthusiasm [33]. This perspective transforms potential sources of resentment into opportunities for ministry and service.

The wife's support for her husband's calling also extends to helping him recognize and develop his gifts and abilities. Through her close observation and intimate knowledge of his character and capabilities, she often sees potential that he might miss or underestimate [34]. Her encouragement and affirmation can provide the confidence he needs to step into new opportunities and embrace greater responsibilities.

Contributing Unique Gifts and Perspectives

While the wife's role includes supporting her husband's leadership and calling, it also encompasses contributing her own unique gifts and perspectives to family construction. God has given every woman specific abilities, insights, and strengths that are meant to be utilized in building strong families [35]. The wise wife identifies these gifts and finds appropriate ways to contribute them to family life.

These unique contributions might include creative abilities that enhance family celebrations and traditions, organizational skills that improve household efficiency, relational gifts that strengthen family bonds and community connections, or spiritual insights that deepen family faith and devotion [36]. The key is recognizing these gifts as valuable contributions to family construction rather than personal hobbies or individual interests.

Contributing unique gifts also requires wisdom in timing and presentation. The wife who understands her supportive role will offer her contributions in ways that strengthen rather than undermine her husband's leadership [37]. This might involve presenting ideas as suggestions rather than demands, offering assistance rather than taking control, or providing input privately rather than publicly challenging decisions.

The goal of contributing unique gifts is to enhance family effectiveness and create a more complete reflection of God's character through the combined strengths of both spouses. When wives embrace this understanding, they can contribute their gifts with confidence while maintaining the relational harmony that characterizes godly families [38].

Building Techniques for Partnership

"She opens her mouth with wisdom, and the teaching of kindness is on her tongue" (Proverbs 31:26). The Proverbs 31 woman provides a comprehensive model of how wives can contribute to family construction through wise words and kind actions. Her example reveals that effective partnership in marriage requires both wisdom to know what to say and kindness to know how to say it [39]. These qualities work together to create an atmosphere where family members feel valued, encouraged, and motivated to grow in their relationships with God and each other.

Honoring Husband in Public and Private

The foundation of the wife's partnership-building technique involves consistently honoring her husband in both public and private settings. This honor goes beyond mere politeness or social convention to reflect a deep understanding of God's design for marriage and a commitment to building Family by the Book: How to Build the Family God Intended [40]. When wives consistently demonstrate honor toward their husbands, they create an atmosphere of respect that strengthens the entire family structure.

Public honor involves speaking positively about her husband to others, supporting his decisions even when she might have handled situations differently, and presenting a united front in parenting and family matters [41]. This does not mean that wives must pretend their husbands are perfect or hide legitimate concerns, but rather that they choose to focus on positive qualities and address concerns privately rather than publicly undermining his authority or reputation.

Private honor often proves more challenging because it requires maintaining respectful attitudes and behaviors even when no one else is watching. This involves treating her husband with courtesy and consideration during everyday interactions, expressing appreciation for his efforts and contributions, and avoiding criticism or complaints that tear down rather than build up [42]. Private honor creates the foundation of trust and respect that enables public honor to feel genuine rather than artificial.

The practice of honor also extends to how wives speak about their husbands to their children. When mothers consistently speak respectfully about fathers, they teach children to honor authority and respect leadership [43]. When they criticize or belittle fathers in front of children, they undermine the family structure and create confusion about appropriate responses to authority. The wife's words about her husband significantly influence how children view both parents and authority in general.

Honoring her husband also involves recognizing and acknowledging his efforts to lead and provide for the family, even when those efforts fall short of expectations or desires. The wife who focuses on her husband's intentions and efforts rather than only on results creates an environment where he feels encouraged to continue growing and improving [44]. This encouragement often proves more effective than criticism in motivating positive change and growth.

Supporting Leadership While Contributing Skills

One of the most delicate aspects of the wife's partnership role involves learning to support her husband's leadership while contributing her own skills and perspectives to family decisions and activities. This balance requires wisdom, humility, and clear communication to ensure that her contributions strengthen rather than undermine his leadership position [45]. When wives master this balance, they create partnerships that utilize the full range of family resources while maintaining proper authority structures.

Supporting leadership while contributing skills often involves offering input and suggestions in private settings where husbands can consider them carefully without feeling challenged or undermined publicly. The wise wife learns to present her ideas as additional information for consideration rather than as corrections to poor decisions [46]. This approach allows husbands to incorporate their wives' insights while maintaining their leadership role and authority.

This balance also requires wives to understand the difference between offering counsel and making demands. Counsel involves sharing perspectives, raising questions, and providing information that helps husbands make better decisions [47]. Demands involve insisting on specific outcomes or threatening consequences if preferences are not followed. The wife who offers counsel while respecting her husband's authority to make final decisions creates an environment where her input is valued and sought.

The timing of input and suggestions also affects how well wives can support leadership while contributing skills. Wise wives learn to recognize when their husbands are open to discussion and when they need space to process decisions independently [48]. They understand that offering input at the wrong time can create resistance even when the suggestions themselves are valuable and appropriate.

Supporting leadership while contributing skills also involves recognizing areas where wives possess greater expertise or ability than their husbands and finding appropriate ways to utilize those strengths for family benefit. This might involve taking primary responsibility for areas where she excels while keeping her husband informed and involved in major decisions [49]. The key is utilizing her strengths in ways that complement rather than compete with his leadership role.

Building Him Up Through Words and Actions

The power of words to build up or tear down cannot be overstated in marriage relationships. The wife who understands her role in family construction recognizes that her words can either strengthen her husband's confidence and motivation or undermine his sense of competence and worth [50]. When wives consistently choose words that build up rather than tear down, they create an atmosphere where their husbands feel encouraged to grow and improve rather than defensive and discouraged.

Building up through words involves more than avoiding criticism or negative comments. It requires actively looking for opportunities to affirm positive qualities, acknowledge efforts and improvements, and express appreciation for contributions both large and small [51]. The wife who makes a habit of noticing and commenting on her husband's positive actions creates an environment where those actions are more likely to continue and multiply.

The timing and specificity of affirming words significantly affect their impact. General statements like "you're a good husband" carry less weight than specific observations like "I really appreciated how patiently you helped Johnny with his homework tonight" [52]. Specific affirmations demonstrate that the wife is paying attention to her husband's efforts and genuinely appreciates his contributions to family life.

Building up through actions involves demonstrating respect and appreciation through behavior as well as words. This might include preparing his favorite meals, maintaining an attractive appearance, creating a peaceful home environment, or finding other ways to show that she values him and their relationship [53]. These actions communicate love and respect in ways that words alone cannot accomplish.

The wife's actions also build up her husband when she demonstrates confidence in his abilities and decisions. When she trusts his judgment, follows his leadership, and supports his choices, she communicates that she believes in his competence and character [54]. This confidence often becomes self-fulfilling as husbands rise to meet the expectations that their wives' trust and respect create.

Creating an Atmosphere of Respect and Encouragement

The overall atmosphere of the home significantly influences every family member's emotional and spiritual health. The wife's role in creating this atmosphere cannot be overstated, as her attitudes, words, and actions set the tone for family interactions and relationships [55]. When wives intentionally work to create atmospheres of respect and encouragement, they provide the emotional climate where family members can flourish and grow.

Creating an atmosphere of respect begins with the wife's own attitude toward her husband and family. When she approaches family relationships with gratitude, appreciation, and positive expectations, those attitudes influence how other family members view each other and their relationships [56]. When she focuses on problems, complaints, and negative aspects of family life, those attitudes also spread throughout the family system.

The atmosphere of respect also depends on how conflicts and disagreements are handled within the family. When wives model respectful communication during disagreements, express their concerns without attacking character, and work toward solutions rather than dwelling on problems, they teach family members healthy ways to handle conflict [57]. This modeling often proves more influential than formal instruction in shaping how family members treat each other.

Encouragement involves recognizing and celebrating progress rather than focusing only on problems and failures. The wife who creates an encouraging atmosphere notices when family members make efforts to improve, acknowledges small steps toward larger goals, and expresses confidence in their ability to continue growing [58]. This encouragement creates motivation for continued growth and improvement.

The physical environment of the home also contributes to the overall atmosphere of respect and encouragement. When wives create homes that are clean, organized, and welcoming, they demonstrate respect for family members and provide environments where positive interactions are more likely to occur [59]. The effort invested in creating pleasant physical environments communicates that family relationships are valuable and worth the investment of time and energy.

Navigating Building Challenges

"A soft answer turns away wrath, but a harsh word stirs up anger" (Proverbs 15:1). Every marriage and family faces challenges that test the strength of relationships and the effectiveness of family construction techniques. The wife's response to these challenges significantly influences whether they become opportunities for growth and strengthening or sources of division and weakness [60]. When wives learn to navigate challenges with wisdom and grace, they contribute to building families that can withstand difficulties and emerge stronger from trials.

When Husbands Make Poor Decisions

One of the most difficult challenges that wives face involves responding appropriately when their husbands make decisions that seem unwise or harmful to family interests. The natural human response often involves criticism, resistance, or attempts to take control of the situation [61]. However, the wife who is committed to building *Family by the Book: How to Build the Family God Intended* must find ways to respond that honor God's design while protecting family welfare.

The first step in handling poor decisions involves careful evaluation to determine whether the decision is actually harmful or simply different from what the wife would have chosen. Many conflicts arise not from genuinely poor decisions but from different preferences, priorities, or approaches [62]. The wise wife learns to distinguish between decisions that require intervention and those that simply require adjustment and support.

When decisions are genuinely harmful or unwise, the wife's response should begin with a private conversation that expresses concerns respectfully and offers alternative perspectives for consideration. This conversation should focus on the potential consequences of the decision rather than attacking the husband's character or competence [63]. The goal is to provide additional information that might lead to reconsideration rather than to force a change through pressure or manipulation.

If private conversation does not result in reconsideration, the wife may need to seek counsel from trusted advisors such as pastors, mentors, or mature Christian friends who can provide an objective perspective and guidance [64]. This counsel should focus on how to respond appropriately rather than on how to change the husband's mind or override his authority.

In extreme situations where decisions threaten serious harm to family members, wives may need to take protective action while continuing to honor their husband's position as family leader. This might involve seeking help from church leaders, professional counselors, or appropriate authorities [65]. The key is taking necessary protective action while maintaining as much respect for the marriage relationship as possible under the circumstances.

Maintaining Respect During Conflicts

Conflict is inevitable in any close relationship, and marriage is no exception. The way conflicts are handled often determines whether they strengthen or weaken the relationship over time [66]. The wife who learns to maintain respect during conflicts contributes significantly to building a marriage that can handle disagreements without damaging the fundamental relationship.

Maintaining respect during conflict begins with controlling emotional responses and choosing words carefully. When wives respond to conflict with anger, sarcasm, or personal attacks, they escalate tensions and make resolution more difficult [67]. When they respond with calm voices, respectful language, and focus on issues rather than personalities, they create environments where productive discussion can occur.

The timing of conflict discussions also affects their outcome significantly. Wise wives learn to recognize when emotions are too high for productive conversation and suggest postponing discussions until both parties can approach them more calmly [68]. This delay often allows for better perspective and more thoughtful responses that lead to better outcomes.

Maintaining respect during conflict also involves listening carefully to understand the husband's perspective rather than simply waiting for opportunities to present counterarguments. When wives demonstrate genuine interest in understanding their husbands' viewpoints, they often discover underlying concerns or motivations that help explain seemingly unreasonable positions [69]. This understanding can lead to creative solutions that address both parties' concerns.

The goal of conflict resolution should be mutual understanding and improved relationships rather than winning arguments or proving points. When wives approach conflicts with the goal of strengthening their marriage rather than getting their way, they often find solutions that satisfy both parties and improve their overall relationship [70]. This approach requires humility and a willingness to compromise, but it produces much better long-term results than adversarial approaches.

The Limits of Partnership and Submission

While biblical submission is an important aspect of the wife's role in family construction, it has limits that must be understood and respected. Submission does not require wives to participate in sinful activities, enable destructive behaviors, or remain silent about serious problems that threaten family welfare [71]. Understanding these limits helps wives respond appropriately to difficult situations while maintaining their commitment to biblical principles.

The primary limit of submission involves situations where husbands ask wives to participate in activities that clearly violate biblical principles or moral standards. In such situations, wives must choose to obey God rather than their husbands, while doing so in ways that maintain as much respect for the marriage relationship as possible [72]. This might involve explaining their concerns, suggesting alternatives, or simply refusing to participate while continuing to show respect in other areas.

Another important limit involves situations where submission would enable destructive behaviors such as addiction, abuse, or financial irresponsibility. In these situations, wives may need to refuse to enable the destructive behavior while continuing to show love and respect for their husbands as a person [73]. This might involve setting boundaries, seeking help, or taking protective action while maintaining hope for restoration and healing.

The limits of submission also apply to situations where wives possess expertise or knowledge that their husbands lack. While wives should offer their expertise respectfully and supportively, they should not remain silent when their knowledge could prevent serious mistakes or harm [74]. The key is offering expertise in ways that support rather than undermine their husband's leadership role.

Understanding the limits of submission helps wives maintain their integrity and protect their families while continuing to honor God's design for marriage. These limits are not excuses for rebellion or selfishness but protective boundaries that ensure submission serves its intended purpose of building strong families rather than enabling destructive patterns [75].

Seeking Help When Needed

The wife's role in family construction includes recognizing when problems exceed her ability to handle them alone and seeking appropriate help from qualified sources. This wisdom to seek help when needed often prevents small problems from becoming major crises and provides resources for building stronger families [76]. The key is knowing when help is needed, where to find it, and how to utilize it effectively.

Professional counseling may be needed when family problems involve complex psychological, emotional, or relational issues that require specialized expertise. This might include marriage counseling when communication patterns become destructive, family counseling when children develop serious behavioral problems, or individual counseling when family members struggle with depression, anxiety, or other mental health issues [77]. Seeking professional help demonstrates wisdom and commitment to family health rather than failure or weakness.

Pastoral counseling provides another valuable resource for families facing spiritual or moral challenges. Pastors can offer a biblical perspective on family problems, provide spiritual guidance for difficult decisions, and help families apply biblical principles to specific situations [78]. Many family problems have spiritual dimensions that require spiritual solutions, making pastoral counsel an important resource for Christian families.

Mentoring relationships with older, more experienced couples can provide ongoing guidance and support for building strong marriages and families. These relationships offer opportunities to learn from others' experiences, receive encouragement during difficult times, and gain perspective on normal family challenges [79]. The wisdom gained from mentoring relationships often prevents problems and provides practical solutions for common family issues.

Support groups for specific challenges, such as financial difficulties, parenting struggles, or marriage problems, can provide both practical help and emotional encouragement. These groups offer opportunities to learn from others facing similar challenges and to receive support from people who understand the specific difficulties involved [80]. The combination of practical help and emotional support often proves more effective than either element alone.

The key to seeking help effectively is approaching it with humility, openness, and commitment to implementing suggested changes. Help is most effective when families are willing to acknowledge their need for assistance, listen carefully to advice and counsel, and make necessary changes to improve their situation [81]. This approach transforms help-seeking from a sign of weakness into a tool for building stronger, healthier families that reflect God's design and bring glory to His name.

Chapter 5
Children as Willing Helpers

Learning to Build "In the Lord"

Having explored the husband's foundational leadership and the wife's essential support structure, we now turn our attention to the third crucial element in building a *Family by the Book: How to Build the Family God Intended* - the children who serve as willing helpers in the construction process. Just as any major building project requires not only skilled craftsmen and support beams but also eager apprentices who learn while they contribute, the family construction project depends on children who embrace their role as junior builders under parental guidance and authority.

In every construction project, willing helpers make the difference between a project that drags on indefinitely and one that progresses smoothly toward completion. These helpers may not possess the skills of master craftsmen, but their eagerness to learn, willingness to follow direction, and commitment to the shared vision enable the entire team to accomplish far more than any individual could achieve alone. When the wife provides her support structure as we discussed in the previous chapter, she creates an environment where children can flourish as willing helpers, learning essential building skills while contributing their unique energy and perspective to the overall family construction effort.

The apostle Paul provides the blueprint for this helper relationship when he writes, *"Children, obey your parents in the Lord, for this is right"* (Ephesians 6:1). This instruction reveals that children's participation in family building is not merely about following rules or maintaining order, but about learning to work within God's design for relationships and authority [1]. When children understand their role as willing helpers rather than reluctant participants, they discover that obedience becomes a pathway to growth, maturity, and meaningful contribution to family life.

The phrase "in the Lord" transforms the entire dynamic of parent-child relationships. It elevates simple obedience from mere behavioral compliance to spiritual formation, connecting earthly relationships to heavenly realities [2]. When children learn to obey their parents "in the Lord," they are simultaneously learning to submit to God's authority and participate in His larger purposes for their lives and families. This spiritual dimension gives meaning and purpose to what might otherwise seem like arbitrary restrictions or burdensome expectations.

Understanding children as willing helpers also transforms how parents approach their role in family construction. Rather than viewing children as obstacles to overcome or problems to solve, parents who embrace this perspective see their children as junior partners in the building process [3]. This approach requires patience, wisdom, and intentional training, but it produces children who feel valued, purposeful, and eager to contribute to family success rather than resentful of family expectations. When families commit to building a Family by the Book: How to Build the Family God Intended, they recognize that every family member has a vital role to play in the construction process.

The beauty of God's design becomes evident when we observe how children's natural characteristics align with their role as willing helpers. Their energy, enthusiasm, and desire to please create ideal conditions for learning and growth when properly channeled [4]. Their questions, observations, and fresh perspectives often provide insights that more experienced builders might miss. When families learn to harness these natural qualities while providing appropriate guidance and structure, they create environments where everyone can flourish and contribute meaningfully to building a Family by the Book: How to Build the Family God Intended.

The Fifth Commandment in Building

"Honor your father and mother (this is the first commandment with a promise), that it may go well with you and that you may live long in the land" (Ephesians 6:2-3). The fifth commandment provides the foundational principle that governs children's participation in family construction. This commandment is unique among the Ten Commandments because it comes with a specific promise, highlighting the importance that God places on proper family relationships and the benefits that flow from honoring parental authority [5].

Honor vs. Obedience: Understanding the Distinction

The distinction between honor and obedience represents one of the most important concepts for children to understand as they learn their role in family building. While obedience involves compliance with specific instructions and expectations, honor encompasses a broader attitude of respect, appreciation, and recognition of parental authority and sacrifice [6]. Understanding this distinction helps children develop appropriate responses to their parents throughout different stages of life and changing circumstances, contributing to the lifelong success of building a *Family by the Book: How to Build the Family God Intended.*

Obedience is primarily behavioral and focuses on specific actions and compliance with rules and expectations. Young children demonstrate obedience by following instructions promptly, accepting parental decisions without argument, and conforming their behavior to family standards [7]. This obedience serves important purposes in early childhood development, establishing patterns of respect for authority and creating safe environments where children can learn and grow without constant conflict or negotiation.

Honor, however, is primarily attitudinal and encompasses the heart motivations that drive behavior. Children who honor their parents demonstrate respect through their words, appreciation for parental sacrifice

102

and provision, and recognition of their parents' God-given authority [8]. This honor continues throughout life, even when specific obedience may no longer be required or appropriate. Adult children honor their parents by showing respect, providing care when needed, and acknowledging the foundation that their parents provided for their lives.

The relationship between honor and obedience becomes particularly important during adolescence, when children are developing independence while still living under parental authority. Teenagers who understand the distinction can demonstrate honor even when they disagree with specific decisions, maintaining respectful attitudes while expressing their perspectives appropriately [9]. This understanding helps families navigate the challenging transition from childhood dependence to adult independence without destroying the fundamental relationship of respect and love.

Teaching children to understand this distinction requires ongoing conversation and modeling from parents. When parents explain the reasons behind their expectations, acknowledge their own imperfections, and demonstrate honor toward their own parents, they help children develop a mature understanding of what it means to honor authority [10]. This teaching prepares children for lifelong success in relationships with employers, government officials, church leaders, and ultimately with God Himself.

The Promise Attached to Honoring Parents

The promise attached to the fifth commandment - "that it may go well with you and that you may live long in the land" - reveals God's heart for family relationships and His design for human flourishing [11]. This promise is not merely a reward for good behavior but a natural consequence of living according to God's design for family relationships. When children learn to honor their parents, they develop character qualities and relational skills that serve them well throughout their lives.

The promise that "it may go well with you" encompasses far more than material prosperity or external success. It includes the development of character qualities such as respect, humility, gratitude, and self-control that enable individuals to build healthy relationships and make wise decisions [12]. Children who learn to honor their parents typically develop better relationships with peers, teachers, employers, and eventually their own spouses and children. These relational skills contribute significantly to overall life satisfaction and success.

The promise of long life in the land also extends beyond mere longevity to include the quality and fruitfulness of life. Children who honor their parents often avoid many of the destructive behaviors and poor decisions that can shorten or diminish life [13]. They learn to value wisdom, seek counsel, and make decisions based on long-term consequences rather than immediate gratification. These patterns of thinking and decision-making contribute to both longer and more fulfilling lives.

Understanding this promise helps children see that honoring their parents serves their own best interests rather than merely satisfying parental expectations. When children recognize that God designed family relationships for their benefit and protection, they can embrace their role as willing helpers with enthusiasm rather than resentment [14]. This perspective transforms obedience from external compliance to internal motivation, creating the foundation for lifelong character development and spiritual growth.

The promise also provides encouragement for parents who sometimes wonder whether their efforts to train and guide their children will produce positive results. God's promise assures parents that children who learn to honor authority will experience His blessing and protection throughout their lives [15]. This assurance motivates parents to persist in their training efforts even when immediate results are not visible or encouraging.

104

Lifelong Application of This Building Principle

The principle of honoring parents extends far beyond childhood and adolescence to encompass the entire lifespan. Adult children continue to have opportunities and obligations to honor their parents, even when specific obedience is no longer required or appropriate [16]. Understanding the lifelong nature of this commandment helps families maintain strong relationships across generations and creates patterns of respect that benefit entire family systems.

Young adult children honor their parents by maintaining respectful communication, seeking counsel on major decisions, and expressing gratitude for the foundation their parents provided [17]. Even when they disagree with parental advice or choose different paths than their parents might prefer, they can demonstrate honor through their attitude and approach to these differences. This honor helps maintain family unity while allowing for individual growth and development, ensuring that the principles learned in building a *Family by the Book: How to Build the Family God Intended* continue across generations.

Middle-aged adults honor their aging parents by providing care, assistance, and emotional support as needs arise. This might involve helping with financial decisions, providing transportation to medical appointments, or simply spending time together to combat loneliness and isolation [18]. The specific forms of honor may change as circumstances change, but the underlying attitude of respect and appreciation remains constant throughout life.

The lifelong application of this principle also extends to how adult children speak about their parents to others, including their own children. When adults consistently speak respectfully about their parents, they model appropriate attitudes for the next generation while honoring the commandment themselves [19]. This modeling teaches children that respect for parents is not merely a childhood requirement but a lifelong value that characterizes mature individuals.

Understanding the lifelong nature of this commandment also helps families navigate difficult situations such as aging, illness, or death. When family members have established patterns of honor and respect, they are better equipped to handle these challenges with grace and unity [20]. The foundation of honor provides stability during times of change and stress, enabling families to support each other through difficult circumstances.

Respect as Foundation for All Authority

Learning to honor parents serves as foundational training for relating appropriately to all forms of legitimate authority throughout life. Children who develop proper attitudes toward parental authority are better prepared to respect teachers, employers, government officials, church leaders, and ultimately God Himself [21]. This foundational training in respect for authority contributes significantly to success in all areas of life and relationships.

The connection between honoring parents and respecting other authorities becomes evident in children's behavior at school, in community activities, and in church settings. Children who have learned to honor their parents typically demonstrate better behavior with teachers, coaches, and other adult leaders [22]. They understand that authority exists for their benefit and protection rather than as an obstacle to their freedom and happiness.

This foundational training also prepares children for future marriage relationships, where mutual submission and respect are essential for success. Children who learn to honor their parents develop an understanding of how authority and submission can coexist with love and respect [23]. This understanding serves them well when they become spouses and parents themselves, enabling them to build families according to God's design rather than cultural patterns that often lead to conflict and dysfunction.

The respect for authority that begins with honoring parents ultimately prepares children for their relationship with God. Children who learn to trust their parents' wisdom and submit to their authority develop patterns of thinking and responding that transfer naturally to their relationship with their heavenly Father [24]. This spiritual foundation becomes the basis for lifelong faith and obedience to God's will and purposes.

Understanding this connection helps parents recognize the eternal significance of their role in training children to honor authority. When parents consistently demonstrate godly authority and require appropriate respect, they are not merely maintaining order in their homes but preparing their children for success in every area of life [25]. This perspective motivates parents to persist in their training efforts even when the process is challenging or the results are not immediately apparent.

Age-Appropriate Building Participation

"Even a child makes himself known by his acts, by whether his conduct is pure and upright" (Proverbs 20:11). Children's participation in family building must be appropriate to their developmental stage, abilities, and understanding. Wise parents recognize that the specific ways children contribute to family construction will change as they grow and mature, but the underlying principles of willing participation and respectful cooperation remain constant [26]. Understanding these developmental stages helps families create appropriate expectations and opportunities for meaningful participation at every age.

Early Childhood: Learning Basic Obedience

The foundation for lifelong participation in family building begins in early childhood with the establishment of basic obedience patterns. Young children between the ages of two and six are naturally self-centered and impulsive, making this stage crucial for establishing patterns of respect for authority and consideration for others [27]. During this stage, children learn fundamental concepts such as immediate compliance with parental instructions, respect for family property and rules, and basic courtesy toward family members and guests. These early lessons become the building blocks for creating a *Family by the Book: How to Build the Family God Intended.*

Early childhood obedience training focuses primarily on external compliance while gradually introducing concepts of heart motivation and character development. Parents during this stage must be consistent, patient, and clear in their expectations while providing appropriate consequences for both obedience and disobedience [28]. The goal is not merely behavioral control but the establishment of patterns that will serve as the foundation for more mature forms of participation as children grow and develop.

Young children contribute to family building through simple tasks such as picking up toys, helping with basic household chores, and showing kindness to siblings and family members. These contributions may seem small, but they teach important lessons about responsibility, cooperation, and the satisfaction that comes from contributing to family welfare [29]. When parents acknowledge and appreciate these contributions, children develop positive associations with helping and serving others.

The spiritual dimension of early childhood participation involves teaching children that their obedience to parents is connected to their relationship with God. Simple concepts such as "God wants children to obey their parents" and "Jesus was obedient to His parents" help young children understand that their behavior has spiritual significance [30]. This foundation prepares them for a more sophisticated understanding of spiritual principles as they mature.1

Discipline during early childhood should focus on training rather than punishment, with the goal of developing internal motivation for appropriate behavior. When children understand that rules exist for their protection and benefit rather than merely to restrict their freedom, they begin to develop the wisdom and self-control that will serve them throughout their lives [31]. This approach to discipline creates willing helpers rather than resentful compliance.

Adolescence: Transitioning to Junior Builder

The adolescent years represent a crucial transition period when children move from simple obedience to more mature forms of participation in family building. Teenagers between the ages of thirteen and eighteen are developing their own identity, values, and decision-making abilities while still living under parental authority [32]. This stage requires careful balance between maintaining appropriate authority and providing opportunities for increased responsibility and independence.

Adolescent participation in family building involves taking on more significant responsibilities, such as managing personal schedules, contributing to family financial discussions, and helping with major family decisions that affect them directly. Teenagers can serve as junior builders by taking initiative in identifying family needs, suggesting solutions to family problems, and taking responsibility for specific areas of family life [33]. This increased participation helps them develop the skills and confidence they will need as adults while contributing meaningfully to current family welfare.

The transition to junior builder status requires ongoing communication between parents and teenagers about expectations, responsibilities, and privileges. Parents must gradually transfer decision-making authority while maintaining appropriate oversight and guidance [34]. This process requires wisdom, patience, and flexibility as both parents and teenagers learn to navigate new roles and relationships within the family structure.

Spiritual development during adolescence involves helping teenagers understand how biblical principles apply to their specific circumstances and decisions. Rather than simply following parental rules, teenagers need to develop personal convictions based on their own understanding of Scripture and relationship with God [35]. This spiritual maturity enables them to make wise decisions even when parents are not present to provide guidance and oversight.

The challenges of adolescence often test family relationships and building principles in new ways. Teenagers may question family values, challenge parental decisions, and struggle with issues of independence and authority [36]. Families that have established strong foundations of love, respect, and communication are better equipped to navigate these challenges while maintaining unity and continuing to build according to God's design.

Young Adulthood: Continuing Honor While Independent

Young adults between the ages of eighteen and twenty-five face the challenge of maintaining honor toward their parents while establishing their own independence and making their own decisions. This stage requires a fundamental shift in the parent-child relationship from authority-based to respect-based interaction [37]. Young adults who successfully navigate this transition maintain strong family relationships while developing the autonomy they need for adult success.

Young adult participation in family building involves contributing their developing skills, perspectives, and resources to family welfare while pursuing their own goals and interests. This might include helping with family business ventures, providing technical assistance with modern technology, or offering fresh perspectives on family challenges and opportunities [38]. Their contributions often bring new energy and ideas that benefit the entire family system.

The honor that young adults show their parents takes different forms from childhood obedience, but remains equally important for family health and individual character development. This honor might involve seeking parental counsel on major decisions, including parents in significant life events, and expressing gratitude for the foundation their parents provided [39]. Young adults who maintain this honor typically experience better relationships with their parents and greater success in their own endeavors.

Financial independence represents a significant milestone in young adult development and affects their participation in family building. Young adults who achieve financial independence gain new freedom to make their own decisions while also gaining new opportunities to contribute to family welfare [40]. This transition requires wisdom and communication to ensure that financial changes strengthen rather than weaken family relationships.

The spiritual dimension of young adult participation involves developing personal faith and convictions that may differ in some ways from their parents' beliefs while maintaining respect for their parents' spiritual influence. Young adults need freedom to explore their own relationship with God while honoring the spiritual foundation their parents provided [41]. This balance enables them to develop authentic faith while maintaining family unity and respect.

Mature Adulthood: Caring for Aging Parents

Mature adults face the privilege and responsibility of caring for aging parents who may need increasing levels of assistance and support. This stage represents the culmination of lifelong honor toward parents and provides opportunities to demonstrate gratitude for the care and sacrifice parents provided during their children's formative years [42]. The specific forms of care will vary depending on parents' needs and adult children's circumstances, but the underlying principle of honor remains constant.

Caring for aging parents might involve providing financial assistance, helping with household maintenance, offering transportation to medical appointments, or simply spending time together to combat loneliness and isolation. Adult children who approach these responsibilities with honor and gratitude often find that caring for aging parents becomes a source of blessing rather than a burden [43]. This perspective transforms necessary duties into opportunities for ministry and relationship building.

The challenges of caring for aging parents often require adult children to make difficult decisions about living arrangements, medical care, and financial management. These decisions require wisdom, patience, and often professional guidance to ensure that parents receive appropriate care while maintaining their dignity and autonomy as much as possible [44]. Adult children who have maintained relationships of honor and respect are better positioned to navigate these challenges successfully.

The spiritual dimension of caring for aging parents involves recognizing this responsibility as an opportunity to demonstrate Christian love and fulfill biblical obligations. Adult children who view parent care as ministry rather than mere duty often experience God's blessing and provision in unexpected ways [45]. This perspective also provides comfort and strength during the difficult seasons that often accompany aging and eventual death.

The example that adult children set in caring for their aging parents significantly influences their own children's understanding of family responsibility and honor. Children who observe their parents caring sacrificially for grandparents learn important lessons about loyalty, gratitude, and the lifelong nature of family commitments [46]. This modeling helps ensure that patterns of honor and respect continue across generations, building strong family legacies that reflect God's design for relationships.

The Motivation for Participation

"And whatever you do, in word or deed, do everything in the name of the Lord Jesus" (Colossians 3:17). The motivation behind children's participation in family building determines both the quality of their contribution and the character development that results from their involvement. When children understand the spiritual, moral, and practical reasons for their participation, they can embrace their role as willing helpers with enthusiasm rather than resentment [47]. This understanding transforms family responsibilities from burdensome obligations into opportunities for growth, service, and blessing.

"In the Lord" - The Spiritual Foundation

The phrase "in the Lord" that appears in Paul's instruction to children reveals the spiritual foundation that should motivate all family relationships and responsibilities. When children learn to obey their parents "in the Lord," they understand that their family participation is connected to their relationship with God and their spiritual development [48]. This spiritual dimension elevates everyday family interactions from mere human relationships to opportunities for worship and spiritual growth.

Understanding the spiritual foundation of family participation helps children see that their obedience to parents is ultimately an expression of their love for God. This perspective transforms compliance from external pressure to internal motivation, creating the foundation for joyful participation rather than grudging cooperation [49]. Children who embrace this spiritual understanding often demonstrate better attitudes and more consistent behavior because their motivation comes from their desire to

113

please God rather than merely to avoid consequences. This spiritual foundation becomes essential for families committed to building a Family by the Book: How to Build the Family God Intended.

The spiritual foundation also provides stability during difficult seasons when family relationships are strained or when parental decisions seem unfair or unreasonable. Children who understand that their participation is "in the Lord" can maintain appropriate attitudes and behavior even when their emotions or circumstances make obedience challenging [50]. This spiritual anchor enables them to respond with grace and maturity rather than rebellion or resentment.

Teaching children to understand the spiritual foundation of family participation requires ongoing conversation about how God views family relationships and how family life connects to broader spiritual realities. Parents can help children see that their family is part of God's larger plan for their lives and that their participation in family building prepares them for future service to God and others [51]. This understanding gives eternal significance to temporal activities and relationships.

The spiritual foundation also helps children understand that their participation in family building is preparation for their future role in building their own families according to God's design. When children see their current family experience as training for future family leadership, they can embrace learning opportunities with greater enthusiasm and purpose [52]. This perspective helps them understand that their current role as willing helpers is preparing them for future roles as family builders and leaders.

"For This is Right" - The Moral Building Code

The declaration that children's obedience to parents is "right" establishes a moral foundation that transcends cultural preferences or personal opinions. This moral dimension helps children understand that their participation in

114

family building is based on unchanging principles of right and wrong rather than arbitrary rules or cultural expectations [53]. Understanding this moral foundation helps children develop convictions that will guide their behavior throughout their lives.

The moral foundation of family participation connects to broader principles of justice, respect, and social order that benefit entire communities and societies. Children who learn to honor their parents contribute to social stability and demonstrate respect for legitimate authority that extends far beyond family relationships [54]. This understanding helps children see that their family participation has implications that reach beyond their immediate family to affect their community and society.

Understanding the moral dimension also helps children navigate situations where they may disagree with specific parental decisions or where they observe imperfections in their parents' behavior. When children understand that honoring parents is morally right regardless of parental perfection, they can maintain appropriate attitudes even when their parents make mistakes [55]. This understanding prevents children from using parental imperfections as excuses for disrespectful or disobedient behavior.

The moral foundation also provides a framework for children to evaluate their own behavior and attitudes toward family participation. When children understand that respect and obedience are morally right, they can assess their own responses and make necessary adjustments without external pressure [56]. This internal moral compass becomes increasingly important as children mature and face situations where external oversight is not available.

Teaching children to understand the moral foundation of family participation involves helping them see how family relationships reflect broader principles of justice, respect, and love that characterize God's character. When children understand that family rules and expectations are based on moral principles rather than arbitrary preferences, they develop respect for authority and understanding of right and wrong that serve them throughout their lives [57].

"That It May Go Well" - The Practical Benefits

The promise that honoring parents will result in things going well provides practical motivation for children's participation in family building. This promise helps children understand that their obedience and respect serve their own best interests rather than merely satisfying parental expectations [58]. Understanding these practical benefits helps children embrace their role as willing helpers with enthusiasm rather than viewing family responsibilities as obstacles to their happiness and success.

The practical benefits of honoring parents include the development of character qualities such as self-control, respect, gratitude, and wisdom that contribute to success in all areas of life. Children who learn to honor their parents typically develop better relationships with teachers, employers, and peers because they understand how to show appropriate respect and cooperation [59]. These relational skills contribute significantly to academic, professional, and personal success throughout their lives.

Honoring parents also provides children with access to wisdom, guidance, and support that can help them avoid many of the mistakes and poor decisions that often characterize young people who reject parental authority. Parents who have lived longer and experienced more of life's challenges can offer valuable perspective and counsel that helps children make better decisions [60]. Children who maintain respectful relationships with their parents benefit from this ongoing source of wisdom and support.

The practical benefits also include the emotional security and stability that come from strong family relationships. Children who honor their parents typically experience greater family harmony, more consistent support during difficult times, and stronger foundations for their own future families [61]. These benefits contribute to overall life satisfaction and emotional well-being that extends far beyond childhood and adolescence.

Understanding the practical benefits helps children see that God's design for family relationships serves their best interests rather than restricting their freedom or happiness. When children recognize that honoring their parents contributes to their own success and well-being, they can embrace family responsibilities with positive attitudes rather than viewing them as burdens [62]. This perspective transforms family participation from obligation to opportunity.

Building Character Through Obedience

The process of learning to obey parents and participate in family building serves as a crucial character development opportunity that shapes children's values, attitudes, and behavior patterns for life. Character qualities such as humility, self-control, perseverance, and respect are developed through the daily practice of family participation rather than through abstract teaching alone [63]. Understanding this character development dimension helps both parents and children appreciate the long-term value of family responsibilities and expectations.

Humility develops as children learn to submit to parental authority and acknowledge that they do not possess all the wisdom and experience necessary to make good decisions independently. This humility protects children from the pride and foolishness that often lead to poor decisions and harmful consequences [64]. Children who develop humility through family participation are better prepared to receive instruction, accept correction, and learn from others throughout their lives.

Self-control develops as children learn to obey even when they would prefer to do something else or when obedience requires sacrifice or effort.

This self-control becomes the foundation for success in academic pursuits, professional endeavors, and personal relationships [65]. Children who learn self-control through family participation develop the ability to delay gratification and make decisions based on long-term consequences rather than immediate desires.

Perseverance develops as children learn to complete family responsibilities even when the tasks are difficult, boring, or unrewarding. This perseverance becomes essential for success in any significant endeavor and helps children develop the determination necessary to achieve their goals and fulfill their commitments [66]. Children who learn perseverance through family participation are better prepared to handle the challenges and setbacks that inevitably arise in adult life.

The character development that occurs through family participation provides a foundation for spiritual growth and maturity that serves children throughout their lives. Children who learn to submit to parental authority develop patterns of thinking and responding that transfer naturally to their relationship with God [67]. This spiritual foundation becomes the basis for lifelong faith and obedience to God's will and purposes, ensuring that the principles learned in building a *Family by the Book: How to Build the Family God Intended* continue to influence their lives long after they leave their parents' home.

Special Building Circumstances

"We must obey God rather than men" (Acts 5:29). While the general principle of honoring parents provides clear guidance for most family situations, children sometimes face circumstances that require wisdom, discernment, and sometimes outside counsel to navigate appropriately. These special circumstances test children's understanding of biblical principles and their ability to maintain honor and respect even in difficult situations [68].

Understanding how to handle these challenges helps children develop mature faith and wisdom that serve them throughout their lives.

When Parents Ask Children to Build Wrongly

One of the most challenging situations children face occurs when parents ask them to participate in activities that clearly violate biblical principles or moral standards. In such situations, children must choose between obedience to parents and obedience to God, understanding that their ultimate allegiance must be to God while maintaining as much respect for their parents as possible [69]. This balance requires spiritual maturity and often outside counsel to navigate successfully.

Children who face requests to lie, steal, or participate in other clearly sinful activities must find ways to refuse while maintaining respectful attitudes toward their parents. This might involve explaining their convictions, suggesting alternatives, or simply declining to participate while continuing to show honor in other areas [70]. The goal is to obey God while preserving family relationships as much as possible under the circumstances.

The approach children take in these situations significantly affects both their character development and their ongoing relationship with their parents. Children who respond with arrogance, disrespect, or self-righteousness often damage their relationships and undermine their witness [71]. Those who respond with humility, respect, and genuine concern for their parents' welfare often maintain better relationships while standing firm in their convictions.

These situations also provide opportunities for children to demonstrate the reality of their faith and the strength of their convictions. When children choose to obey God rather than parents in clear moral issues, they often gain their parents' respect even when their parents disagree with their decisions

[72]. This witness can sometimes lead to positive changes in family dynamics and even parental conversion or spiritual growth.

Seeking wise counsel from pastors, youth leaders, or other mature believers becomes crucial when children face these difficult situations. Outside perspective can help children distinguish between clear moral issues and matters of preference or opinion [73]. This counsel also provides support and encouragement for children who may feel isolated or pressured to compromise their convictions.

Dealing with Imperfect Parent-Builders

All parents are imperfect, and children must learn to honor their parents while recognizing and dealing appropriately with parental weaknesses, mistakes, and failures. This reality requires children to develop a mature understanding of human nature and grace while maintaining appropriate respect for parental authority [74]. Learning to navigate these imperfections prepares children for all future relationships and helps them develop realistic expectations and gracious responses to human weakness.

Children who recognize parental imperfections must resist the temptation to use these weaknesses as excuses for disrespectful or disobedient behavior. Understanding that parents are human and make mistakes does not eliminate children's responsibility to show honor and respect [75]. Instead, this understanding should increase children's compassion and patience while motivating them to pray for their parents and seek to encourage rather than criticize.

The way children respond to parental imperfections significantly affects their own character development and their future relationships. Children who learn to extend grace to imperfect parents develop the ability to maintain healthy relationships despite human weaknesses and failures [76]. This skill becomes essential for success in marriage, friendship, and professional relationships throughout their lives.

Children can sometimes help their parents grow and improve by demonstrating maturity, wisdom, and grace in their responses to parental mistakes. When children respond to parental failures with forgiveness and continued respect, they often motivate their parents toward positive change [77]. This influence must be exercised with humility and patience rather than pride or manipulation.

Understanding parental imperfection also helps children develop realistic expectations for their own future parenting. Children who recognize that their parents did their best despite their limitations are better prepared to extend grace to themselves when they become parents [78]. This understanding helps break cycles of perfectionism and unrealistic expectations that can damage family relationships across generations.

Honoring Parents Who Don't Follow God's Blueprint

Children from non-Christian families or families where parents do not consistently follow biblical principles face unique challenges in learning to honor their parents while developing their own faith and convictions. These children must find ways to show respect and appreciation for their parents while not compromising their own spiritual growth and development [79]. This balance requires wisdom, maturity, and often outside support from church family and mentors.

Children in these situations can honor their parents by expressing gratitude for the good things their parents have provided, showing respect for their parents' efforts and sacrifices, and demonstrating love through their attitudes and actions. This honor does not require agreement with all parental values or decisions but focuses on acknowledging the positive aspects of their parents' care and provision [80].

The witness that children provide through their respectful behavior and changed lives often becomes a powerful testimony to their parents about the reality and value of faith. When children demonstrate love, respect, and maturity that exceeds what their parents expected, they often create curiosity about the source of these positive changes [81]. This witness must be accompanied by patience and prayer rather than pressure or manipulation.

Children from non-Christian families often need additional support and guidance from the church family, youth leaders, and Christian mentors to develop their faith and understanding of biblical principles. This support helps compensate for the lack of spiritual guidance at home while providing models of mature Christian living [82]. These relationships become especially important during adolescence when peer pressure and family pressure may conflict with Christian values.

The long-term goal for children in these situations is to maintain family relationships while developing strong personal faith that can eventually influence their entire family system. Many parents have come to faith through the witness and influence of their children, who learned to honor them while following Christ [83]. This influence requires patience, prayer, and consistent demonstration of Christian character over time.

Seeking Godly Counsel in Difficult Situations

When children face complex family situations that involve conflicting loyalties, unclear moral issues, or abusive treatment, seeking counsel from mature believers becomes essential for navigating these challenges successfully. This counsel provides perspective, support, and guidance that helps children make wise decisions while maintaining their integrity and safety [84]. Learning to seek and receive counsel also prepares children for lifelong patterns of wisdom-seeking that serve them well in all areas of life.

The sources of counsel that children seek should be mature believers who understand biblical principles and have experience in family relationships and child development. Pastors, youth leaders, Christian teachers, and other trusted adults can provide valuable perspective and guidance [85]. Children should seek counsel from multiple sources when facing particularly difficult or complex situations to ensure they receive balanced and wise advice.

The timing of seeking counsel is important, as children should not wait until situations become crisis-level before reaching out for help. Early intervention often prevents small problems from becoming major crises and provides opportunities for positive resolution [86]. Children who develop habits of seeking counsel when they first recognize problems are better equipped to handle difficulties successfully.

The attitude with which children seek counsel affects both the quality of advice they receive and their ability to implement suggested solutions. Children who approach counselors with humility, openness, and a genuine desire for wisdom typically receive more helpful guidance than those who seek counsel primarily to validate their own opinions [87]. This humble approach also demonstrates maturity and wisdom that encourages counselors to invest more deeply in helping them.

The implementation of counsel requires courage, patience, and often ongoing support from those who provided the guidance. Children who receive wise counsel must be willing to follow through with suggested actions even when those actions are difficult or uncomfortable [88]. This follow-through often requires a continued relationship with counselors who can provide encouragement and accountability during the implementation process.

Chapter 6

Parents as Master Builders

Building Character Without Breaking Spirit

As we have explored the husband's foundational leadership, the wife's essential support structure, and the children's role as willing helpers, we now arrive at one of the most crucial aspects of creating a *Family by the Book: How to Build the Family God Intended* - the comprehensive responsibility that parents bear as master builders in shaping the character of the next generation. The transition from understanding individual family roles to examining the parental calling represents a natural progression in our construction project, as parents must integrate all previous principles while adding the specialized skills required for character development and spiritual formation.

The apostle Paul provides the master blueprint for parental building when he declares, *"Fathers, do not provoke your children to anger, but bring them up in the discipline and instruction of the Lord"* (Ephesians 6:4). This foundational verse reveals the delicate balance that master builders must maintain between firm guidance and loving nurture, between high standards and patient grace [1]. The phrase "do not provoke your children to anger" warns against harsh, unreasonable, or inconsistent approaches that damage rather than develop character, while "bring them up in the discipline and instruction of the Lord" establishes the positive goal of character formation according to divine standards.

Understanding parents as master builders transforms how we approach the daily challenges and opportunities of child-rearing. Rather than viewing parenting as a series of behavioral problems to solve or compliance issues to manage, master builders recognize that every interaction with their children represents an opportunity to shape character, teach wisdom, and demonstrate

124

God's love [2]. This perspective requires patience, intentionality, and long-term vision, but it produces children who are equipped not only for temporal success but for eternal significance in God's kingdom purposes.

The master builder approach to parenting recognizes that the goal is not merely to produce well-behaved children who comply with external rules, but to develop internal character qualities that will guide children throughout their lives [3]. This character-focused approach requires parents to address heart issues rather than merely managing surface behaviors, to teach principles rather than simply enforcing rules, and to model the very qualities they want to see developed in their children's lives.

When families commit to building a *Family by the Book: How to Build the Family God Intended*, parents understand that their role as master builders extends far beyond their own children to influence future generations and the broader community. The character qualities they develop in their children today will be passed down to grandchildren and great-grandchildren, creating a legacy that impacts multiple generations [4]. This multigenerational perspective motivates parents to invest deeply in character development, recognizing that their faithful work today will bear fruit for generations to come.

The master builder approach also recognizes that different children require different building techniques while maintaining the same foundational principles and ultimate goals. Just as skilled craftsmen adapt their methods to work with different materials while following the same architectural plans, wise parents adjust their approaches to match their children's unique personalities, learning styles, and developmental needs [5]. This flexibility requires wisdom, observation, and often divine guidance to discern what approaches will be most effective with each child while maintaining consistency in values and expectations across the family.

Balancing Love and Discipline

"For the Lord disciplines the one he loves, and chastises every son whom he receives" (Hebrews 12:6). The foundation of effective parental master building rests on understanding and implementing the proper balance between love and discipline. This balance reflects God's own character and approach to His children, providing both the model and the motivation for how earthly parents should approach their character-building responsibilities [6].

Avoiding Building Extremes of Permissiveness and Harshness

One of the greatest challenges facing parents who want to build character effectively involves avoiding the extremes of permissiveness and harshness that characterize much of contemporary parenting culture. Permissive parenting fails to provide the structure and boundaries that children need for healthy development, while harsh parenting creates fear and resentment that hinder rather than promote character growth [7]. Master builders must find the biblical middle ground that combines firm expectations with loving support.

Permissive parenting often stems from parents' desire to be liked by their children or their fear of damaging their children's self-esteem through correction. However, this approach actually harms children by failing to prepare them for the realities of adult life, where boundaries and consequences are inevitable [8]. Children who grow up without appropriate discipline often struggle with self-control, respect for authority, and personal responsibility throughout their lives.

Harsh parenting, on the other hand, often reflects parents' frustration, impatience, or desire for immediate compliance rather than long-term character development. This approach may produce short-term behavioral compliance but often creates long-term relational damage and fails to develop the internal motivation necessary for mature character [9]. Children who experience harsh parenting often become either rebellious or fearful, neither of which represents the confident, loving obedience that characterizes mature Christian character.

The biblical approach to balancing love and discipline recognizes that both elements are essential for healthy character development and that they must work together rather than in opposition to each other. Love without discipline becomes sentimentality that fails to prepare children for life's challenges, while discipline without love becomes harshness that damages relationships and hinders spiritual growth [10]. When parents successfully integrate love and discipline, they create an environment where children feel both secure and challenged to grow.

This balance requires parents to understand that discipline is actually an expression of love rather than its opposite. When parents discipline their children appropriately, they demonstrate their commitment to their children's long-term welfare rather than their own immediate convenience [11]. Children who understand that discipline flows from love rather than anger are more likely to respond positively to correction and to develop the internal motivation necessary for mature character development.

The Example of God's Building Style

God's approach to disciplining His children provides the perfect model for how earthly parents should balance love and discipline in their character-building efforts. Scripture reveals that God's discipline is always motivated by love, designed for our benefit, and administered with perfect wisdom and timing [12]. When parents study and emulate God's disciplinary approach, they discover principles that enable them to discipline effectively while maintaining strong relationships with their children.

God's discipline is always purposeful rather than reactive. Unlike human parents who sometimes discipline out of frustration or anger, God's correction is always designed to produce specific character qualities and spiritual growth in His children [13]. This purposeful approach helps parents focus on long-term character goals rather than immediate behavioral compliance, leading to more effective and meaningful discipline.

God's discipline is also proportionate to the need and appropriate to the individual. Scripture reveals that God deals with each of His children according to their unique needs, circumstances, and level of maturity [14]. This individualized approach provides a model for parents who want to discipline effectively while recognizing the unique characteristics and needs of each child.

The timing of God's discipline also provides important lessons for earthly parents. God's correction often comes after repeated warnings and opportunities for repentance, demonstrating patience and grace while maintaining clear expectations [15]. However, when discipline is necessary, it comes with certainty and consistency that reinforces the seriousness of moral and spiritual issues.

God's discipline is always redemptive rather than punitive. The goal is always restoration and growth rather than punishment or revenge [16]. This redemptive focus helps parents approach discipline with the right heart attitude and helps children understand that correction is designed for their benefit rather than their harm.

When parents learn to emulate God's disciplinary approach in building a *Family by the Book: How to Build the Family God Intended,* they discover that discipline becomes a tool for building relationships rather than damaging them. Children who experience godly discipline learn to trust their parents' wisdom and love, creating a foundation for lifelong relationships based on mutual respect and affection [17].

Creating an Atmosphere of Grace and Truth

The atmosphere in which discipline takes place significantly affects its effectiveness in building character and maintaining relationships. Jesus was described as being *"full of grace and truth"* (John 1:14), providing a model for the kind of atmosphere that parents should create in their homes [18]. This combination of grace and truth enables parents to maintain high standards while demonstrating unconditional love and acceptance.

Grace in the family atmosphere means that children understand they are loved and accepted regardless of their performance or behavior. This unconditional love provides the security that children need to take risks, admit mistakes, and grow from their failures [19]. When children know they are loved unconditionally, they are more likely to be honest about their struggles and receptive to correction and guidance.

Truth in the family atmosphere means that parents maintain clear expectations and consistent consequences while helping children understand the reasons behind family rules and standards. This commitment to truth helps children develop an understanding of right and wrong and prepares them to make wise decisions when parental guidance is not available [20]. When truth is communicated with grace, children learn to appreciate rather than resent parental standards.

The combination of grace and truth creates an atmosphere where discipline can be effective without damaging relationships. Children who experience both grace and truth learn to see discipline as an expression of love rather than rejection, making them more receptive to correction and more likely to develop internal motivation for good behavior [21].

This atmosphere of grace and truth also enables parents to admit their own mistakes and seek forgiveness when they fail to discipline appropriately. When parents model humility and repentance, they teach their children important lessons about character while strengthening rather than weakening their authority [22]. Children who see their parents acknowledge mistakes and seek forgiveness learn that maturity involves taking responsibility for failures rather than defending or hiding them.

Discipline as Training, Not Punishment

Understanding discipline as training rather than punishment fundamentally changes how parents approach correction and character development. The biblical concept of discipline encompasses both instruction and correction, revealing that effective discipline involves teaching right principles as well as addressing wrong behavior [23]. When parents understand discipline as training, they approach correction with long-term goals and eternal perspective rather than short-term convenience or emotional reaction.

Training-focused discipline emphasizes teaching and learning rather than suffering and punishment. The goal is to help children understand why certain behaviors are wrong and how they can make better choices in the future [24]. This educational approach helps children develop the understanding and motivation necessary for mature character rather than simply creating fear of consequences.

Training-focused discipline also emphasizes the development of internal motivation rather than external compliance. While external consequences may be necessary to get children's attention and demonstrate the seriousness of moral issues, the ultimate goal is to help children develop personal convictions that will guide their behavior when external supervision is not present [25].

The training approach to discipline recognizes that different children may require different methods and approaches while maintaining the same standards and goals. Some children respond well to verbal correction and natural consequences, while others may require more structured intervention [26]. Parents who understand discipline as training are willing to adapt their methods to match their children's needs while maintaining consistency in their expectations and values.

Training-focused discipline also involves helping children learn from their mistakes rather than simply suffering for them. This means taking time to discuss what went wrong, why it was wrong, and how similar situations can be handled better in the future [27]. This processing helps children develop wisdom and discernment that will serve them throughout their lives.

Building Children's Character

"All Scripture is breathed out by God and profitable for teaching, for reproof, for correction, and for training in righteousness" (2 Timothy 3:16). The development of godly character in children represents the ultimate goal of parental master building and requires intentional effort, biblical wisdom, and long-term commitment. Character development goes far beyond behavioral modification to include shaping hearts, minds, and motivations according to God's design and purposes [28].

Scripture's Role in Character Construction

The Word of God provides both the blueprint and the building materials for character development in children's lives. Scripture reveals God's standards for character, provides examples of both godly and ungodly character, and offers the spiritual power necessary for character transformation [29]. When parents make Scripture central to their character-building efforts, they provide their children with an objective standard that transcends cultural expectations and personal preferences.

Regular exposure to Scripture helps children develop a biblical worldview that shapes how they think about themselves, others, and the world around them. This worldview provides the foundation for making wise decisions and developing godly character qualities [30]. When children learn to see life through the lens of Scripture, they are better equipped to resist cultural pressures and maintain biblical values throughout their lives.

Scripture also provides children with examples of character that they can emulate and warnings about character flaws they should avoid. The stories of biblical characters help children understand how character choices affect not only individuals but also families and communities [31]. These examples make abstract character qualities concrete and help children understand the practical importance of developing godly character.

The promises and commands of Scripture provide both motivation and guidance for character development. When children understand that God's commands are designed for their benefit and that His promises provide hope for the future, they develop internal motivation for obedience and character growth [32]. This understanding helps children see character development as a privilege rather than a burden.

Parents who want to use Scripture effectively for character construction must model their own commitment to biblical truth and demonstrate how Scripture applies to daily life decisions and challenges. Children learn more from what they observe than from what they are taught, making parental example crucial for effective character development [33]. When children see their parents turning to Scripture for guidance and strength, they learn that God's Word is practical and relevant for all of life.

The integration of Scripture into character building also requires parents to help children understand and apply biblical principles rather than simply memorizing verses or following rules. This application-focused approach helps children develop the ability to think biblically about new situations and challenges they will encounter throughout their lives [34]. When families commit to building a *Family by the Book: How to Build the Family God Intended*, Scripture becomes the foundation for all character development efforts.

Teaching by Example: Modeling Christian Building

The most powerful tool available to parents for character development is their own example. Children learn character qualities more through observation than instruction, making parental modeling crucial for effective character building [35]. When parents consistently demonstrate the character qualities they want to see developed in their children, they provide compelling motivation for character growth while creating an environment where godly character feels natural and desirable.

Modeling Christian character requires parents to take their own spiritual growth seriously and to pursue godliness with the same intensity they expect from their children. This means regular engagement with Scripture, consistent prayer life, and ongoing commitment to personal character development [36]. Parents who are growing in their own character provide dynamic examples that inspire their children to pursue similar growth.

The authenticity of parental modeling significantly affects its impact on children's character development. Children are remarkably perceptive about whether their parents' public behavior matches their private character [37]. When parents demonstrate consistency between their public and private lives, they teach their children that character is about who you are rather than what you do when others are watching.

Parental modeling also involves demonstrating how to handle failures and mistakes in ways that promote character growth rather than character damage. When parents acknowledge their failures, seek forgiveness, and make necessary changes, they teach their children that character involves taking responsibility for mistakes rather than defending or hiding them [38].

This modeling helps children develop humility and repentance as character qualities.

The modeling of conflict resolution provides particularly important lessons for children's character development. When parents demonstrate how to handle disagreements with grace, seek understanding rather than victory, and work toward reconciliation, they teach their children essential skills for maintaining relationships throughout their lives [39]. Children who observe healthy conflict resolution learn that character involves how you treat others during difficult times, rather than just during pleasant circumstances.

Parents who want their modeling to be effective for character development must also be willing to explain their decision-making processes and help their children understand the character principles that guide their choices. This explanation helps children learn to think about character issues rather than simply imitating behaviors [40]. When children understand the principles behind their parents' choices, they are better equipped to make similar choices when facing their own character challenges.

Age-Appropriate Spiritual Construction

Effective character building requires parents to understand how to adapt their approaches to match their children's developmental stages while maintaining consistent principles and goals. Different ages require different methods for character instruction, but the fundamental character qualities remain the same throughout childhood and adolescence [41].

Early childhood character building focuses primarily on establishing basic patterns of obedience, honesty, and kindness. Young children learn character primarily through repetition, clear expectations, and immediate consequences [42]. Parents who want to build character effectively during early childhood must be willing to invest significant time and energy in establishing routines and responding consistently to both appropriate and inappropriate behavior.

The character instruction most effective during early childhood emphasizes simple, concrete concepts that young children can understand and apply. Abstract character qualities like integrity or perseverance must be broken down into specific behaviors that young children can practice [43]. For example, honesty can be taught through simple expectations about telling the truth, while kindness can be developed through specific instructions about sharing and helping others.

Middle childhood provides opportunities for more sophisticated character instruction as children develop greater cognitive abilities and social awareness. Children at this stage can understand more complex character concepts and can begin to see connections between character choices and their consequences [44]. Parents can engage children in discussions about character issues and help them think through the implications of different choices.

The character development most important during middle childhood involves helping children understand the reasons behind character expectations rather than simply following rules. Children at this stage are capable of understanding why honesty is important, how kindness affects relationships, and why self-control leads to better outcomes [45]. This understanding helps children develop internal motivation for character development rather than simply external compliance.

Adolescent character building focuses on helping teenagers develop personal convictions and the ability to make character-based decisions independently. Teenagers need opportunities to practice character choices while still having access to parental guidance and support [46]. The goal is to

135

help teenagers internalize character principles so they can maintain godly character when parental supervision is not present.

The character challenges most common during adolescence involve peer pressure, identity formation, and preparation for adult responsibilities. Parents who want to build character effectively during this stage must help teenagers understand how character choices affect their identity and future opportunities [47]. This long-term perspective helps teenagers make character-based decisions even when immediate consequences are not obvious.

Developing Internal Motivation for Righteousness

The ultimate goal of character building involves helping children develop internal motivation for righteousness that will sustain them throughout their lives. This internal motivation goes beyond fear of consequences or desire for approval to include genuine love for God and commitment to His standards [48]. When children develop this internal motivation, they are equipped to maintain godly character regardless of external circumstances or pressures.

Internal motivation for righteousness begins with helping children understand God's character and His love for them. When children understand that God's standards flow from His love and are designed for their benefit, they develop positive attitudes toward righteousness rather than viewing it as a burdensome restriction [49]. This understanding provides the foundation for a lifelong commitment to godly character.

The development of internal motivation also requires helping children experience the benefits of godly character in their own lives. When children see that honesty leads to trust, kindness leads to friendship, and self-control leads to success, they develop appreciation for character qualities [50]. These positive experiences provide motivation for continued character development.

Parents can foster internal motivation by helping children understand the connection between character and identity. When children learn that their character defines who they are rather than just what they do, they develop greater commitment to character development [51]. This identity-based approach helps children see character as essential to their personhood rather than optional behavior.

The role of the Holy Spirit in developing internal motivation cannot be overlooked. Parents must pray for their children's spiritual growth and help them understand their need for divine assistance in character development [52]. When children learn to depend on God's strength for character growth, they develop resources that will sustain them throughout their lives.

When families successfully build a *Family by the Book: How to Build the Family God Intended*, children develop internal motivation for righteousness that enables them to maintain godly character in any environment or circumstance. This internal motivation becomes the foundation for lifelong spiritual growth and effective service in God's kingdom [53].

Discipline That Builds

"No discipline seems pleasant at the time, but painful. Later on, however, it produces a harvest of righteousness and peace" (Hebrews 12:11). Effective discipline serves as a crucial tool in the master builder's toolkit for character development, but it must be implemented with wisdom, consistency, and love to achieve its intended purposes. The goal of biblical discipline is always restoration and growth rather than punishment or control [54].

The Purpose: Restoration, Not Destruction

Understanding the proper purpose of discipline fundamentally changes how parents approach correction and character development. Biblical discipline is always designed to restore children to a right relationship with God, family, and others rather than simply to make them suffer for their mistakes [55]. This restorative focus helps parents maintain the right heart attitude during discipline and helps children understand that correction flows from love rather than anger.

Restorative discipline focuses on helping children understand what went wrong, why it was wrong, and how they can make better choices in the future. This educational approach helps children learn from their mistakes rather than simply experiencing consequences [56]. When children understand the reasons behind discipline, they are more likely to develop internal motivation for good behavior rather than simply external compliance.

The restorative approach to discipline also emphasizes the importance of reconciliation after correction has been administered. This means taking time to reaffirm love and acceptance while reinforcing the lessons learned through the disciplinary process [57]. Children who experience this reconciliation learn that discipline is temporary while love is permanent, helping them maintain trust in their parents' love even during difficult times.

Restorative discipline also involves helping children make amends for their wrong choices when appropriate. This might involve apologizing to those who were hurt, making restitution for damage caused, or taking steps to prevent similar problems in the future [58]. These restorative actions help children understand the impact of their choices on others and develop empathy and responsibility.

The goal of restoration also means that discipline should be proportionate to the offense and appropriate to the child's age and maturity level. Excessive discipline can damage rather than restore, while insufficient discipline may fail to communicate the seriousness of moral issues [59]. Parents who focus on restoration seek to use the minimum amount of discipline necessary to achieve the desired character development.

When discipline is truly restorative, it strengthens rather than weakens family relationships. Children who experience restorative discipline learn to trust their parents' wisdom and love, creating a foundation for lifelong relationships based on mutual respect and affection [60]. This relational strength enables families to navigate future challenges with unity and confidence.

Methods That Reflect God's Character

The methods parents use for discipline should reflect God's character and demonstrate the same qualities they want to develop in their children. This means that discipline should be administered with patience, kindness, justice, and love rather than anger, frustration, or convenience [61]. When parents discipline in ways that reflect God's character, they provide their children with a picture of how God deals with His children.

Patience in discipline means taking time to understand the situation fully before responding and avoiding hasty reactions that may be inappropriate or excessive. This patience demonstrates to children that their parents care enough to seek understanding rather than simply reacting to behavior [62]. Children who experience patient discipline learn that their parents are committed to justice rather than convenience.

Kindness in discipline means maintaining a loving attitude even while administering correction. This kindness is demonstrated through tone of voice, facial expressions, and overall demeanor during disciplinary interactions [63]. Children who experience kind discipline learn that correction can coexist with love and that their parents' commitment to their welfare extends even to difficult times.

Justice in discipline means ensuring that consequences are fair and proportionate to the offense. This justice helps children understand that discipline is not arbitrary or capricious but is based on clear standards and consistent application [64]. Children who experience just discipline develop respect for authority and understanding of cause-and-effect relationships.

Love in discipline means that all correction is motivated by concern for the child's welfare rather than parental convenience or satisfaction. This love is demonstrated through the goals of discipline, the methods used, and the follow-up provided after correction [65]. Children who experience loving discipline learn that their parents are committed to their long-term growth rather than short-term compliance.

The methods of discipline should also be appropriate to the specific child and situation. Some children respond well to verbal correction and natural consequences, while others may require more structured intervention [66]. Parents who reflect God's character in their discipline are willing to adapt their methods to match their children's needs while maintaining consistency in their standards and goals.

When parents discipline in ways that reflect God's character, they teach their children important lessons about God's nature while building character and maintaining relationships. This godly approach to discipline becomes a powerful tool for spiritual formation as well as character development [67].

Helping Children Learn from Building Mistakes

One of the most important aspects of effective discipline involves helping children process their mistakes in ways that promote learning and growth rather than shame or discouragement. This learning-focused approach recognizes that mistakes are inevitable parts of the character

140

development process and can become valuable opportunities for growth when handled appropriately [68].

Helping children learn from mistakes begins with creating an atmosphere where children feel safe to admit their failures without fear of excessive punishment or rejection. This safety enables children to be honest about their struggles and receptive to guidance and correction [69]. When children know they will be treated with grace even when they fail, they are more likely to seek help when facing character challenges.

The learning process also involves helping children understand the connection between their choices and the consequences they experience. This cause-and-effect understanding helps children develop wisdom and discernment that will serve them throughout their lives [70]. When children understand how their choices affect themselves and others, they are better equipped to make wise decisions in the future.

Parents can facilitate learning by asking questions that help children think through their mistakes rather than simply telling them what they did wrong. Questions like "What do you think went wrong?" and "How could you handle this differently next time?" help children develop critical thinking skills and personal responsibility [71]. This questioning approach helps children become active participants in their character development rather than passive recipients of correction.

The learning process also involves helping children understand the broader principles behind specific rules and expectations. When children understand why certain behaviors are wrong and how they conflict with godly character, they develop the ability to apply these principles to new situations [72]. This principle-based understanding helps children make wise choices even when facing unfamiliar circumstances.

Helping children learn from mistakes also requires parents to model how to handle their own failures appropriately. When parents acknowledge their mistakes, seek forgiveness, and make necessary changes, they demonstrate that learning from failure is a lifelong process [73]. This modeling helps children develop resilience and the ability to grow from their mistakes rather than being defeated by them.

When families successfully help children learn from their mistakes while building a Family by the Book: How to Build the Family God Intended, they create an environment where character development can flourish naturally and joyfully. Children who learn to view mistakes as learning opportunities develop the resilience and wisdom necessary for lifelong character growth [74].

Natural Consequences vs. Imposed Punishment

Understanding the difference between natural consequences and imposed punishment helps parents discipline more effectively while teaching children important lessons about responsibility and decision-making. Natural consequences flow directly from children's choices and help them understand the real-world implications of their behavior, while imposed punishment is administered by parents to address moral or character issues [75].

Natural consequences provide powerful learning opportunities because they demonstrate the connection between choices and outcomes in ways that children can easily understand. When children experience the natural results of their decisions, they learn important lessons about responsibility without parents having to impose artificial consequences [76]. For example, a child who refuses to wear a coat may become cold, teaching the importance of preparation and wise decision-making.

The use of natural consequences also helps children develop internal motivation for wise choices rather than simply external compliance with parental expectations. When children understand that their choices affect their own welfare, they develop personal investment in making good decisions [77]. This internal motivation is more sustainable than external pressure and better prepares children for independent adult living.

However, natural consequences are not always sufficient for character development, particularly when moral or spiritual issues are involved. Some behaviors may not have immediate natural consequences but still require correction because they violate biblical standards or damage character [78]. In these situations, parents must impose appropriate consequences to communicate the seriousness of moral issues.

Imposed consequences should be designed to reinforce the lessons that natural consequences might teach and to address character issues that natural consequences might not address. These consequences should be logical, proportionate, and designed to promote character growth rather than simply to punish [79]. When imposed consequences are thoughtfully designed, they can be as effective as natural consequences for promoting character development.

The combination of natural and imposed consequences provides children with a comprehensive understanding of how choices affect both immediate circumstances and long-term character development. This understanding helps children develop wisdom and discernment that will serve them throughout their lives [80]. When children understand both the practical and moral implications of their choices, they are better equipped to make decisions that honor God and benefit themselves and others.

Preparing for Independent Building

"When I was a child, I spoke like a child, I thought like a child, I reasoned like a child. When I became a man, I gave up childish ways" (1 Corinthians 13:11). The ultimate goal of parental master building involves preparing children for independent adult living while maintaining strong family relationships based on mutual respect and love. This preparation requires gradually transferring responsibility and decision-making authority to children as they demonstrate maturity and wisdom [81].

Teaching Decision-Making: Building Skills

One of the most important responsibilities of parental master builders involves teaching children how to make wise decisions based on biblical principles rather than cultural pressures or personal preferences. This decision-making training goes far beyond rule-following to include developing discernment, understanding consequences, and learning to seek God's guidance in all areas of life [82].

The foundation of decision-making training involves helping children understand that all of life is spiritual and that God's principles apply to every decision and relationship they will encounter. This comprehensive worldview helps children see that their choices in areas such as friendships, entertainment, academics, and future planning all have spiritual significance and eternal consequences [83]. When children develop this perspective through the consistent teaching found in building a *Family by the Book: How to Build the Family God Intended*, they are more likely to seek God's guidance and apply biblical principles to their decision-making processes throughout their lives.

Practical decision-making training involves teaching children how to evaluate options, consider consequences, and seek counsel when facing important choices. Parents can provide this training through family

144

discussions about current events, hypothetical scenarios, and real-life situations that arise in their children's experience [84]. These conversations help children develop critical thinking skills and learn to apply biblical principles to practical situations they will encounter as they mature.

Chapter 7
Building in Community

Living as Salt and Light

Having explored the foundational roles of husbands, wives, children, and parents in creating godly families, we now turn our attention to how these well-built families function within the broader community as witnesses to God's design and grace. The transition from internal family construction to external community engagement represents a natural progression in our journey through *Family by the Book: How to Build the Family God Intended*, as families that have been built according to biblical principles become powerful testimonies to the watching world about the beauty and effectiveness of God's design for human relationships.

Jesus provides the foundational blueprint for family community engagement when He declares, *"You are the salt of the earth… You are the light of the world"* (Matthew 5:13-14). These metaphors reveal that Christian families are not meant to exist in isolation from their communities but are called to be preserving and illuminating influences that demonstrate God's character and advance His kingdom purposes [1]. The salt metaphor emphasizes the family's role in preserving moral and spiritual values in society, while the light metaphor highlights the family's responsibility to illuminate truth and provide guidance for those who are lost in darkness.

Understanding families as salt and light transforms how we approach community engagement and cultural interaction. Rather than viewing the broader community as a threat to be avoided or an enemy to be defeated, families built according to biblical principles recognize their calling to be positive influences that attract others to Christ through the beauty of their relationships and the integrity of their character [2]. This perspective requires

146

families to maintain their distinctiveness while remaining engaged with their communities in ways that demonstrate God's love and truth.

The salt and light calling also reveals that effective community engagement flows naturally from healthy family construction rather than being an additional burden or responsibility. When families have been built according to God's design, their witness becomes an overflow of their internal health and spiritual vitality [3]. This organic approach to community engagement enables families to serve as authentic witnesses rather than performing artificial religious activities that lack genuine spiritual power.

When families commit to building a *Family by the Book: How to Build the Family God Intended*, they understand that their community engagement serves multiple purposes in God's kingdom economy. Their witness provides hope and guidance for struggling families, demonstrates the practical benefits of biblical principles, and creates opportunities for gospel conversations that can lead to eternal transformation [4]. This multi-faceted impact motivates families to take their community calling seriously while maintaining their primary focus on internal spiritual health and relational strength.

The community engagement of biblical families also serves as a form of spiritual warfare against the forces that seek to destroy marriage, family, and society. When families consistently demonstrate love, faithfulness, integrity, and service, they provide a powerful counter-narrative to the cultural messages that promote selfishness, materialism, and moral relativism [5]. This positive witness becomes a form of resistance against destructive cultural trends while offering constructive alternatives that point toward God's better way.

Family's Witness to Society

"Let your light shine before others, so that they may see your good works and give glory to your Father who is in heaven" (Matthew 5:16). The witness that Christian families provide to their communities represents one of the most powerful forms of evangelism and cultural influence available to the church. This witness goes beyond verbal proclamation to include the demonstration of God's character through daily family life and community interaction [6].

Being Different Without Being Isolated

One of the greatest challenges facing Christian families in contemporary culture involves maintaining biblical distinctiveness while remaining engaged with their communities in meaningful ways. This balance requires wisdom, discernment, and ongoing commitment to both spiritual growth and cultural engagement [7]. Families that successfully navigate this balance become powerful witnesses to the possibility of living according to biblical principles in a secular world.

Biblical distinctiveness begins with families that order their priorities, relationships, and decisions according to Scripture rather than cultural expectations or personal preferences. This distinctiveness becomes evident in how families handle conflict, make financial decisions, raise their children, and treat one another during both pleasant and difficult circumstances [8]. When families consistently demonstrate biblical values in these areas, they provide compelling evidence that God's ways are both practical and beneficial.

However, biblical distinctiveness must be balanced with genuine love and concern for the broader community. Families that isolate themselves from their communities in an attempt to maintain purity often fail to fulfill their calling as salt and light [9]. True biblical distinctiveness involves being different in character and values while remaining engaged in relationships and service that demonstrate God's love for all people.

The key to maintaining this balance involves understanding that biblical families are called to be in the world but not of the world. This means participating in community activities, building relationships with non-Christian neighbors, and contributing to the common good while maintaining clear boundaries around activities and relationships that would compromise biblical convictions [10]. This engaged distinctiveness requires ongoing wisdom and discernment but produces powerful witness opportunities.

Families that successfully maintain biblical distinctiveness while remaining engaged often find that their differences become conversation starters rather than barriers to the relationship. When neighbors observe how Christian families handle stress, resolve conflicts, and support one another, they often become curious about the source of such stability and love [11]. This curiosity creates natural opportunities for sharing the gospel and explaining how faith makes a practical difference in family life.

The goal of being different without being isolated is to create relationships and opportunities where the gospel can be shared naturally and authentically. When families demonstrate genuine love and concern for their neighbors while maintaining clear biblical convictions, they earn the right to speak into others' lives during times of crisis or questioning [12]. This relational foundation makes gospel conversations more effective and meaningful than impersonal evangelistic efforts.

Demonstrating God's Love Through Family Life

The daily interactions and relationships within Christian families provide powerful demonstrations of God's character and love that often speak more loudly than verbal presentations of the gospel. When families consistently demonstrate forgiveness, patience, kindness, and sacrificial love, they provide their communities with tangible examples of how God relates to His children [13].

The demonstration of God's love through family life becomes particularly powerful during times of crisis or difficulty. When Christian families face challenges with faith, hope, and unity rather than despair, anger, or division, they provide compelling evidence that their faith is both real and practical [14]. These demonstrations often have a profound impact on neighbors and friends who are facing similar challenges without the resources that faith provides.

Marriage relationships within Christian families provide especially powerful witnesses to God's design for human relationships. When husbands and wives demonstrate sacrificial love, mutual respect, and lifelong commitment, they offer hope to couples who are struggling with conflict, infidelity, or divorce [15]. This witness becomes particularly important in communities where healthy marriages are rare and divorce is common.

Parent-child relationships also provide important demonstrations of God's character and love. When parents discipline with love rather than anger, forgive quickly and completely, and invest sacrificially in their children's welfare, they demonstrate how God relates to His children [16]. Children who experience this kind of parenting often become powerful witnesses themselves as they demonstrate the security and confidence that comes from being loved unconditionally.

The hospitality that Christian families extend to others provides another important demonstration of God's love and character. When families regularly welcome guests, serve those in need, and open their homes for ministry purposes, they demonstrate that their resources belong to God and exist to serve His purposes [17]. This hospitality often provides opportunities for deeper relationships and gospel conversations that might not occur in other settings.

The consistency of these demonstrations over time significantly affects their impact on the community. When neighbors observe Christian families demonstrating God's love consistently through both good times and difficult seasons, they develop trust in the authenticity of their faith [18]. This long-term consistency often proves more influential than dramatic but isolated acts of service or kindness.

When families successfully demonstrate God's love through their daily interactions while building a Family by the Book: How to Build the Family God Intended, they create powerful testimonies that attract others to Christ and provide hope for struggling families in their communities [19].

The Power of Godly Homes' Testimony

The testimony of a godly home extends far beyond the immediate family to influence extended family members, neighbors, friends, and even strangers who observe the family's character and relationships. This testimony becomes particularly powerful because it demonstrates the practical benefits of biblical principles in ways that are observable and verifiable [20].

The power of a godly home's testimony often becomes most evident during times of crisis or challenge. When Christian families face difficulties with faith, hope, and unity, they provide compelling evidence that their beliefs are more than mere intellectual concepts [21]. Neighbors and friends who observe how Christian families handle job loss, illness, death, or other crises often become curious about the source of their strength and stability.

The testimony of godly homes also becomes powerful through the character and behavior of the children who are raised in these environments. When children from Christian families demonstrate respect, responsibility, kindness, and integrity in their interactions with others, they provide evidence of the effectiveness of biblical parenting principles [22]. These character qualities often make Christian children attractive friends and desirable employees, creating opportunities for their families to share about their faith and values.

The financial stewardship demonstrated by Christian families also provides powerful testimony to their communities. When families live within their means, give generously to others, and avoid the debt and materialism that characterize much of contemporary culture, they demonstrate alternative approaches to money and possessions [23]. This financial wisdom often attracts the attention of neighbors who are struggling with financial pressures and seeking practical guidance.

The longevity and stability of Christian marriages provide another important aspect of godly homes' testimony. In communities where divorce is common and marriage is viewed as temporary, couples who demonstrate lifelong commitment and growing love provide hope and inspiration for others [24]. These stable marriages often become sources of counsel and encouragement for couples who are facing marital difficulties.

The service and generosity that flow from godly homes also contribute to their powerful testimony. When families consistently serve others, contribute to community needs, and demonstrate concern for the welfare of their neighbors, they provide evidence that their faith produces practical benefits for the broader community [25]. This service often opens doors for deeper relationships and gospel conversations.

The cumulative effect of these various aspects of testimony creates a comprehensive witness that demonstrates the beauty and effectiveness of God's design for family life. When communities observe families that consistently demonstrate love, stability, generosity, and service, they often become curious about the source of such character and blessing [26].

Attracting Others to Christ Through Family Witness

The ultimate goal of family witness involves attracting others to Christ through the demonstration of His character and the proclamation of His gospel. This attraction occurs most effectively when families combine authentic Christian living with genuine relationships and clear gospel communication [27].

The attraction process often begins with curiosity about the differences that others observe in Christian families. When neighbors notice that Christian families handle stress differently, resolve conflicts more effectively, or demonstrate unusual stability and love, they often become curious about the source of these differences [28]. This curiosity creates natural opportunities for families to share about their faith and explain how the gospel has transformed their relationships.

The relational foundation that Christian families build with their neighbors significantly affects their ability to attract others to Christ. When families invest in genuine friendships, demonstrate consistent care and concern, and prove themselves trustworthy over time, they earn the right to speak into others' lives during times of crisis or questioning [29]. These established relationships make gospel conversations more natural and effective than impersonal evangelistic efforts.

The timing of gospel conversations often proves crucial for their effectiveness. Christian families who are sensitive to the Holy Spirit's leading and attentive to their neighbors' circumstances can often identify optimal times for sharing the gospel [30]. These times might include periods of crisis, major life transitions, or seasons when neighbors are asking spiritual questions or expressing dissatisfaction with their current circumstances.

The manner in which families share the gospel also significantly affects its reception. When gospel conversations flow naturally from established relationships and demonstrated love, they are more likely to be received positively than when they feel forced or artificial [31]. Families who have earned trust and demonstrated genuine care can often share difficult truths about sin and salvation in ways that are received as expressions of love rather than judgment.

The follow-up and ongoing support that Christian families provide to those who express interest in the gospel often determines whether initial interest develops into genuine faith. When families are willing to invest in discipleship relationships, answer questions, and provide ongoing encouragement, they significantly increase the likelihood that gospel conversations will result in lasting spiritual transformation [32].

The multiplication effect of family witness can extend far beyond immediate neighbors to influence entire communities over time. When families consistently attract others to Christ through their witness, those new believers often become witnesses themselves, creating expanding circles of gospel influence [33]. This multiplication demonstrates the strategic importance of family witness in God's plan for advancing His kingdom.

Navigating Cultural Pressures

"Do not be conformed to this world, but be transformed by the renewal of your mind" (Romans 12:2). Christian families living in contemporary culture face constant pressure to conform to values, priorities, and practices that conflict with biblical principles. Successfully navigating these pressures requires wisdom, courage, and ongoing commitment to biblical truth while maintaining love and grace toward those who hold different values [34].

Maintaining Biblical Values in a Secular World

The challenge of maintaining biblical values in a secular world begins with helping family members understand the fundamental differences

154

between biblical and cultural worldviews. This understanding provides the foundation for making wise decisions about which cultural practices to embrace, which to modify, and which to reject entirely [35].

Biblical worldview training must begin early and continue throughout children's development as they encounter increasingly sophisticated challenges to their faith and values. Parents who want to prepare their children for cultural engagement must help them understand not only what the Bible teaches but also why biblical principles are superior to cultural alternatives [36]. This apologetic foundation enables children to maintain their convictions even when facing intellectual or social pressure to compromise.

The practical application of biblical values often requires families to make difficult choices about entertainment, education, career opportunities, and social relationships. These choices become particularly challenging when biblical values conflict with financial opportunities, social acceptance, or personal preferences [37]. Families that successfully maintain biblical values develop decision-making processes that prioritize spiritual considerations over temporal benefits.

The consistency with which families apply biblical values significantly affects their credibility and influence in their communities. When families demonstrate that their values are more than mere preferences but are deeply held convictions that guide all areas of life, they earn respect even from those who disagree with their beliefs [38]. This consistency requires ongoing commitment and often involves sacrifice, but it produces powerful witness opportunities.

The grace with which families maintain their biblical values also affects their community relationships and witness effectiveness. When families demonstrate that it is possible to hold strong convictions while treating others with love and respect, they provide compelling examples of how faith can be both principled and gracious [39]. This gracious firmness often attracts others who are seeking authentic spirituality that combines truth and love.

The long-term perspective that guides biblical families helps them maintain their values even when immediate consequences seem negative. When families understand that their primary goal is to honor God and build His kingdom rather than to achieve temporal success or social acceptance, they can make difficult choices with confidence [40]. This eternal perspective provides strength and motivation for maintaining biblical values regardless of cultural pressures.

When families successfully maintain biblical values while building a *Family by the Book: How to Build the Family God Intended*, they provide powerful testimonies to the possibility of living according to God's design in any cultural context [41].

Teaching Children Biblical Thinking About Culture

One of the most important responsibilities of Christian parents involves teaching their children how to think biblically about cultural issues and challenges. This training goes beyond simply telling children what to believe to include helping them develop the analytical skills necessary to evaluate cultural messages according to biblical standards [42].

Biblical thinking about culture begins with helping children understand that all cultural practices and values must be evaluated according to Scripture rather than popular opinion or personal preference. This scriptural foundation provides an objective standard for making decisions about cultural engagement [43]. Children who learn to use Scripture as their primary filter for cultural evaluation are better equipped to maintain their faith in challenging environments.

The development of critical thinking skills enables children to analyze cultural messages and identify the worldview assumptions that underlie them.

When children learn to ask questions like "What does this assume about human nature?" or "How does this conflict with biblical truth?" they develop the ability to think independently about cultural issues [44]. These analytical skills become increasingly important as children encounter more sophisticated challenges to their faith.

The historical perspective that biblical education provides helps children understand that cultural values and practices change over time while biblical truth remains constant. This understanding helps children recognize that contemporary cultural practices are not necessarily superior to traditional approaches simply because they are newer [45]. This historical awareness provides stability and confidence for maintaining biblical convictions in changing cultural contexts.

The practical application of biblical thinking requires children to practice evaluating real cultural issues and making decisions based on biblical principles. Parents can provide this practice through family discussions about current events, entertainment choices, and social situations that arise in their children's experience [46]. These discussions help children develop confidence in their ability to apply biblical principles to practical situations.

The modeling that parents provide significantly affects their children's development of biblical thinking about culture. When children observe their parents consistently applying biblical principles to cultural decisions, they learn that faith is practical and relevant to all areas of life [47]. This modeling often proves more influential than formal instruction in shaping children's approaches to cultural engagement.

The goal of teaching children biblical thinking about culture is to prepare them to engage their communities as effective witnesses while maintaining their spiritual integrity. When children develop the ability to think biblically about cultural issues, they are equipped to be salt and light in their generation [48].

Standing Firm While Showing Grace

The balance between standing firm on biblical convictions and showing grace to those who hold different values represents one of the most challenging aspects of Christian family life in contemporary culture. This balance requires wisdom, maturity, and ongoing dependence on the Holy Spirit's guidance [49].

Standing firm on biblical convictions begins with having a clear understanding of which issues are matters of biblical principle and which are matters of personal preference or cultural tradition. This distinction enables families to focus their energy on truly important issues while demonstrating flexibility on matters that are not clearly addressed in Scripture [50]. This discernment helps families avoid unnecessary conflicts while maintaining their witness on essential issues.

The manner in which families communicate their convictions significantly affects how those convictions are received by others. When families explain their positions with humility, respect, and genuine concern for others' welfare, they are more likely to be heard than when they communicate with arrogance, judgment, or hostility [51]. This gracious communication often opens doors for meaningful dialogue rather than creating defensive reactions.

The consistency with which families live according to their stated convictions affects their credibility and influence. When families demonstrate that their convictions are more than mere words but are principles that guide their daily decisions and relationships, they earn respect even from those who disagree with their beliefs [52]. This consistency requires ongoing commitment and often involves personal sacrifice.

The love that families demonstrate toward those who hold different values provides powerful evidence of the transforming power of the gospel. When families show genuine care and concern for neighbors, coworkers, and community members who live according to different principles, they demonstrate that their faith produces love rather than judgment [53]. This love often creates opportunities for deeper relationships and gospel conversations.

The patience that families demonstrate when facing opposition or misunderstanding reflects their confidence in God's sovereignty and timing. When families respond to criticism or persecution with grace rather than defensiveness, they provide compelling evidence of their spiritual maturity [54]. This patient's response often surprises critics and creates opportunities for witnesses that would not otherwise exist.

The goal of standing firm while showing grace is to maintain biblical integrity while building relationships that create opportunities for gospel influence. When families successfully achieve this balance, they become powerful witnesses to the possibility of combining truth and love in ways that honor God and bless others [55].

Engaging Culture Without Compromising Truth

The challenge of engaging culture without compromising truth requires families to develop a sophisticated understanding of how to participate in community life while maintaining their spiritual integrity. This engagement involves strategic thinking about which activities to embrace, which to modify, and which to avoid entirely [56].

Cultural engagement begins with understanding that Christians are called to be in the world but not of the world. This means participating in community activities, building relationships with non-Christian neighbors, and contributing to the common good while maintaining clear boundaries around activities that would compromise biblical convictions [57]. This engaged distinctiveness requires ongoing wisdom and discernment.

The selection of community activities requires families to evaluate each opportunity according to biblical principles and family priorities. Some activities may be clearly beneficial and appropriate, while others may be clearly inappropriate for Christian participation [58]. Many activities fall into a gray area that requires careful consideration of factors such as the activity's purpose, the relationships involved, and the potential impact on family spiritual health.

The modification of cultural practices enables families to participate in community life while maintaining their distinctive values. For example, families might participate in community celebrations while avoiding aspects that conflict with their beliefs, or they might host alternative activities that accomplish similar social goals through different means [59]. This creative adaptation enables families to remain engaged while maintaining their integrity.

The contribution that Christian families make to their communities often provides the most effective form of cultural engagement. When families consistently serve others, contribute to community needs, and work for the common good, they demonstrate that their faith produces practical benefits for society [60]. This service often earns respect and creates opportunities for deeper relationships and gospel conversations.

The boundaries that families establish around cultural engagement help them maintain their spiritual health while remaining involved in community life. These boundaries might involve time limits on certain activities, restrictions on particular types of entertainment, or guidelines for social relationships [61]. Clear boundaries enable families to engage confidently while protecting their spiritual integrity.

When families successfully engage culture without compromising truth while building a Family by the Book: How to Build the Family God Intended, they provide powerful examples of how faith can be both relevant and distinctive in contemporary society [62].

Family's Role in Church Community

"And let us consider how to stir up one another to love and good works" (Hebrews 10:24). The relationship between individual families and the broader church community represents a crucial aspect of biblical family life that affects both family health and church effectiveness. Well-built families contribute significantly to church vitality while receiving essential support and encouragement for their own spiritual growth [63].

Supporting Other Building Families

One of the most important contributions that established Christian families can make to their church communities involves supporting and encouraging other families who are working to build according to biblical principles. This support takes many forms and provides essential encouragement for families who are facing challenges or seeking to grow in their understanding of God's design [64].

Practical support for other families often involves sharing resources, providing childcare, offering meals during difficult times, and helping with household tasks when families are facing crises. This practical assistance demonstrates the love of Christ in tangible ways while providing relief that enables struggling families to focus on their spiritual and relational priorities [65]. Such support often proves more valuable than formal counseling or advice because it meets immediate needs while demonstrating genuine care.

Emotional support for other families involves providing encouragement, listening to concerns, and offering hope during difficult seasons. Many

161

families face challenges that seem overwhelming when faced alone, but become manageable when shared with caring friends who understand similar struggles [66]. This emotional support often proves crucial for helping families persevere through difficult times without compromising their biblical convictions.

Spiritual support for other families involves praying together, sharing biblical insights, and providing accountability for spiritual growth and family priorities. When families commit to supporting each other's spiritual development, they create networks of encouragement that strengthen everyone involved [67]. This spiritual support often proves essential for maintaining a long-term commitment to biblical family building.

Educational support for other families involves sharing knowledge, resources, and experiences that can help others grow in their understanding of biblical principles and practical applications. Experienced families can provide valuable guidance about child-rearing, marriage enrichment, financial stewardship, and other aspects of family life [68]. This educational support helps newer families avoid common mistakes while learning from others' successes and failures.

The modeling that established families provide for newer families often proves as valuable as direct instruction or assistance. When newer families observe how mature Christian families handle conflicts, make decisions, and maintain their priorities, they gain practical understanding of how biblical principles work in real-life situations [69

]. This modeling provides hope and direction for families who are still learning how to apply biblical principles effectively.

The reciprocal nature of family support within church communities creates networks of mutual encouragement that benefit everyone involved. Even families that are primarily giving support often receive unexpected blessings and insights from those they are helping [70]. This mutual support creates strong church communities where families can thrive spiritually and relationally.

Mentoring Younger Families in Construction

The formal and informal mentoring relationships that develop between established and newer families provide crucial support for successful family building according to biblical principles. These mentoring relationships transfer wisdom, provide accountability, and create lasting bonds that strengthen both families involved [71].

Formal mentoring programs within churches can provide structured opportunities for experienced families to share their knowledge and insights with newer families. These programs often include regular meetings, specific curriculum or discussion topics, and clear expectations for both mentors and mentees [72]. Formal programs ensure that mentoring relationships develop systematically and that important topics are addressed comprehensively.

Informal mentoring relationships often develop naturally through church activities, neighborhood connections, or shared interests. These relationships may be less structured than formal programs but can be equally effective for transferring wisdom and providing support [73]. Informal mentoring often feels more natural and comfortable for both families involved while still providing valuable guidance and encouragement.

The content of family mentoring typically includes practical guidance about marriage enrichment, child-rearing, financial stewardship, spiritual disciplines, and community engagement. Experienced families can share what they have learned through both successes and failures, helping newer families avoid common mistakes while learning effective strategies [74]. This practical wisdom often proves more valuable than theoretical knowledge because it has been tested in real-life situations.

The timing of mentoring conversations often proves crucial for their effectiveness. Experienced mentors learn to recognize when newer families are facing specific challenges or transitions that create teachable moments [75]. These timely conversations can provide crucial guidance and support when families are most receptive to learning and most in need of encouragement.

The relationship building that occurs through mentoring often extends far beyond the formal mentoring period to create lasting friendships that benefit both families for years to come. These relationships provide ongoing support, accountability, and encouragement that help families maintain their commitment to biblical principles [76]. The mutual blessing that flows from these relationships often surprises both mentors and mentees.

The multiplication effect of effective mentoring creates expanding networks of families who are committed to building according to biblical principles. When families who have been mentored become mentors themselves, they create ongoing cycles of support and encouragement that strengthen entire church communities [77].

Contributing to Local Church Health

The active participation of well-built families significantly affects the overall health and effectiveness of local church communities. These families provide leadership, service, and stability that enable churches to fulfill their mission while creating environments where other families can flourish [78].

Leadership contributions from mature families often include serving in various church ministries, teaching classes, and providing oversight for church programs and activities. These leadership roles enable experienced families to share their gifts and insights while helping to maintain the church's commitment to biblical principles [79]. The stability and wisdom that mature families bring to leadership positions often prove crucial for church health and effectiveness.

Service contributions from families include volunteering for various church activities, supporting church programs, and using their skills and resources to meet church needs. When families consistently serve others within the church community, they demonstrate the love of Christ while contributing to the church's ability to minister effectively [80]. This service often provides examples that encourage other families to become more involved in church life.

Financial contributions from committed families provide essential resources for church ministry while demonstrating stewardship principles that encourage others to give generously. When families consistently support their church financially, they enable the church to maintain its programs and expand its ministry [81]. The generosity that characterizes biblical families often inspires others to develop similar patterns of giving.

Stability contributions from established families provide continuity and consistency that help churches weather difficult seasons and maintain their focus on biblical priorities. When families remain committed to their church through both good times and challenging periods, they provide examples of faithfulness that encourage others [82]. This stability often proves crucial for maintaining church health during pastoral transitions or other significant changes.

Evangelistic contributions from families include bringing friends and neighbors to church activities, supporting outreach programs, and creating welcoming environments for visitors. When families actively invite others to participate in church life, they contribute significantly to church growth and evangelistic effectiveness [83]. The relationships that families build in their communities often provide the most effective means for attracting new people to church.

When families successfully contribute to local church health while building a *Family by the Book: How to Build the Family God Intended*, they create positive cycles where strong families build strong churches, which in turn support and encourage strong families [84].

Chapter 8

Building Through Difficulties

When Construction Gets Challenging

As we have explored the foundational principles of biblical family construction through examining individual roles, parental responsibilities, and community engagement, we now turn our attention to one of the most crucial aspects of creating a Family by the Book: How to Build the Family God Intended - navigating the inevitable difficulties and challenges that arise during the construction process. The transition from understanding ideal family functioning to addressing real-world challenges represents a necessary progression in our building project, as even the most well-constructed families will face trials that test their foundations and require wisdom, faith, and perseverance to overcome.

The apostle James provides essential guidance for families facing difficulties when he declares, *"Count it all joy, my brothers, when you meet trials of various kinds"* (James 1:2). This foundational verse reveals that difficulties are not signs of construction failure but are inevitable aspects of life in a fallen world that can actually strengthen family bonds and spiritual maturity when handled according to biblical principles [1]. The phrase "count it all joy" does not suggest that families should enjoy suffering, but rather that they should recognize the potential for growth and blessing that can emerge from properly navigated challenges.

Understanding difficulties as opportunities for growth rather than threats to family stability transforms how families approach the inevitable challenges they will face. Rather than viewing conflicts, crises, and pressures as evidence that their family construction has failed, families built according to biblical principles recognize that these challenges provide opportunities to

168

demonstrate the strength of their foundations and to develop greater maturity and unity [2]. This perspective requires faith, patience, and long-term vision, but it enables families to emerge from difficulties stronger and more unified than before.

The reality of difficulties in family life also reveals the importance of building strong foundations during peaceful seasons. Families that have invested in developing biblical principles, strong relationships, and spiritual disciplines during good times are better equipped to weather the storms that inevitably arise [3]. This preparation involves more than simply learning biblical concepts; it requires developing the character qualities and relational skills that enable families to respond to challenges with wisdom and grace.

When families commit to building a *Family by the Book: How to Build the Family God Intended*, they understand that difficulties serve multiple purposes in God's plan for their growth and development. These challenges test the strength of their foundations, reveal areas that need additional construction work, and provide opportunities to demonstrate their faith to watching family members and community observers [4]. This multi-faceted understanding helps families maintain perspective during difficult seasons while remaining committed to biblical principles and family unity.

The approach that families take to difficulties significantly affects both the immediate outcomes and the long-term impact on family relationships and spiritual growth. Families that respond to challenges with blame, anger, or despair often find that difficulties create lasting damage to relationships and spiritual health [5]. However, families that respond with faith, unity, and biblical wisdom often discover that challenges become catalysts for deeper relationships and stronger spiritual foundations.

The community support that families receive during difficult seasons often proves crucial for the successful navigation of challenges. Families that have invested in building relationships with other believers and have remained connected to their church communities typically find greater resources and encouragement during times of crisis [6]. This support network provides practical assistance, emotional encouragement, and spiritual guidance that can make the difference between families that thrive through difficulties and those that are overwhelmed by them.

Dealing with Family Conflicts

"If your brother sins against you, go and tell him his fault, between you and him alone" (Matthew 18:15). Conflict represents one of the most common and challenging aspects of family life, arising inevitably from the interaction of imperfect people living in close proximity with different personalities, preferences, and perspectives. Understanding how to handle family conflicts biblically is essential for maintaining healthy relationships and creating environments where all family members can flourish [7].

The Inevitability of Conflict in Building Relationships

Recognizing that conflict is inevitable in family relationships helps families prepare for challenges rather than being surprised or discouraged when disagreements arise. This understanding begins with acknowledging that all family members are fallen human beings who will sometimes make mistakes, act selfishly, or misunderstand one another [8]. When families accept this reality, they can approach conflicts as normal aspects of family life rather than as threats to family unity.

The sources of family conflict are numerous and varied, ranging from simple misunderstandings and personality differences to more serious issues involving values, priorities, and behavioral choices. Understanding these various sources helps families respond appropriately to different types of conflicts [9]. Some conflicts arise from external pressures such as financial stress or schedule demands, while others emerge from internal dynamics such as sibling rivalry or generational differences.

The frequency of conflicts in family life often surprises new families who expected that love and good intentions would prevent most disagreements. However, the reality is that families who spend significant time together and care deeply about one another will inevitably experience conflicts as they navigate the complexities of daily life [10]. This frequency does not indicate family failure but rather reflects the normal challenges of building intimate relationships among imperfect people.

The intensity of family conflicts often exceeds that of conflicts in other relationships because family members feel safer expressing their true feelings and because the stakes feel higher when disagreements involve people we love most deeply. This intensity can be both beneficial and challenging for family relationships [11]. While it enables families to address issues honestly and thoroughly, it can also create emotional wounds that require careful attention and healing.

The impact of unresolved conflicts on family relationships can be devastating over time, creating patterns of resentment, withdrawal, and dysfunction that undermine family unity and spiritual health. Families that fail to develop effective conflict resolution skills often find that small disagreements escalate into major crises that threaten family stability [12]. This cumulative effect demonstrates the importance of addressing conflicts promptly and biblically rather than allowing them to fester.

The opportunity that conflicts provide for family growth and deeper relationships often goes unrecognized by families who view disagreements only as problems to be solved. However, conflicts that are handled biblically can actually strengthen family bonds by increasing understanding, demonstrating forgiveness, and building confidence in the family's ability to work through challenges together [13]. This transformative potential makes conflict resolution skills essential for successful family building.

Biblical Principles for Conflict Resolution

The Bible provides comprehensive guidance for resolving conflicts in ways that honor God, restore relationships, and promote spiritual growth. These principles apply to all types of family conflicts, from minor disagreements to major crises, and provide frameworks for addressing issues constructively rather than destructively [14].

The principle of direct communication, outlined in Matthew 18:15, requires family members to address conflicts directly with the people involved rather than talking to others about the problem or allowing resentment to build. This direct approach prevents gossip, reduces misunderstandings, and demonstrates respect for the relationship [15]. When family members consistently practice direct communication, they create environments where issues can be resolved quickly before they escalate into major problems.

The principle of gentle confrontation emphasizes the importance of addressing conflicts with love and humility rather than anger or accusation. Galatians 6:1 instructs believers to restore those who are caught in sin *"in a spirit of gentleness,"* recognizing their own vulnerability to similar failures [16]. This gentle approach increases the likelihood that confrontation will be received positively and lead to genuine resolution rather than defensive reactions.

The principle of listening before speaking, emphasized in James 1:19, requires family members to seek understanding before trying to be understood. This listening involves more than simply waiting for one's turn to talk; it requires genuine effort to understand the other person's perspective, feelings, and concerns [17]. When family members practice active listening, they often discover that conflicts are based on misunderstandings that can be easily resolved through better communication.

The principle of confession and forgiveness provides the foundation for restoring relationships after conflicts have been resolved. This involves acknowledging personal contributions to the conflict, seeking forgiveness for mistakes or sins, and extending forgiveness to others who have caused hurt [18]. The practice of confession and forgiveness prevents conflicts from creating lasting resentment and enables families to move forward with restored relationships.

The principle of seeking wise counsel, outlined in Proverbs 15:22, encourages families to seek outside perspectives when they are unable to resolve conflicts on their own. This counsel might come from pastors, mature friends, or professional counselors who can provide objective insights and biblical guidance [19]. The willingness to seek help demonstrates humility and commitment to resolution rather than pride or stubbornness.

The principle of focusing on solutions rather than blame helps families move beyond simply identifying problems to developing practical strategies for preventing similar conflicts in the future. This solution-focused approach requires families to work together toward common goals rather than trying to determine who is at fault [20]. When families consistently focus on solutions, they develop problem-solving skills that serve them well in all areas of life.

When families successfully apply these biblical principles while building a Family by the Book: How to Build the Family God Intended, they discover that conflicts become opportunities for growth rather than threats to family unity [21].

Forgiveness and Reconciliation in Family Building

Forgiveness represents one of the most crucial elements in successful family conflict resolution, yet it is often misunderstood or inadequately practiced by families who want to restore relationships after disagreements. Biblical forgiveness goes beyond simply forgetting offenses to include genuine release of resentment and commitment to a restored relationship [22].

Understanding forgiveness as a choice rather than a feeling helps family members extend forgiveness even when they do not feel emotionally ready to do so. This understanding recognizes that forgiveness is an act of obedience to God and commitment to family relationships rather than an emotional response that must be waited for [23]. When family members choose to forgive regardless of their feelings, they often find that emotional healing follows their obedient choice.

The process of forgiveness often requires time and may involve multiple steps rather than a single decision. This process might include acknowledging the hurt that was caused, choosing to release resentment, communicating forgiveness to the offending party, and working toward restoring trust and relationship [24]. Understanding forgiveness as a process helps families be patient with themselves and others as they work toward complete reconciliation.

The distinction between forgiveness and trust helps families navigate the restoration process wisely. While forgiveness can be extended immediately upon repentance, trust must often be rebuilt gradually through demonstrated change and consistent behavior [25]. This distinction enables families to forgive quickly while still maintaining appropriate boundaries and expectations for behavioral change.

The role of repentance in the forgiveness process cannot be overlooked, as genuine repentance demonstrates acknowledgment of wrongdoing and commitment to change. This repentance involves more than simply saying "I'm sorry" but includes taking responsibility for one's actions and making necessary changes to prevent similar problems in the future [26]. When family members practice genuine repentance, they create environments where forgiveness can be extended confidently and relationships can be restored completely.

The benefits of forgiveness extend beyond the immediate resolution of conflicts to include improved family emotional health, stronger relationships, and powerful modeling for children about God's character and grace. Families that practice forgiveness consistently create environments where family members feel safe to admit mistakes and seek help when needed [27]. This safety enables families to address problems early before they become major crises.

The multiplication effect of forgiveness within families often extends beyond the immediate family to influence extended family relationships and community interactions. When children observe their parents practicing forgiveness consistently, they learn valuable lessons about grace, humility, and relationship restoration that serve them throughout their lives [28]. This modeling often proves more influential than formal instruction in shaping children's approaches to conflict resolution.

Teaching Children Healthy Conflict Resolution

One of the most important responsibilities of parents involves teaching their children how to handle conflicts in ways that honor God and strengthen relationships. This training provides children with essential life skills while creating family environments where conflicts can be resolved constructively [29].

Age-appropriate conflict resolution training begins in early childhood with simple concepts such as sharing, taking turns, and using words instead of physical aggression to express frustration. Young children need concrete guidance about how to handle disagreements with siblings and friends [30]. This early training provides the foundation for more sophisticated conflict resolution skills that develop throughout childhood and adolescence.

The modeling that parents provide during their own conflicts significantly affects their children's development of conflict resolution skills. When children observe their parents handling disagreements with respect, seeking understanding, and working toward resolution, they learn that conflicts can be resolved without damaging relationships [31]. This modeling often proves more influential than formal instruction in shaping children's approaches to conflict.

The practice opportunities that parents provide for children to resolve their own conflicts help develop confidence and competence in conflict resolution skills. Rather than immediately intervening in sibling disputes, parents can guide children through the process of working out their own disagreements [32]. This guided practice helps children develop the skills they will need for handling conflicts throughout their lives.

The biblical principles that parents teach during conflict resolution training help children understand that conflict resolution is not merely a practical skill but a spiritual discipline that reflects God's character. When children learn to apply biblical principles such as forgiveness, humility, and love during conflicts, they develop spiritual maturity alongside practical skills [33]. This spiritual foundation provides motivation and guidance for handling conflicts throughout their lives.

The consequences that parents establish for inappropriate conflict resolution help children understand the importance of handling disagreements constructively. These consequences should be designed to teach rather than simply punish, helping children understand why certain approaches to conflict are harmful and encouraging them to develop better strategies [34]. When consequences are administered with love and clear explanation, they become valuable learning opportunities.

The celebration that families engage in when conflicts are resolved successfully helps reinforce positive conflict resolution patterns and creates positive associations with the hard work of relationship restoration. This celebration might involve acknowledging the effort that family members put into resolving disagreements or expressing gratitude for restored relationships [35]. These positive reinforcements encourage family members to continue investing in healthy conflict resolution.

When Marriages Face Crisis

"What therefore God has joined together, let not man separate" (Mark 10:9). Marriage crises represent some of the most challenging difficulties that families can face, threatening not only the relationship between spouses but also the stability and security of the entire family unit. Understanding how to navigate marriage crises biblically is essential for preserving families and demonstrating God's design for lifelong commitment [36].

Biblical Principles for Marriage Restoration

The foundation of marriage restoration rests on understanding marriage as a covenant relationship that reflects God's faithfulness to His people rather than simply a contract based on mutual satisfaction or compatibility. This covenant perspective provides motivation and framework for working through difficulties that might otherwise seem insurmountable [37].

The principle of unconditional commitment provides the foundation for marriage restoration by establishing that the goal is always to restore and strengthen the relationship rather than to determine whether the marriage should continue. This commitment recognizes that marriage vows include promises to remain faithful "for better or worse" and that difficulties are opportunities to demonstrate covenant love [38]. When both spouses maintain this commitment, they create environments where restoration becomes possible even after serious failures.

The principle of personal responsibility requires each spouse to focus on their own contributions to marriage problems rather than simply blaming their partner for difficulties. This responsibility involves honest self-examination, acknowledgment of personal failures, and commitment to personal change regardless of what the other spouse does [39]. When spouses take personal responsibility, they create positive momentum toward restoration rather than defensive cycles that perpetuate problems.

The principle of grace and truth, modeled by Jesus in His relationships, requires spouses to combine honest communication about problems with loving acceptance and forgiveness. This balance enables couples to address serious issues without destroying hope or damaging self-worth [40]. When spouses practice grace and truth consistently, they create environments where both accountability and healing can occur.

The principle of seeking God's guidance through prayer, Scripture study, and wise counsel provides essential resources for marriage restoration that go beyond human wisdom and effort. This spiritual dimension recognizes that marriage restoration often requires supernatural intervention and that God is committed to helping couples succeed in their covenant relationships [41]. When couples consistently seek God's guidance, they often discover solutions and strength that they could not find through their own efforts.

The principle of patience and perseverance acknowledges that marriage restoration typically requires time and sustained effort rather than quick fixes or immediate solutions. This patience enables couples to work through complex issues systematically while maintaining hope for eventual restoration

[42]. When couples commit to long-term restoration processes, they often discover that their marriages become stronger than they were before the crisis occurred.

The principle of professional help recognizes that some marriage crises require assistance from trained counselors, pastors, or other professionals who can provide an objective perspective and specialized expertise. This willingness to seek help demonstrates humility and commitment to restoration rather than pride or stubbornness [43]. When couples seek appropriate professional help, they often gain insights and tools that enable them to work through issues more effectively.

When to Seek Pastoral and Professional Help

Recognizing when marriage difficulties require outside assistance represents an important skill for couples who want to address problems before they become crises. This recognition involves understanding the difference between normal marriage challenges that couples can handle on their own and serious problems that require professional intervention [44].

Warning signs that indicate the need for professional help include persistent communication problems that couples cannot resolve on their own, recurring conflicts that escalate rather than improve over time, and emotional or physical withdrawal that threatens the basic connection between spouses. These patterns often indicate underlying issues that require professional insight and intervention [45]. Early recognition of these warning signs enables couples to seek help before problems become entrenched and more difficult to resolve.

The presence of destructive behalviors such as verbal abuse, physical violence, substance abuse, or infidelity typically requires immediate professional intervention to ensure safety and begin restoration processes. These behaviors often involve complex psychological and spiritual issues that

179

require specialized expertise to address effectively [46]. Couples facing these challenges should seek help immediately rather than trying to handle them independently.

Mental health issues such as depression, anxiety, or other psychological conditions often require professional treatment that goes beyond marriage counseling to address underlying medical or psychological factors. These conditions can significantly affect marriage relationships and may require specialized treatment before marriage restoration can be effective [47]. Understanding the connection between mental health and marriage health helps couples seek appropriate help for all aspects of their difficulties.

The selection of appropriate professional help requires careful consideration of the counselor's qualifications, approach, and commitment to biblical principles. Couples should seek counselors who understand and support the covenant nature of marriage and who are committed to restoration rather than simply helping couples feel better about their decisions [48]. This careful selection ensures that professional help supports rather than undermines biblical approaches to marriage restoration.

The timing of professional intervention often affects its effectiveness, with earlier intervention typically producing better outcomes than waiting until crises become severe. Couples who seek help at the first signs of serious problems often find that restoration is easier and more complete than when they wait until damage has become extensive [49]. This early intervention requires humility and wisdom, but it often prevents more serious problems from developing.

The integration of professional help with church support and personal spiritual disciplines creates comprehensive approaches to marriage restoration that address all aspects of the relationship. This integration recognizes that marriage restoration involves spiritual, emotional, and practical dimensions that require different types of support and intervention [50]. When couples successfully integrate these various resources, they often experience more complete and lasting restoration.

The Church's Role in Supporting Struggling Marriages

The local church community plays a crucial role in supporting marriages through both preventive ministry and crisis intervention. This support reflects the church's commitment to God's design for marriage and provides essential resources for couples who are working toward restoration [51].

Preventive marriage ministry involves providing ongoing education, support, and encouragement for couples before serious problems develop. This ministry might include marriage enrichment classes, mentoring programs, and regular opportunities for couples to connect with other married couples who can provide encouragement and accountability [52]. These preventive measures help couples develop strong foundations that enable them to weather inevitable challenges.

Crisis Intervention Ministry provides immediate support and resources for couples who are facing serious marriage difficulties. This intervention might include pastoral counseling, referrals to professional counselors, practical assistance during difficult times, and ongoing prayer and encouragement [53]. The availability of immediate help often makes the difference between couples who work through their problems and those who give up on their marriages.

Marriage mentoring programs connect struggling couples with mature couples who have successfully navigated similar challenges and can provide practical guidance and encouragement. These mentoring relationships often provide hope and practical wisdom that professional counseling alone cannot offer [54]. The personal connection and ongoing support that mentoring provides often proves crucial for successful marriage restoration.

Support groups for couples facing specific challenges, such as infidelity, addiction, or communication problems, provide opportunities for couples to connect with others who understand their struggles and can offer encouragement and practical advice. These groups often provide hope and practical strategies that couples cannot find elsewhere [55]. The community support that these groups provide often proves essential for long-term restoration success.

Practical assistance during marriage crises might include childcare, meals, financial support, or other forms of help that enable couples to focus on restoration without being overwhelmed by practical concerns. This assistance demonstrates the church's commitment to marriage restoration and provides tangible evidence of God's love and care [56]. The practical support that churches provide often enables couples to invest in restoration processes that they could not otherwise afford.

Long-term follow-up and accountability help ensure that marriage restoration efforts produce lasting change rather than temporary improvement. This follow-up might include ongoing mentoring relationships, regular check-ins with pastoral staff, and continued participation in marriage support programs [57]. The long-term commitment that churches demonstrate often provides the ongoing support necessary for sustained marriage health.

Hope for Rebuilding After Breakdown

Even marriages that have experienced a serious breakdown can be restored when couples are willing to commit to biblical restoration processes and seek appropriate help and support. This hope is based on God's power to transform hearts and relationships rather than simply on human effort or good intentions [58].

The possibility of restoration exists even after serious failures such as infidelity, abandonment, or other covenant violations because God's grace is sufficient to overcome any sin, and His power is able to transform any heart. This possibility does not minimize the seriousness of covenant violations but recognizes that God's redemptive power extends to all areas of human brokenness [59]. When couples understand this possibility, they often find motivation to pursue restoration even when circumstances seem hopeless.

The process of rebuilding after a breakdown typically requires more time and effort than preventing problems in the first place, but it can result in marriages that are stronger and more intimate than they were before the crisis occurred. This rebuilding process often involves addressing underlying issues that contributed to the breakdown while developing new patterns of communication and relationship [60]. The depth of restoration that can occur often surprises couples who commit to thorough rebuilding processes.

The role of forgiveness in rebuilding cannot be overstated, as genuine restoration requires both spouses to extend and receive forgiveness for the failures that led to the breakdown. This forgiveness often must be renewed repeatedly as couples work through the complex emotions and practical challenges involved in restoration [61]. The practice of ongoing forgiveness creates environments where healing can occur and trust can be rebuilt gradually.

The importance of accountability and ongoing support during rebuilding processes helps ensure that couples develop sustainable patterns rather than simply returning to previous dysfunctional dynamics. This accountability might involve regular meetings with counselors or mentors, participation in support groups, and ongoing commitment to personal growth and change [62]. The external support that couples receive often provides the motivation and guidance necessary for successful rebuilding.

When marriages are successfully rebuilt after breakdown, while families work toward building a *Family by the Book: How to Build the Family God Intended*, they often become powerful testimonies to God's redemptive power and provide hope and encouragement for other couples who are facing similar challenges [63].

Financial Pressures and Harmony

"But godliness with contentment is great gain" (1 Timothy 6:6). Financial pressures represent one of the most common sources of family stress and conflict, affecting not only practical aspects of family life but also relationships, spiritual health, and overall family harmony. Understanding how to handle financial challenges biblically is essential for maintaining family unity and demonstrating trust in God's provision [64].

Biblical Money Management Building Principles

The foundation of biblical financial management rests on understanding that all resources belong to God and that families are stewards rather than owners of their financial resources. This stewardship perspective transforms how families approach earning, spending, saving, and giving decisions [65]. When families embrace this stewardship mindset, they often find that financial decisions become clearer and that conflicts over money decrease significantly.

The principle of contentment, emphasized in 1 Timothy 6:6, provides essential protection against the materialism and debt that create financial pressure for many families. This contentment involves learning to be satisfied with God's provision rather than constantly striving for more possessions or higher income [66]. When families practice contentment, they often discover that they have sufficient resources for their needs and can avoid the debt and stress that characterize many contemporary families.

184

The principle of diligent work, outlined in 2 Thessalonians 3:10, establishes that families should work hard to provide for their needs rather than expecting others to support them or relying on get-rich-quick schemes. This diligence involves developing skills, maintaining good work habits, and taking responsibility for family financial needs [67]. When families practice diligent work, they often find that God blesses their efforts and provides for their needs in unexpected ways.

The principle of generous giving, emphasized throughout Scripture, requires families to prioritize giving to God's work and helping others even when their own resources seem limited. This generosity demonstrates trust in God's provision and creates opportunities for God to bless families financially [68]. When families practice generous giving, they often discover that God provides for their needs in ways that exceed their expectations.

The principle of wise planning, illustrated in Proverbs 21:5, encourages families to develop budgets, save for future needs, and make thoughtful decisions about major purchases rather than living impulsively or without financial goals. This planning enables families to avoid debt, prepare for emergencies, and work toward long-term financial stability [69]. When families practice wise planning, they often find that they can accomplish more with their resources than they thought possible.

The principle of avoiding debt, warned against in Proverbs 22:7, protects families from the financial bondage that creates stress and limits their ability to be generous and responsive to God's leading. This debt avoidance requires families to live within their means and save for major purchases rather than borrowing money for wants or even some needs [70]. When families avoid debt, they often experience greater financial freedom and reduced stress.

Working Together Toward Financial Goals

The unity that couples demonstrate in their financial decision-making significantly affects both their financial success and their marriage relationship. This unity requires ongoing communication, shared values, and mutual commitment to family financial goals [71].

The development of shared financial goals requires couples to discuss their values, priorities, and dreams while working together to establish realistic and achievable objectives. These goals might include debt elimination, saving for children's education, purchasing a home, or increasing charitable giving [72]. When couples develop shared goals, they create motivation for working together rather than competing with each other over financial decisions.

The creation of family budgets provides practical frameworks for achieving financial goals while ensuring that all family needs are met appropriately. These budgets should reflect family values and priorities while providing realistic guidelines for spending and saving [73]. When families create and follow budgets consistently, they often find that they can accomplish their financial goals more quickly than they expected.

The assignment of financial responsibilities within families should reflect each spouse's gifts, interests, and availability while ensuring that both spouses remain informed about the family's financial status. Some couples work best when one spouse handles most financial management, while others prefer to share responsibilities more equally [74]. The key is finding approaches that work for each specific family while maintaining unity and communication.

The regular review of family financial status helps couples stay on track toward their goals while identifying problems early before they become crises. These reviews might occur monthly or quarterly and should include assessment of income, expenses, savings, and progress toward goals [75].

When couples review their finances regularly, they often catch problems early and can make adjustments before difficulties become serious.

The celebration of financial milestones helps families maintain motivation for their financial goals while acknowledging God's provision and blessing. These celebrations might involve special meals, family activities, or expressions of gratitude when families reach savings goals, eliminate debt, or achieve other financial objectives [76]. When families celebrate financial progress, they often find increased motivation for continued financial discipline.

The flexibility that families maintain in their financial planning enables them to adjust their goals and strategies when circumstances change or when God provides unexpected opportunities or challenges. This flexibility requires families to hold their plans loosely while remaining committed to biblical principles [77]. When families maintain appropriate flexibility, they often find that they can respond to changing circumstances without abandoning their financial goals.

Teaching Children About Money and Generosity

One of the most important responsibilities of parents involves teaching their children biblical principles about money, work, and generosity that will guide them throughout their lives. This training provides children with essential life skills while helping them develop character qualities that honor God [78].

Age-appropriate money management training begins in early childhood with simple concepts such as the difference between needs and wants, the importance of work, and the joy of giving to others. Young children can learn these concepts through allowances, chores, and opportunities to give to church or charity [79]. This early training provides the foundation for more sophisticated financial understanding that develops throughout childhood and adolescence.

The modeling that parents provide in their own financial decisions significantly affects their children's development of money management skills and attitudes. When children observe their parents making wise financial decisions, working diligently, and giving generously, they learn that money is a tool for serving God and others rather than an end in itself [80]. This modeling often proves more influential than formal instruction in shaping children's financial attitudes and behaviors.

The practice opportunities that parents provide for children to manage money help develop confidence and competence in financial decision-making. These opportunities might include allowances, earnings from chores or jobs, and guidance in making spending and saving decisions [81]. When children practice money management with parental guidance, they develop skills and wisdom that serve them throughout their lives.

The biblical principles that parents teach during money management training help children understand that financial decisions are spiritual issues that reflect their relationship with God. When children learn to apply biblical principles such as stewardship, contentment, and generosity to their financial decisions, they develop spiritual maturity alongside practical skills [82]. This spiritual foundation provides motivation and guidance for handling money throughout their lives.

Chapter 9
Building a Legacy

Generational Construction

As we have explored the foundational principles of biblical family construction through examining individual roles, parental responsibilities, community engagement, and navigating difficulties, we now turn our attention to one of the most profound aspects of creating a *Family by the Book: How to Build the Family God Intended* - the multigenerational impact that well-built families have on future generations and the broader community. The transition from focusing on immediate family construction to understanding long-term legacy building represents the culmination of our building project, as families that have been constructed according to biblical principles become launching pads for successive generations of godly families.

The psalmist provides the foundational blueprint for generational construction when he declares, *"We will not hide them from their children, but tell to the coming generation the glorious deeds of the Lord, and his might, and the wonders that he has done"* (Psalm 78:4). This foundational verse reveals that the ultimate purpose of family construction extends far beyond the immediate family to include the intentional transfer of faith, values, and wisdom to future generations [1]. The phrase "we will not hide them" emphasizes the active responsibility that each generation bears for ensuring that God's truth and character are passed down to their children and grandchildren.

Understanding families as generational construction projects transforms how we approach the daily decisions and long-term planning that shape family life. Rather than viewing family building as a project that ends when children reach adulthood, families built according to biblical principles recognize that their construction work creates foundations that will support multiple generations of descendants [2]. This multigenerational perspective requires patience, intentionality, and eternal vision, but it produces families that impact th0eir communities and advance God's kingdom for generations to come.

The legacy that families build through their construction efforts extends far beyond material inheritance to include spiritual heritage, character qualities, relationship patterns, and kingdom values that shape how future generations approach life, marriage, parenting, and service. This comprehensive legacy affects not only direct descendants but also the broader community as successive generations of godly families contribute to society's moral and spiritual health [3]. When families understand the scope of their potential legacy, they often find greater motivation for the daily sacrifices and long-term commitments required for successful family construction.

When families commit to building a *Family by the Book: How to Build the Family God Intended*, they understand that their legacy-building serves multiple purposes in God's economy. Their faithful construction provides hope and direction for struggling families, demonstrates the practical benefits of biblical principles across multiple generations, and creates expanding networks of influence that advance God's kingdom purposes [4]. This multi-faceted impact motivates families to take their legacy building seriously while maintaining their focus on faithful obedience rather than visible results.

The intentionality required for effective legacy building involves more than simply hoping that children will follow their parents' example. It requires deliberate planning, consistent modeling, systematic teaching, and ongoing investment in relationships that will continue long after parents are no longer present to provide direct guidance [5]. This intentional approach recognizes that legacy building is both a privilege and a responsibility that requires wisdom, commitment, and dependence on God's grace.

191

The community impact of generational construction often extends far beyond what individual families can see or measure. When multiple families in a community commit to biblical construction principles, they create cultural momentum that influences schools, businesses, churches, and civic organizations for generations [6]. This cumulative effect demonstrates the strategic importance of family legacy building in God's plan for transforming communities and advancing His kingdom purposes.

Understanding Generational Impact

"A good man leaves an inheritance to his children's children" (Proverbs 13:22). The impact that families have on future generations extends far beyond what most parents realize, affecting not only their immediate children but also grandchildren, great-grandchildren, and even descendants they will never meet. Understanding this generational impact helps families recognize the eternal significance of their daily choices and long-term commitments [7].

The Ripple Effect of Family Choices

Every decision that families make creates ripple effects that extend far beyond the immediate circumstances, influencing patterns of thinking, relating, and living that can persist for multiple generations. These ripple effects operate according to spiritual and psychological principles that amplify both positive and negative influences over time [8].

Positive family choices create expanding circles of blessing that benefit not only immediate family members but also future generations who inherit the benefits of wise decisions made by their ancestors. These positive choices might include commitments to biblical principles, investments in education and character development, patterns of generous giving, and traditions of faithful service [9]. When families consistently make positive choices, they create momentum that makes it easier for future generations to continue in similar patterns.

The modeling that parents provide through their daily choices significantly affects their children's understanding of what constitutes normal family life. Children who observe their parents making wise decisions, handling conflicts constructively, and maintaining biblical priorities often assume that such patterns are natural and expected [10]. This modeling creates positive expectations that influence how children approach their own marriages, parenting, and life decisions.

Negative family choices also create ripple effects that can persist for multiple generations, establishing patterns of dysfunction, poor decision-making, and spiritual compromise that become increasingly difficult to break over time. These negative patterns might include addictive behaviors, financial irresponsibility, relationship dysfunction, or spiritual apathy [11]. Understanding the potential negative impact of poor choices motivates families to seek help when needed and to break destructive patterns before they become entrenched.

The cumulative effect of family choices over time often produces results that far exceed what individual decisions might suggest. Small positive choices made consistently over many years can produce dramatic positive outcomes, while small negative choices can accumulate into serious problems [12]. This cumulative principle helps families understand the importance of consistency in their construction efforts and motivates them to persevere even when immediate results are not visible.

The multiplication effect of family choices occurs as children who have been influenced by their parents' decisions go on to influence their own children, creating expanding networks of impact that can affect entire communities over time. This multiplication demonstrates the strategic importance of family construction in God's plan for advancing His kingdom [13]. When families understand this multiplication potential, they often find greater motivation for the sacrifices required for faithful family building.

The redemptive potential that exists within generational impact provides hope for families who recognize negative patterns in their heritage. While negative influences can persist across generations, positive changes can also create new patterns that benefit future generations [14]. This redemptive potential motivates families to pursue biblical construction even when their own family backgrounds include dysfunction or spiritual compromise.

Breaking Negative Generational Patterns

One of the most important aspects of legacy building involves identifying and breaking negative patterns that have been passed down from previous generations. This pattern-breaking requires wisdom, courage, and often professional help, but it can create new trajectories that benefit multiple future generations [15].

Recognizing negative generational patterns begins with an honest assessment of family history and current family dynamics to identify recurring problems or dysfunctional behaviors that have persisted across multiple generations. These patterns might include addiction, abuse, financial irresponsibility, relationship dysfunction, or spiritual compromise [16]. The willingness to acknowledge these patterns honestly provides the foundation for breaking them effectively.

Understanding the sources of negative patterns helps families address root causes rather than simply managing symptoms. Many negative patterns originate from unresolved trauma, spiritual compromise, or learned behaviors that were adaptive in previous circumstances but have become destructive in current contexts [17]. This understanding enables families to develop comprehensive strategies for change that address underlying issues.

194

Developing strategies for pattern-breaking often requires families to seek help from pastors, counselors, or other professionals who can provide an objective perspective and specialized expertise. These strategies might include counseling, support groups, accountability relationships, and systematic efforts to develop new patterns of thinking and behaving [18]. The willingness to seek help demonstrates humility and commitment to change rather than pride or denial.

Implementing new patterns requires sustained effort and often involves setbacks and challenges that test families' commitment to change. This implementation process typically requires several years of consistent effort before new patterns become established and natural [19]. The patience and perseverance required for successful pattern-breaking often prove challenging but produce lasting benefits for multiple generations.

Teaching children about negative family patterns helps them understand their heritage while empowering them to make different choices for their own families. This teaching should be age-appropriate and should emphasize hope and redemption rather than shame or despair [20]. When children understand their family history honestly, they are better equipped to avoid repeating negative patterns while building on positive aspects of their heritage.

Celebrating progress in pattern-breaking helps families maintain motivation for continued change while acknowledging God's grace and power in transformation. This celebration might involve recognizing milestones in recovery, acknowledging improved relationships, or expressing gratitude for new opportunities [21]. When families celebrate progress regularly, they often find increased motivation for continued growth and change.

The long-term perspective that guides pattern-breaking efforts helps families persevere through difficult seasons while maintaining hope for future generations. This perspective recognizes that pattern-breaking is often a multi-generational process that requires sustained effort across several generations [22]. When families maintain this long-term perspective, they often find the strength to continue their efforts even when immediate results are limited.

Creating Positive Generational Momentum

While breaking negative patterns represents an important aspect of legacy building, creating positive generational momentum involves the proactive development of beneficial patterns that will bless future generations. This momentum-building requires intentional effort and long-term vision but produces expanding benefits over time [23].

Establishing positive family traditions creates recurring opportunities for families to reinforce their values, strengthen relationships, and create positive memories that children will want to continue with their own families. These traditions might include regular family devotions, annual service projects, holiday celebrations, or special recognition of family milestones [24]. When families establish meaningful traditions, they create positive momentum that often continues for multiple generations.

Developing family mission statements or value systems helps families articulate their priorities and commitments in ways that can guide decision-making across multiple generations. These statements should reflect biblical principles while addressing the specific calling and circumstances of each family [25]. When families develop clear mission statements, they provide direction and motivation for future generations who want to continue their family's legacy.

Investing in education and character development creates advantages that benefit not only immediate children but also future generations who inherit the benefits of improved knowledge, skills, and character qualities.

These investments might include formal education, character training, skill development, or spiritual formation [26]. When families prioritize education and character development, they often create upward mobility that benefits multiple generations.

Building financial stability and generosity patterns creates resources that can benefit future generations while demonstrating biblical principles of stewardship and giving. This financial legacy might include debt-free living, generous giving patterns, wise investment strategies, or business development [27]. When families build positive financial patterns, they often provide opportunities and security for future generations.

Maintaining strong relationships with extended family members creates networks of support and influence that can benefit multiple generations. These relationships provide children with additional role models, support systems, and opportunities for learning and growth [28]. When families invest in extended family relationships, they often create resources that benefit their children throughout their lives.

Documenting family history and lessons learned helps preserve wisdom and insights that can benefit future generations who face similar challenges and opportunities. This documentation might include written family histories, recorded interviews with older family members, or systematic recording of important family decisions and their outcomes [29]. When families document their experiences thoughtfully, they provide valuable resources for future generations.

When families successfully create positive generational momentum while building a Family by the Book: How to Build the Family God Intended, they establish trajectories that can influence multiple generations and contribute significantly to God's kingdom purposes [30].

Building Traditions That Last

"These words that I command you today shall be on your heart. You shall teach them diligently to your children" (Deuteronomy 6:6-7). The traditions that families establish provide powerful vehicles for transferring values, creating memories, and strengthening relationships across multiple generations. Understanding how to build meaningful traditions that will endure requires wisdom, intentionality, and commitment to biblical principles [31].

Creating Meaningful Family Rituals

Family rituals serve as regular opportunities for families to reinforce their values, strengthen relationships, and create positive memories that children will associate with their family heritage. These rituals become particularly powerful when they combine biblical truth with practical application and emotional connection [32].

Daily family rituals provide consistent opportunities for families to connect with one another and with God while reinforcing important values and priorities. These daily rituals might include family devotions, shared meals, bedtime prayers, or regular expressions of affection and appreciation [33]. When families establish meaningful daily rituals, they create stability and security that children often carry into their own families.

Weekly family rituals create opportunities for more extended connection and deeper spiritual formation while providing regular rhythms that help families maintain their priorities despite busy schedules. These weekly rituals might include family worship, service projects, special meals, or recreational activities that bring the family together [34]. When families establish consistent weekly rituals, they often find that these times become highlights that family members anticipate and protect.

Monthly family rituals provide opportunities for special celebrations, extended activities, or focused attention on particular aspects of family life that require more time and planning. These monthly rituals might include extended family gatherings, special outings, service projects, or celebrations of family milestones [35]. When families establish meaningful monthly rituals, they create special memories that often become treasured family stories.

Annual family rituals create opportunities for major celebrations, extended planning, and significant family experiences that mark the passage of time and create lasting memories. These annual rituals might include holiday celebrations, family vacations, anniversary commemorations, or special recognition of family achievements [36]. When families establish meaningful annual rituals, they often create traditions that children eagerly anticipate and want to continue with their own families.

The flexibility that families maintain in their rituals enables them to adapt to changing circumstances while preserving the essential elements that make the rituals meaningful. This flexibility might involve modifying activities to accommodate different ages, adjusting schedules to fit changing circumstances, or adapting traditions to reflect family growth and development [37]. When families maintain appropriate flexibility, they often find that their rituals remain relevant and meaningful across multiple generations.

The intentionality that families bring to their rituals significantly affects their long-term impact and sustainability. This intentionality involves thinking carefully about the purposes of each ritual, planning activities that support those purposes, and regularly evaluating whether rituals are achieving their intended goals [38]. When families approach their rituals intentionally, they often create more meaningful experiences that have a lasting impact.

Passing Down Faith and Values

The systematic transfer of faith and values from one generation to the next represents one of the most important responsibilities of family construction and requires more than simply hoping that children will absorb family beliefs through observation. This transfer requires deliberate planning, consistent modeling, and ongoing investment in relationships [39].

Formal faith instruction provides children with a systematic understanding of biblical truth, Christian doctrine, and practical application of faith principles to daily life. This instruction might include family devotions, Bible study, catechism training, or participation in church education programs [40]. When families provide consistent formal instruction, they help children develop solid foundations for their own faith development.

Informal faith modeling occurs through the daily demonstration of faith principles in family decision-making, conflict resolution, financial stewardship, and relationship management. This modeling often proves more influential than formal instruction because it demonstrates the practical relevance of faith to all areas of life [41]. When parents consistently model authentic faith, they provide compelling evidence of faith's value and importance.

Storytelling traditions enable families to share their spiritual heritage, family history, and important lessons learned through previous generations' experiences. These stories help children understand their place in God's larger story while providing examples of faith in action [42]. When families develop rich storytelling traditions, they often create powerful connections between past, present, and future generations.

Value clarification activities help families articulate their priorities and commitments while providing opportunities for children to understand and embrace family values. These activities might include family discussions about current events, decision-making processes that involve the whole family, or regular evaluation of family priorities and goals [43]. When families engage in regular value clarification, they help children develop a clear understanding of what their family stands for.

Mentoring relationships within the family provide opportunities for older family members to invest individually in younger members while transferring wisdom, skills, and spiritual insights. These relationships might involve grandparents mentoring grandchildren, older siblings mentoring younger ones, or parents providing specialized guidance for individual children [44]. When families develop strong mentoring relationships, they often create lasting bonds that continue throughout life.

Service opportunities enable families to demonstrate their values through action while providing children with practical experience in living out their faith. These opportunities might include regular volunteer work, support for missionaries, assistance to needy families, or participation in church ministries [45]. When families serve together regularly, they often create powerful memories while demonstrating the practical importance of their faith and values.

The consistency that families maintain in their faith and value transfer efforts significantly affects their long-term success. This consistency requires families to prioritize these activities even when schedules become busy or when immediate results are not visible [46]. When families maintain consistency in their faith transfer efforts, they often see significant results in their children's spiritual development and character formation.

Holiday and Celebration Traditions

The holidays and celebrations that families observe provide powerful opportunities for reinforcing faith, strengthening relationships, and creating positive memories that children will want to continue with their own families. These celebrations become particularly meaningful when they combine biblical truth with family heritage and cultural appreciation [47].

Christmas traditions provide opportunities for families to celebrate the incarnation of Christ while creating meaningful memories and reinforcing the importance of giving, family relationships, and spiritual reflection. These traditions might include Advent celebrations, special meals, gift-giving patterns, or service activities [48]. When families develop meaningful Christmas traditions, they often create some of their most treasured family memories.

Easter traditions enable families to celebrate the resurrection of Christ while emphasizing themes of new life, hope, and redemption that apply to all areas of family life. These traditions might include special worship services, family meals, symbolic activities, or service projects [49]. When families develop meaningful Easter traditions, they often create powerful connections between their faith and their family celebrations.

Birthday traditions provide opportunities for families to celebrate individual family members while reinforcing themes of God's blessing, personal growth, and family love. These traditions might include special meals, meaningful gifts, expressions of appreciation, or spiritual reflection on God's faithfulness [50]. When families develop meaningful birthday traditions, they often create special memories that make each family member feel valued and loved.

Anniversary traditions enable families to celebrate marriage relationships while reinforcing the importance of commitment, love, and God's blessing on family life. These traditions might include special meals, renewal of vows, expressions of gratitude, or reflection on family growth and development [51]. When families develop meaningful anniversary traditions, they often strengthen marriage relationships while providing positive examples for children.

Achievement celebrations provide opportunities for families to recognize accomplishments, character growth, and spiritual development while reinforcing the importance of hard work, perseverance, and God's blessing. These celebrations might include special recognition, meaningful rewards, expressions of pride, or reflection on lessons learned [52]. When families develop meaningful achievement celebrations, they often motivate continued growth while creating positive memories.

Cultural heritage celebrations enable families to appreciate their ethnic or cultural backgrounds while maintaining their primary identity as followers of Christ. These celebrations might include traditional foods, cultural activities, historical education, or connections with extended family [53]. When families develop meaningful cultural celebrations, they often help children appreciate their heritage while maintaining their spiritual priorities.

The balance that families maintain between religious and cultural elements in their celebrations helps children understand the relationship between their faith and their cultural heritage. This balance enables families to appreciate cultural traditions while ensuring that spiritual priorities remain central [54]. When families achieve appropriate balance in their celebrations, they often create rich traditions that honor both their faith and their heritage.

Preparing Children for Their Own Building

"Train up a child in the way he should go; even when he is old he will not depart from it" (Proverbs 22:6). The ultimate goal of family construction involves preparing children to build their own godly families while maintaining strong relationships with their family of origin. This preparation requires systematic

training, gradual transfer of responsibility, and ongoing support as children transition to independence [55].

Teaching Life Skills for Independent Living

The practical skills that children need for successful independent living extend far beyond academic knowledge to include domestic skills, financial management, relationship abilities, and spiritual disciplines that will enable them to build their own godly families. This skill development requires intentional training and practice opportunities throughout childhood and adolescence [56].

Domestic skills training prepares children to manage households effectively while demonstrating the importance of creating environments that support family spiritual and relational health. These skills might include cooking, cleaning, home maintenance, organization, and hospitality [57]. When children develop strong domestic skills, they are better prepared to create homes that support their own family construction efforts.

Financial management training provides children with essential skills for stewardship, budgeting, saving, and giving that will enable them to avoid debt and build financial stability for their own families. This training should begin early with age-appropriate concepts and progress to a sophisticated understanding of biblical financial principles [58]. When children develop strong financial skills, they are better equipped to avoid financial pressures that threaten many families.

Relationship skills training helps children develop the communication, conflict resolution, and emotional intelligence necessary for building strong marriages and family relationships. These skills include active listening, empathy, forgiveness, and the ability to work through disagreements constructively [59]. When children develop strong relationship skills, they are better prepared for the interpersonal challenges of marriage and parenting.

Spiritual discipline training provides children with personal practices that will sustain their faith and spiritual growth throughout their lives. These disciplines might include personal Bible study, prayer, worship, service, and fellowship with other believers [60]. When children develop consistent spiritual disciplines, they are better equipped to maintain their faith during challenging seasons and to lead their own families spiritually.

Work ethic development helps children understand the importance of diligence, responsibility, and excellence in all areas of life while preparing them for career success and financial stability. This development might include chores, part-time jobs, volunteer work, or academic responsibilities [61]. When children develop strong work ethics, they are better prepared to provide for their own families while contributing positively to their communities.

Decision-making skills training helps children learn to evaluate options, consider consequences, and make wise choices based on biblical principles rather than cultural pressures or personal preferences. This training should include both formal instruction and practical opportunities to make increasingly important decisions [62]. When children develop strong decision-making skills, they are better equipped to navigate the complex choices they will face as adults.

The gradual transfer of responsibility from parents to children enables young people to develop confidence and competence in managing their own lives while still having access to parental guidance and support. This transfer should be systematic and age-appropriate, increasing responsibility as children demonstrate maturity [63]. When parents successfully transfer responsibility gradually, they often raise children who are well-prepared for independent living.

Spiritual Formation for the Next Generation

The spiritual formation of children represents the most important aspect of preparing them for their own family construction and requires more than simply teaching biblical knowledge or ensuring church attendance. This formation involves developing personal relationships with God, internal motivation for righteousness, and the ability to apply biblical principles to all areas of life [64].

Personal relationship development with God provides the foundation for all other aspects of spiritual formation and requires children to move beyond simply knowing about God to experiencing personal connection with Him through prayer, worship, and obedience. This relationship development often occurs gradually throughout childhood and adolescence [65]. When children develop genuine personal relationships with God, they are better equipped to lead their own families spiritually.

Biblical worldview formation helps children understand how Scripture applies to all areas of life, including relationships, work, finances, entertainment, and social issues. This worldview formation requires systematic teaching combined with practical application opportunities [66]. When children develop biblical worldviews, they are better equipped to make wise decisions and resist cultural pressures throughout their lives.

Character development focuses on helping children internalize biblic1al virtues such as integrity, compassion, self-control, and perseverance that w1ill guide their behavior regardless of external circumstances. This character development requires both instruction and practice opportunities in real-life situations [67]. When children develop strong character, they are better prepared to handle the challenges and temptations they will face as adults.

Ministry involvement provides children with opportunities to serve others while developing their spiritual gifts and understanding their role in

God's kingdom purposes. This involvement might include church ministries, community service, or mission activities [68]. When children develop patterns of ministry involvement, they often continue serving throughout their lives while teaching their own children the importance of service.

Apologetics training helps children understand the intellectual foundations of their faith while preparing them to defend their beliefs in academic and professional environments that may be hostile to Christianity. This training should be age-appropriate and should emphasize both intellectual understanding and personal conviction [69]. When children receive solid apologetics training, they are better equipped to maintain their faith in challenging environments.

Evangelism preparation helps children understand their responsibility to share the gospel with others while developing the skills and confidence necessary for effective witness. This preparation should include both formal training and practical opportunities to share their faith [70]. When children develop evangelistic skills and passion, they often become effective witnesses who influence their communities for Christ.

The mentoring relationships that children develop with mature believers provide additional sources of spiritual guidance and support that supplement parental influence. These relationships might involve grandparents, church leaders, family friends, or other mature Christians who can provide different perspectives and insights [71]. When children develop strong mentoring relationships, they often receive valuable guidance that helps them navigate challenging seasons.

Launching Adult Children Successfully

The transition from dependent childhood to independent adulthood represents one of the most challenging aspects of family construction and requires careful planning, gradual implementation, and ongoing support as children establish their own households and potentially their own families [72].

Educational preparation involves helping children develop the knowledge, skills, and credentials necessary for career success while ensuring that their education supports rather than undermines their spiritual and moral development. This preparation might include academic planning, career exploration, college selection, or vocational training [73]. When children receive appropriate educational preparation, they are better equipped to support their own families financially while contributing positively to their communities.

Career guidance helps children understand their gifts, interests, and calling while exploring career options that will enable them to support their families while serving God's kingdom purposes. This guidance should consider both practical factors, such as income potential, and spiritual factors such as ministry opportunities [74]. When children receive wise career guidance, they often find fulfilling work that supports their family goals while advancing God's kingdom.

Marriage preparation provides children with an understanding of biblical marriage principles, practical relationship skills, and wisdom for selecting appropriate spouses who share their faith and values. This preparation should begin early and should include both formal instruction and practical modeling [75]. When children receive thorough marriage preparation, they are better equipped to build strong marriages that honor God and bless their communities.

Financial independence training helps children develop the skills and resources necessary to support themselves and eventually their own families without ongoing dependence on their parents. This training should include budgeting, career development, debt avoidance, and saving strategies [76].

When children achieve appropriate financial independence, they are better positioned to build their own families successfully.

Ongoing relationship maintenance enables families to continue providing support and encouragement for adult children while respecting their independence and decision-making authority. This relationship maintenance requires wisdom, flexibility, and clear boundaries [77]. When families successfully maintain relationships with adult children, they often provide valuable support during challenging seasons while enjoying the benefits of lifelong family connections.

Grandparent preparation helps parents understand their future role in supporting their children's families while avoiding interference or inappropriate involvement. This preparation should include understanding appropriate boundaries, supportive roles, and opportunities for positive influence [78]. When parents prepare appropriately for grandparenthood, they often become valuable resources for their children's family construction efforts.

When families successfully prepare and launch their children while building a *Family by the Book: How to Build the Family God Intended*, they often create expanding networks of godly families that influence their communities for multiple generations [79].

The Multigenerational Vision

"He established a testimony in Jacob and appointed a law in Israel, which he commanded our fathers to teach to their children, that the next generation might know them" (Psalm 78:5-6). The ultimate vision for family construction extends beyond individual families to encompass multiple generations working together to advance God's kingdom purposes while supporting and encouraging one another in their construction efforts [80].

Building Family Networks That Span Generations

The development of strong relationships among multiple generations within extended families creates networks of support, wisdom, and influence that benefit all family members while advancing God's kingdom purposes. These networks require intentional cultivation and ongoing investment but produce benefits that extend far beyond individual families [81].

Extended family relationships provide children with additional role models, sources of wisdom, and support systems that supplement parental influence while connecting them to their family heritage and identity. These relationships might involve grandparents, aunts and uncles, cousins, or other extended family members who can provide different perspectives and insights [82]. When families invest in extended family relationships, they often create resources that benefit multiple generations.

Family reunion traditions create opportunities for extended families to maintain connections, share family history, and reinforce family values across multiple generations. These reunions might include annual gatherings, special celebrations, or regular communication that keeps family members connected despite geographic distance [83]. When families develop meaningful reunion traditions, they often strengthen family bonds while creating positive memories for all generations.

Mentoring relationships between generations enable older family members to share their wisdom and experience with younger members while providing opportunities for mutual blessing and learning. These relationships might involve formal mentoring programs or informal connections that develop naturally through family interactions [84]. When families develop strong intergenerational mentoring, they often create powerful bonds that benefit both mentors and mentees.

Family business or ministry partnerships provide opportunities for multiple generations to work together toward common goals while sharing resources, skills, and vision. These partnerships might involve family businesses, ministry organizations, or service projects that engage multiple family members [85]. When families develop successful partnerships, they often create lasting legacies while strengthening family relationships.

The documentation of family history and lessons learned helps preserve wisdom and insights that can benefit future generations who face similar challenges and opportunities. This documentation might include written family histories, recorded interviews, or systematic recording of important family decisions and their outcomes [86]. When families document their experiences thoughtfully, they provide valuable resources for future generations.

Communication systems that connect multiple generations enable families to maintain relationships and share important information despite busy schedules and geographic distance. These systems might include regular family newsletters, social media groups, or scheduled communication that keeps family members connected [87]. When families develop effective communication systems, they often maintain stronger relationships across multiple generations.

Chapter 10

The Completed Construction

Living in the Finished Family

As we reach the culmination of our journey through the principles and practices of biblical family construction, having explored foundational roles, navigated challenges, built community connections, and established generational legacies, we now arrive at the profound joy and responsibility of living in a family that has been built according to God's design. The transition from active construction to ongoing stewardship represents not an ending but a new beginning, as families that have been established according to the principles found in Family by the Book: How to Build the Family God Intended discover the deep satisfaction and eternal significance that comes from dwelling in structures that reflect God's character and advance His kingdom purposes.

The apostle Paul provides the perfect framework for understanding completed family construction when he declares, *"So then you are no longer strangers and aliens, but you are fellow citizens with the saints and members of the household of God, built on the foundation of the apostles and prophets, Christ Jesus himself being the cornerstone"* (Ephesians 2:19-20). This foundational passage reveals that the ultimate goal of family construction is not merely to create functional households but to establish communities that reflect the character of God's eternal family and serve as foretastes of the heavenly reality that awaits all believers [1].

Understanding families as completed constructions that reflect God's household transforms how we approach the daily rhythms and long-term stewardship of family life. Rather than viewing family construction as a project that ends when certain milestones are reached, families built according to biblical principles recognize that completion brings new opportunities for worship, service, and witness that demonstrate the beauty and effectiveness of God's design [2]. This perspective requires ongoing gratitude, faithful stewardship, and continued commitment to the principles that made successful construction possible.

The completion of family construction also reveals the interconnectedness of all the elements we have explored throughout our building project. The husband's foundational leadership, the wife's essential support, the children's willing participation, the parents' character-building efforts, the community engagement, the difficulty navigation, and the legacy building all work together to create families that function as integrated wholes rather than collections of separate parts [3]. This integration demonstrates the wisdom of God's design and the importance of attending to all aspects of family construction rather than focusing on isolated elements.

When families successfully complete their construction according to the principles of *Family by the Book: How to Build the Family God Intended*, they discover that their finished families become sources of blessing not only for their immediate members but also for their extended families, communities, and future generations. This expanding influence reflects the multiplication principle that characterizes God's kingdom work, where faithful obedience in one area produces benefits that extend far beyond the original investment [4].

The stewardship responsibilities that come with completed family construction require families to maintain their structures, continue growing together, and use their stability and strength to serve others who are still in the construction process. This stewardship involves both preservation of what has been built and ongoing development of new capacities for service and influence [5]. When families embrace these stewardship responsibilities, they often discover that their greatest years of impact and satisfaction come after their basic construction has been completed.

The eternal perspective that guides completed families helps them understand that their earthly family construction serves as preparation for the eternal family relationships that await all believers in God's kingdom. This perspective provides motivation for continued faithfulness while offering hope and comfort during the inevitable transitions and losses that affect all earthly families [6]. When families maintain this eternal perspective, they often find greater peace and purpose in their daily family life.

Celebrating What God Has Built

"Unless the Lord builds the house, those who build it labor in vain" (Psalm 127:1). The recognition and celebration of what God has accomplished through faithful family construction represent an essential aspect of completed family life that honors God's grace while providing motivation for continued faithfulness and service. This celebration involves both gratitude for God's blessing and recognition of the privilege of participating in His construction work [7].

Recognizing God's Grace in Family Construction

The foundation of proper celebration rests on understanding that successful family construction results primarily from God's grace rather than human effort, wisdom, or goodness. This recognition prevents pride while fostering genuine gratitude for the undeserved blessings that God has provided through faithful obedience to His design principles [8].

Acknowledging God's provision throughout the construction process helps families understand that their success has depended on divine resources rather than merely human capabilities. This provision has included wisdom for difficult decisions, strength for challenging seasons, resources for family needs, and grace for failures and mistakes [9]. When families regularly acknowledge God's provision, they develop a deeper appreciation for His faithfulness while maintaining proper perspective on their own contributions.

Understanding God's timing in family development enables families to appreciate how He has orchestrated circumstances, relationships, and opportunities to accomplish His purposes in their family construction. This timing often becomes apparent only in retrospect, as families recognize how seemingly difficult seasons contributed to their growth and how unexpected blessings advanced their construction goals [10]. When families understand God's timing, they often develop greater trust in His sovereignty and wisdom.

Recognizing God's protection during vulnerable seasons helps families appreciate how He has shielded them from dangers, temptations, and destructive influences that could have derailed their construction efforts. This protection has often been invisible and unrecognized at the time, but becomes apparent as families reflect on their journey and recognize potential disasters that were avoided [11]. When families recognize God's protection, they often develop deeper gratitude and stronger faith in His continuing care.

Appreciating God's redemption of failures and mistakes demonstrates His ability to bring good from even the most difficult circumstances and poor decisions that families have made during their construction process. This redemption often involves using failures as learning opportunities, bringing families closer together through shared struggles, or creating testimonies that encourage other families [12]. When families appreciate God's redemptive work, they often develop greater confidence in His ability to continue working in their lives.

Celebrating God's faithfulness across multiple generations helps families understand that their construction success builds on the faithful obedience of previous generations while creating foundations for future generations.

This multigenerational perspective reveals how God works through families across time to accomplish His purposes [13]. When families celebrate God's multigenerational faithfulness, they often develop a greater appreciation for their place in His larger story.

The humility that characterizes proper celebration prevents families from taking credit for what God has accomplished while enabling them to enjoy the blessings He has provided. This humility recognizes that successful family construction requires both divine grace and human obedience, with grace being the primary factor [14]. When families maintain proper humility, they often experience greater joy in their celebrations while avoiding the pride that can undermine their continued success.

Gratitude for Family Relationships

The deep appreciation that completed families develop for their relationships reflects their understanding of the precious gift that God has given them through family bonds that have been strengthened and refined through the construction process. This gratitude encompasses both the relationships themselves and the shared experiences that have created lasting bonds [15].

Marriage relationship gratitude recognizes the profound blessing of having a spouse who has shared the construction journey and contributed to the family's success through faithful partnership, sacrificial love, and mutual support. This gratitude appreciates both the spouse's contributions and the growth that has occurred in the marriage relationship through the construction process [16]. When couples develop deep gratitude for their marriage relationships, they often experience renewed appreciation and affection that continues to strengthen their bonds.

Parent-child relationship gratitude acknowledges the privilege of raising children according to biblical principles while appreciating the unique

216

personalities, gifts, and contributions that each child has brought to the family construction process. This gratitude recognizes both the joy of watching children grow and develop and the satisfaction of seeing them embrace family values and principles [17]. When parents develop genuine gratitude for their relationships with their children, they often find greater enjoyment in their ongoing interactions and deeper satisfaction in their parenting accomplishments.

Sibling relationship gratitude celebrates the bonds that have developed among children through shared family experiences, mutual support during challenges, and participation in family construction efforts. These relationships often become sources of lifelong friendship and support that extend far beyond the immediate family [18]. When families foster gratitude for sibling relationships, they often create lasting bonds that provide ongoing support and encouragement throughout life.

Extended family relationship gratitude appreciates the contributions that grandparents, aunts, uncles, and other relatives have made to the family construction process through their support, wisdom, and encouragement. These relationships often provide additional resources and perspectives that enrich the family construction experience [19]. When families develop gratitude for extended family relationships, they often strengthen these bonds while creating networks of support that benefit multiple generations.

Community relationship gratitude recognizes the blessing of friends, neighbors, church members, and other community connections who have supported and encouraged the family construction process. These relationships often provide practical assistance, spiritual encouragement, and social connections that enhance family life [20]. When families appreciate their community relationships, they often develop stronger connections that continue to benefit all involved.

The expression of gratitude through words, actions, and ongoing investment in relationships helps families communicate their appreciation while strengthening the bonds they celebrate. This expression might include regular affirmations, special celebrations, thoughtful gifts, or increased time and attention devoted to important relationships [21]. When families consistently express their gratitude, they often find that their relationships continue to grow stronger and more satisfying.

Sharing Testimonies of God's Faithfulness

The responsibility that completed families bear for sharing their testimonies with others reflects their understanding that God's blessings are intended not only for their own enjoyment but also for the encouragement and instruction of other families who are still in the construction process. This sharing provides hope and practical guidance while giving glory to God for His faithfulness [22].

Personal testimony sharing involves families telling their own stories of God's faithfulness during their construction process, including both the challenges they faced and the ways God provided wisdom, strength, and blessing. These testimonies often encourage other families while demonstrating the practical benefits of biblical family construction [23]. When families share their testimonies regularly, they often find that their own faith is strengthened while others receive valuable encouragement.

Practical wisdom sharing enables families to pass along the lessons they have learned through their construction experience, including both successful strategies and mistakes to avoid. This wisdom sharing often proves more valuable than theoretical instruction because it has been tested in real-life situations [24]. When families share their practical wisdom generously, they often help other families avoid common pitfalls while accelerating their construction progress.

218

Resource sharing involves families using their stability and strength to provide practical assistance to other families who are facing challenges or lacking resources needed for successful construction. This assistance might include financial support, childcare, meals, or other forms of practical help [25]. When families share their resources generously, they often create networks of mutual support that benefit entire communities.

Mentoring relationships enable completed families to provide ongoing guidance and encouragement to families who are earlier in their construction process. These relationships often involve regular meetings, accountability, and systematic sharing of wisdom and experience [26]. When families engage in mentoring relationships, they often find that they receive as much blessing as they provide while creating lasting bonds with other families.

Church ministry involvement provides opportunities for completed families to use their stability and experience to serve their church communities through teaching, leadership, and service roles. This involvement often enables families to influence multiple other families while contributing to the overall health of their church communities [27]. When families engage actively in church ministry, they often find meaningful ways to use their construction success for kingdom purposes.

Community service activities enable families to demonstrate their values while contributing to the welfare of their broader communities. This service might involve volunteer work, civic involvement, or support for community organizations that align with family values [28]. When families engage in community service together, they often strengthen their own bonds while making positive contributions to their communities.

When families faithfully share their testimonies while living as examples of *Family by the Book: How to Build the Family God Intended*, they often become powerful witnesses that attract others to biblical family construction principles [29].

Maintaining the Family Structure

"Be watchful, stand firm in the faith, act like men, be strong" (1 Corinthians 16:13). The ongoing maintenance of family structures that have been built according to biblical principles requires vigilance, commitment, and continued application of the same principles that made successful construction possible. This maintenance involves both preservation of what has been built and adaptation to changing circumstances and seasons of life [30].

Ongoing Spiritual Disciplines

The spiritual disciplines that sustained families during their construction process become even more important for maintaining the spiritual health and vitality of completed families. These disciplines provide the ongoing connection with God that enables families to continue growing while maintaining their spiritual foundations [31].

Family worship practices create regular opportunities for completed families to acknowledge God's lordship, express gratitude for His blessings, and seek His continued guidance and blessing. These practices might include daily devotions, weekly family worship times, or seasonal celebrations that focus on spiritual themes [32]. When families maintain consistent worship practices, they often find that their spiritual unity and vitality continue to grow even after their basic construction is complete.

Prayer disciplines enable families to maintain their dependence on God while seeking His guidance for ongoing decisions and challenges. These disciplines might include individual prayer times, family prayer sessions, or special prayer focuses during particular seasons or circumstances [33]. When families maintain strong prayer disciplines, they often find that their relationship with God continues to deepen while their unity as a family is strengthened.

Scripture study practices provide ongoing spiritual nourishment and guidance for families while ensuring that their decisions and priorities continue to align with biblical principles. These practices might include individual Bible study, family Bible reading, or systematic study of particular biblical themes or books [34]. When families maintain consistent Scripture study, they often find that their understanding of God's will continues to grow while their commitment to biblical principles is reinforced.

Service disciplines create opportunities for families to express their faith through action while contributing to God's kingdom purposes. These disciplines might include regular volunteer work, support for missions, or involvement in church ministries [35]. When families maintain consistent service disciplines, they often find that their faith becomes more practical and meaningful while their impact on others increases.

Fellowship disciplines enable families to maintain connections with other believers while receiving encouragement and accountability for their spiritual growth. These disciplines might include regular church attendance, participation in small groups, or involvement in Christian community activities [36]. When families maintain strong fellowship disciplines, they often find that their spiritual growth is accelerated while their sense of belonging and purpose is strengthened.

Stewardship disciplines help families continue to manage their resources according to biblical principles while using their blessings to serve others and advance God's kingdom. These disciplines might include regular giving, wise financial management, or generous hospitality [37]. When families maintain faithful stewardship disciplines, they often find that their resources are blessed while their impact on others is multiplied.

The consistency that families maintain in their spiritual disciplines significantly affects their long-term spiritual health and effectiveness. This consistency requires ongoing commitment and often involves adjusting practices to accommodate changing circumstances while maintaining core commitments [38]. When families maintain consistency in their spiritual disciplines, they often find that these practices become natural and enjoyable rather than burdensome obligations.

Protecting Against Complacency

One of the greatest dangers facing completed families involves the temptation to become complacent about the principles and practices that made their construction successful. This complacency can gradually undermine family health and effectiveness if not actively resisted through ongoing vigilance and commitment [39].

Recognizing complacency warning signs helps families identify potential problems before they become serious threats to family health. These warning signs might include decreased attention to spiritual disciplines, reduced investment in family relationships, or gradual compromise of family values and standards [40]. When families learn to recognize these warning signs early, they can often address problems before they cause significant damage.

Maintaining accountability relationships with other families or individuals provides an external perspective and encouragement that helps families avoid complacency while continuing to grow. These relationships might involve formal mentoring arrangements, informal friendships, or participation in accountability groups [41]. When families maintain strong accountability relationships, they often receive valuable feedback and encouragement that helps them continue growing.

Regular family evaluation sessions create opportunities for families to assess their spiritual health, relationship quality, and adherence to their values and goals. These sessions might occur annually or seasonally and should include honest discussion of both strengths and areas needing improvement [42]. When families conduct regular evaluations, they often identify issues early while celebrating progress and maintaining motivation for continued growth.

Continuing education and growth activities help families stay current with new insights and resources while preventing stagnation in their understanding and application of biblical principles. These activities might include reading, conferences, seminars, or discussions with other families [43]. When families commit to continuing education, they often discover new insights and strategies that enhance their family life while preventing complacency.

Setting new goals and challenges provides families with ongoing motivation for growth while preventing the stagnation that can result from achieving previous objectives. These goals might involve new areas of service, relationship improvements, or spiritual growth targets [44]. When families regularly set new goals, they often maintain momentum and excitement about their family development while continuing to grow in new areas.

Embracing new seasons and transitions helps families adapt their practices and priorities to changing circumstances while maintaining their core commitments and values. These transitions might involve children leaving home, career changes, or aging parents requiring care [45]. When families embrace transitions positively, they often discover new opportunities for growth and service while maintaining their family unity and purpose.

Adapting to Life Changes

The ability to adapt family structures and practices to accommodate changing life circumstances while maintaining core principles and relationships represents a crucial skill for long-term family success. This adaptation requires wisdom, flexibility, and ongoing commitment to family priorities [46].

Empty nest transitions require families to adjust their daily routines, relationship patterns, and service opportunities while maintaining strong connections with adult children and discovering new purposes for their marriage relationship. This transition often provides opportunities for couples to rediscover their relationship while finding new ways to serve others [47]. When families navigate empty nest transitions successfully, they often find that their marriage relationship is strengthened while their capacity for service is expanded.

Aging parent care responsibilities require families to balance their obligations to aging parents with their ongoing commitments to their own families while demonstrating the honor and respect that characterize biblical family relationships. This responsibility often involves difficult decisions about care arrangements, financial support, and time allocation [48]. When families handle aging parent care responsibilities well, they often strengthen intergenerational relationships while modeling important values for their own children.

Career transitions and changes require families to adapt their financial planning, time management, and service commitments while maintaining their priorities and values. These transitions might involve job changes, retirement, or new career directions that affect family dynamics and opportunities [49]. When families handle career transitions wisely, they often discover new opportunities for service and growth while maintaining their family stability and unity.

Health challenges and crises require families to adjust their expectations, routines, and goals while maintaining their faith and unity during difficult circumstances. These challenges often test family foundations while providing opportunities for deeper relationships and stronger faith [50]. When families handle health challenges well, they often emerge with stronger relationships and deeper appreciation for God's faithfulness.

Financial changes and pressures require families to adapt their lifestyle, spending patterns, and giving practices while maintaining their stewardship principles and family priorities. These changes might involve both positive developments, such as increased income, and challenging circumstances, such as job loss [51]. When families handle financial changes wisely, they often strengthen their stewardship practices while maintaining their family unity and values.

Geographic relocations require families to establish new community connections, find new service opportunities, and adapt to different cultural contexts while maintaining their family identity and values. These relocations often provide opportunities for growth and new ministry while testing family adaptability [52]. When families handle relocations well, they often discover new opportunities for service and growth while strengthening their family bonds.

When families successfully adapt to life changes while maintaining the principles found in Family by the Book: How to Build the Family God Intended, they often discover that their flexibility and resilience enable them to thrive in any circumstances [53].

Continuing to Grow Together

"But grow in the grace and knowledge of our Lord and Savior Jesus Christ" (2 Peter 3:18). The completion of basic family construction does not mark the end of family growth but rather creates stable foundations for continued development in spiritual maturity, relational depth, and service effectiveness. This ongoing growth requires intentional effort and commitment to lifelong learning and development [54].

Deepening Relationships Over Time

The relationships that have been established through successful family construction provide foundations for continued growth in intimacy, understanding, and mutual support that can continue developing throughout life. This deepening requires ongoing investment and intentional effort to maintain and strengthen family bonds [55].

Marriage relationship deepening involves couples continuing to invest in their relationship through regular communication, shared experiences, and mutual support while discovering new dimensions of intimacy and partnership. This deepening often accelerates after children leave home and couples have more time and energy to focus on their relationship [56]. When couples commit to ongoing relationship deepening, they often find that their later years together are among their most satisfying and intimate.

Parent-adult child relationship development requires families to navigate the transition from parent-child authority relationships to adult friendships based on mutual respect and shared values. This development often involves learning new communication patterns and establishing appropriate boundaries [57]. When families successfully develop adult relationships, they often find that their connections become deeper and more satisfying while providing ongoing support and encouragement.

Grandparent relationship building provides opportunities for older family members to invest in new generations while sharing their wisdom and experience. These relationships often become sources of great joy and satisfaction while providing valuable support for younger families [58]. When families develop strong grandparent relationships, they often create lasting bonds that benefit multiple generations while strengthening family unity.

Extended family connection strengthening enables families to maintain and develop relationships with aunts, uncles, cousins, and other relatives who can provide ongoing support and encouragement. These connections often become more important as families age and seek to maintain their heritage and identity [59]. When families invest in extended family connections, they often create networks of support that benefit all involved while preserving family history and traditions.

Friendship development with other families provides opportunities for mutual encouragement, shared experiences, and community building that enriches family life while creating support networks. These friendships often develop through church involvement, community activities, or shared interests and values [60]. When families develop strong friendships with other families, they often find that their social connections enhance their family life while providing valuable support and encouragement.

Mentoring relationship participation enables families to both give and receive guidance and support through relationships with families at different stages of development. These relationships often provide opportunities for mutual learning and growth while strengthening community connections [61]. When families engage in mentoring relationships, they often find that both giving and receiving guidance enriches their family experience while contributing to community health.

Learning New Things Together

The commitment to lifelong learning and growth helps families continue developing new capacities, interests, and skills while maintaining their curiosity and enthusiasm for life. This learning often strengthens family bonds while providing new opportunities for service and enjoyment [62].

Educational pursuits enable family members to continue developing their knowledge and skills while pursuing interests that contribute to personal growth and family enrichment. These pursuits might include formal education, professional development, or personal interest learning [63]. When families support each other's educational pursuits, they often find that individual growth contributes to overall family development while creating new opportunities for service and contribution.

Skill development activities provide opportunities for families to learn new practical abilities while spending time together and supporting each other's growth. These activities might include hobbies, crafts, sports, or other skills that family members can enjoy together [64]. When families engage in skill development together, they often strengthen their relationships while developing new capacities for enjoyment and service.

Travel and cultural experiences enable families to broaden their perspectives while creating shared memories and learning about different cultures and ways of life. These experiences often strengthen family bonds while increasing appreciation for God's creation and human diversity [65]. When families engage in meaningful travel and cultural experiences, they often develop broader perspectives while creating lasting memories and stronger relationships.

Service learning opportunities enable families to develop new capacities for helping others while learning about different needs and challenges in their communities and world. These opportunities might include volunteer work, mission involvement, or community service projects [66]. When families engage in service learning together, they often develop greater compassion and understanding while strengthening their commitment to serving others.

Creative pursuits provide opportunities for families to explore artistic and creative expressions while developing new forms of enjoyment and self-expression. These pursuits might include music, art, writing, or other creative activities that family members can share [67]. When families engage in creative pursuits together, they often discover new dimensions of enjoyment and expression while strengthening their relationships.

Spiritual growth activities enable families to continue developing their understanding of God and their relationship with Him while exploring new dimensions of faith and service. These activities might include Bible study, theological education, or spiritual formation practices [68]. When families commit to ongoing spiritual growth, they often find that their faith continues to deepen while their capacity for service and witness increases.

The Eternal Perspective

"For here we have no lasting city, but we seek the city that is to come" (Hebrews 13:14). The ultimate significance of completed family construction lies not in earthly achievements but in its contribution to eternal purposes and its preparation for the heavenly family relationships that await all believers. This eternal perspective provides both motivation for continued faithfulness and comfort during the inevitable transitions and losses that affect all earthly families [69].

Preparing for Eternal Family Relationships

The family relationships that have been built according to biblical principles serve as preparation and foretaste of the eternal family relationships that all believers will enjoy in God's kingdom. This preparation involves developing character qualities and relationship patterns that reflect heavenly realities [70].

Understanding heavenly family dynamics helps earthly families appreciate how their relationships point toward and prepare them for the eternal relationships they will enjoy with God and other believers. These dynamics include perfect love, complete unity, and joyful service that characterize life in God's kingdom [71]. When families understand these heavenly realities, they often find greater motivation for developing godly relationships while gaining comfort about the temporary nature of earthly separations.

Developing eternal character qualities enables family members to become more like Christ while preparing for the perfect character that will characterize all believers in heaven. These qualities include love, joy, peace, patience, kindness, goodness, faithfulness, gentleness, and self-control [72]. When families focus on developing eternal character qualities, they often find that their earthly relationships improve while they become better prepared for heavenly relationships.

Practicing heavenly values in earthly relationships helps families align their priorities and behaviors with eternal realities while demonstrating kingdom principles to watching observers. These values include sacrificial love, humble service, generous giving, and faithful obedience [73]. When families practice heavenly values consistently, they often find that their earthly relationships become more satisfying while their witness becomes more effective.

Building eternal treasures through faithful family construction enables families to invest in things that will last beyond earthly life while finding true satisfaction and meaning in their family relationships. These treasures include spiritual growth, character development, and kingdom service [74]. When families focus on building eternal treasures, they often find greater satisfaction in their family life while developing a proper perspective on temporary earthly concerns.

Anticipating eternal reunions provides comfort and hope for families facing the inevitable separations that result from death while maintaining confidence in the permanent nature of relationships built on spiritual foundations. This anticipation recognizes that earthly family relationships that are grounded in faith will continue in heavenly contexts [75]. When families maintain this eternal perspective, they often find greater peace during difficult transitions while maintaining hope for future reunions.

Leaving a Legacy That Honors God

The ultimate goal of family construction involves creating legacies that honor God and advance His kingdom purposes while providing foundations for future generations to build upon. This legacy building requires families to think beyond their immediate circumstances to consider their long-term impact [76].

Spiritual legacy development involves families passing down faith, values, and spiritual practices that will influence future generations while contributing to the advancement of God's kingdom. This legacy includes both formal instruction and practical modeling of authentic faith [77]. When families successfully develop spiritual legacies, they often influence multiple generations while contributing significantly to kingdom purposes.

Character legacy building enables families to pass down integrity, wisdom, and moral strength that will guide future generations while contributing to community health and stability. This legacy involves both teaching and modeling character qualities that reflect God's nature [78]. When families build strong character legacies, they often influence their communities while providing foundations for future family success.

Service legacy creation involves families establishing patterns of generous giving and faithful service that will inspire future generations while contributing to community welfare and kingdom advancement. This legacy demonstrates the practical importance of faith while creating positive community impact [79]. When families create strong service legacies, they often influence their communities while inspiring continued service from future generations.

Wisdom legacy preservation enables families to document and pass down the lessons they have learned through their construction experience while providing guidance for future generations facing similar challenges. This legacy might include written records, recorded conversations, or systematic teaching of important principles [80]. When families preserve their wisdom effectively, they often provide valuable resources for future generations while ensuring that important lessons are not lost.

When families successfully complete their construction while maintaining eternal perspective and building lasting legacies according to the principles of Family by the Book: How to Build the Family God Intended, they discover the deep satisfaction that comes from participating in God's eternal purposes while enjoying the blessings of relationships that reflect His character and advance His kingdom [81].

Conclusion
The Master Builder's Masterpiece

Living in the Family God Built

As we reach the end of our comprehensive journey through the principles and practices of biblical family construction, having explored God's original blueprint, examined each family member's essential role, navigated the challenges and opportunities of community engagement, weathered the inevitable difficulties, built lasting legacies, and celebrated the joy of completed construction, we now stand at a place of profound gratitude and renewed commitment. The transition from learning about family construction to living as a completed masterpiece represents not an ending but a glorious new beginning [1]. Families that have been built according to the timeless principles found in Family by the Book: How to Build the Family God Intended discover the deep satisfaction and eternal significance that comes from dwelling in structures that reflect the Master Builder's perfect design [2]. These families advance His kingdom purposes throughout the world while serving as beacons of hope to other families who are still in the construction process.

The apostle Paul provides the perfect framework for understanding our families as God's masterpieces when he declares, *"For we are his workmanship, created in Christ Jesus for good works, which God prepared beforehand, that we should walk in them"* (Ephesians 2:10). This foundational verse reveals that our families are not merely human constructions built through our own wisdom and effort [3]. Instead, they are divine masterpieces crafted by the Master Builder Himself, designed to display His glory and accomplish His eternal purposes [4]. These purposes extend far beyond our immediate understanding or observation, encompassing both present blessings and future impact that may not become visible until eternity.

Understanding our families as God's workmanship transforms how we view both our construction journey and our ongoing stewardship responsibilities. Rather than taking credit for what has been accomplished, we recognize that the Master Builder continues His work in and through our families [5]. He uses both our faithful obedience and our failures as materials in His perfect construction project [6]. This perspective brings both humility about our contributions and confidence in His ability to complete what He has begun, preventing both pride during successful seasons and despair during challenging times.

The phrase "created in Christ Jesus for good works" emphasizes that our family construction serves purposes far greater than our own happiness or success. Our families extend to the advancement of God's kingdom and the blessing of others who observe our families [7]. They are drawn to the Master Builder through our witness, creating expanding circles of influence that often exceed our expectations [8]. This eternal perspective provides both motivation for continued faithfulness and comfort during seasons when our construction efforts seem to produce limited visible results.

When families embrace their identity as the Master Builder's masterpieces while living according to the principles of *Family by the Book: How to Build the Family God Intended*, they discover that their greatest joy comes not from achieving perfect family life but from participating in God's eternal purposes. They experience the deep satisfaction that results from aligning their construction efforts with His perfect design [9]. This discovery often marks the beginning of their most fruitful and satisfying years of family life [10]. The good works that God has prepared beforehand for our families encompass both the internal construction that builds strong relationships and character, and the external witness that demonstrates the beauty and effectiveness of biblical principles to watching communities.

The community impact of families that have been built as God's masterpieces often extends across multiple generations and geographic boundaries. Their witness influences other families to pursue biblical construction [11]. Their children carry forward the principles and practices they have learned, creating multiplication effects that demonstrate the strategic importance of family construction in God's plan for advancing His kingdom throughout the world [12].

The Central Theme Revisited

"Submitting to one another out of reverence for Christ" (Ephesians 5:21). As we reflect on the comprehensive journey we have taken through the principles of biblical family construction, from understanding God's original blueprint to celebrating completed construction, one central theme emerges as the foundation that makes all other principles possible. This foundation is the mutual submission that flows from reverence for Christ [13]. It enables family members to serve one another with joy rather than seeking their own interests, creating an atmosphere where all other biblical principles can flourish [14].

How Biblical Building Creates Beautiful Relationships

The beauty that characterizes families built according to biblical principles results not from the absence of conflict or challenge, but from the presence of Christ-centered relationships where each family member seeks to serve others rather than demanding to be served. This beauty becomes visible through the daily interactions, conflict resolution patterns, and sacrificial love [15]. These qualities mark families as distinctly different from those built according to worldly principles, creating attractive testimonies that draw others to biblical family construction [16].

Marriage relationships that have been built on the foundation of mutual submission demonstrate the beauty of complementary roles working together in harmony. Husbands provide loving leadership while wives offer respectful support [17]. This creates partnerships that reflect the relationship between Christ and His church, providing children with positive models for their own future relationships [18]. The beauty of these marriages attracts others to biblical marriage principles while demonstrating the practical benefits of following God's design for family relationships.

Parent-child relationships that have been shaped by biblical submission principles demonstrate the beauty of authority exercised with love and respect received with joy. Parents provide guidance and discipline motivated by genuine care [19]. Children respond with honor and obedience that flows from trust rather than fear, creating family atmospheres where all members feel valued and secure [20]. This beauty teaches important lessons about relating to authority throughout life while preparing children for their own future leadership responsibilities.

Sibling relationships that have been influenced by mutual submission principles demonstrate the beauty of cooperation and mutual support. Children learn to prefer one another's interests while resolving conflicts through forgiveness and reconciliation [21]. This approach replaces competition and resentment with genuine care and concern for one another [22]. This beauty often produces lifelong friendships among siblings while teaching important lessons about community relationships that extend far beyond the immediate family.

Extended family relationships that reflect biblical submission principles demonstrate the beauty of multigenerational cooperation and mutual respect. Older and younger family members honor one another while sharing wisdom, resources, and support across generational lines [23]. This beauty strengthens family networks while providing children with additional sources of guidance and encouragement [24]. The consistency that families maintain in applying submission principles across all their relationships creates coherent family cultures where biblical values are demonstrated rather than merely discussed.

The Holy Spirit's Role in Enabling Construction

The recognition that successful family construction depends ultimately on the Holy Spirit's power rather than human effort provides both humility about our limitations and confidence in God's ability to accomplish His purposes through our faithful obedience. This recognition prevents both pride in success and despair during challenging seasons [25]. Understanding the Holy Spirit as the divine contractor who enables family construction helps families recognize that their role involves cooperation with His work [26]. This cooperation requires sensitivity to His leading, obedience to His direction, and dependence on His power for both daily decisions and long-term planning.

The Holy Spirit's work in individual family members creates the character transformation that makes biblical family relationships possible. He produces love, joy, peace, patience, kindness, goodness, faithfulness, gentleness, and self-control in those who yield to His influence [27]. This character transformation often occurs gradually over many years but produces lasting changes that benefit entire families [28]. The Holy Spirit's work in family relationships enables forgiveness, reconciliation, and restoration that would be impossible through human effort alone.

The Holy Spirit softens hearts, provides wisdom for difficult conversations, and creates opportunities for healing and growth [29]. This supernatural work often produces breakthroughs in relationships that seemed hopeless while demonstrating God's power to restore what has been broken [30]. The Holy Spirit's work through families extends their influence beyond their immediate households, using their witness to draw others to Christ while providing them with opportunities to serve and encourage other families.

Well-Built Christian Families as Witnesses

The witness that well-built Christian families provide to their communities often proves more powerful than formal evangelistic efforts. Their relationships demonstrate the practical benefits of biblical principles [31]. Their joy and stability attract others who are struggling with family challenges, creating natural opportunities for sharing both faith and practical wisdom [32]. An authentic witness emerges naturally from families that have been genuinely transformed by biblical principles rather than those who merely attempt to appear successful while struggling with hidden problems.

This authenticity requires families to be honest about their challenges while demonstrating how biblical principles provide resources for addressing difficulties [33]. Consistent witness involves families demonstrating biblical principles across all areas of their lives rather than compartmentalizing their faith to certain activities or relationships [34]. This consistency includes their business dealings, community involvement, entertainment choices, and responses to both success and failure.

An attractive witness draws others to biblical principles through the obvious benefits that these principles produce in family relationships, financial stability, character development, and community contribution. This attraction often leads to opportunities for families to share their faith [35]. They provide practical guidance for family construction while maintaining humility that acknowledges family success results from God's grace rather than human superiority [36]. When families serve as effective witnesses while building according to the principles of Family by the Book: How to Build the Family God Intended, they often discover that their greatest ministry opportunities come through their family relationships rather than through formal church programs.

Review of Key Principles: God's Design Through Christ's Power

As we review the comprehensive journey we have taken through biblical family construction, several key principles emerge as foundational to successful building that honors God while blessing family members and communities. These principles work together to create integrated approaches to family life [37]. They reflect God's character and advance His purposes while providing practical frameworks for daily family decisions [38].

God's sovereignty in family construction reminds us that He initiates, guides, and completes the building process while using our faithful obedience as instruments in His perfect plan. This sovereignty provides both comfort during difficult seasons and motivation for continued faithfulness [39]. Christ's lordship over family relationships establishes the authority structure that enables all other principles to function effectively [40]. Family members submit to His leadership while serving one another in His name, preventing both authoritarianism and chaos while creating environments where all family members can flourish.

Biblical role clarity enables family members to understand their unique contributions to family construction while avoiding both role confusion and role competition. This clarity includes understanding complementary rather than competitive relationships [41]. Character development priority emphasizes that successful family construction focuses primarily on developing godly character rather than achieving external success or avoiding all difficulties [42]. This priority guides decision-making while providing criteria for evaluating family progress.

Relationship investment commitment recognizes that strong family bonds require ongoing time, attention, and effort rather than assuming that relationships will automatically remain strong without intentional cultivation. This commitment includes regular communication, shared experiences, and mutual support [43]. Community engagement responsibility acknowledges that well-built families have obligations to serve and influence their communities rather than focusing exclusively on their own needs and interests [44]. Legacy building vision motivates families to consider the long-term impact of their construction efforts on future generations and communities rather than focusing only on immediate concerns.

Daily Application of Biblical Principles

"Therefore, encourage one another and build one another up, just as you are doing" (1 Thessalonians 5:11). The transformation of biblical knowledge into daily family life requires intentional application of construction principles through regular routines, consistent responses to challenges, and ongoing encouragement. This application builds family unity while demonstrating God's character to watching observers [45]. The daily choices that families make either reinforce or undermine their construction efforts [46]. Making biblical principles practical requires both systematic planning and flexible adaptation to changing circumstances.

Starting Where You Are: Small Building Steps

The journey toward biblical family construction begins not with dramatic changes or perfect implementation of all principles simultaneously, but with small, consistent steps that gradually build momentum. These steps create positive patterns that can be expanded over time [47]. This approach prevents overwhelming family members while establishing foundations for continued growth [48]. Identifying current family strengths provides positive starting points for construction efforts while building confidence and motivation for addressing areas that need improvement.

These strengths might include existing patterns of communication, service, worship, or relationship investment that can be enhanced and expanded [49]. Recognizing areas needing improvement enables families to prioritize their construction efforts while avoiding the discouragement that can result from attempting to address all challenges simultaneously [50]. This recognition should be honest but hopeful, acknowledging problems while maintaining confidence in God's ability to bring change.

Setting realistic goals helps families make steady progress while avoiding the frustration that results from unrealistic expectations or overly ambitious timelines. These goals should be specific, measurable, and achievable within reasonable timeframes [51]. Celebrating small victories maintains motivation and momentum while acknowledging God's faithfulness in bringing positive changes to family life [52]. Building accountability systems helps families maintain their commitments while receiving encouragement and guidance from others who share their values and goals.

Morning Routines That Set a Godly Tone

The way families begin each day significantly affects the atmosphere and interactions that characterize their entire day. Morning routines become important opportunities for establishing godly priorities [53]. They prepare family members for the challenges and opportunities they will face while reinforcing family unity and spiritual focus [54]. Family worship time provides opportunities for families to acknowledge God's lordship while seeking His guidance and blessing for the day ahead.

This worship might include Bible reading, prayer, singing, or devotional discussions that connect family members with God and with one another [55]. Prayer for individual family members demonstrates care and concern while inviting God's blessing and protection on each person's activities and relationships [56]. Affirmation and encouragement expressions help family members begin their day with confidence and security while reinforcing their value and importance to the family.

Goal setting and planning discussions help families coordinate their activities while ensuring that individual schedules support rather than undermine family priorities and relationships [57]. Character focus reminders help family members maintain awareness of biblical principles while preparing them to apply these principles in their daily interactions and decisions [58]. The consistency that families maintain in their morning routines creates stability and security while establishing patterns that can continue even during busy or challenging seasons.

Handling Everyday Conflicts with Grace

The way families respond to the inevitable conflicts and disagreements that arise in daily life provides important opportunities for demonstrating biblical principles. These responses teach valuable lessons about forgiveness, reconciliation, and problem-solving [59]. Conflict prevention strategies help families minimize unnecessary disagreements while creating environments where differences can be discussed constructively [60]. Biblical conflict resolution principles provide frameworks for addressing disagreements in ways that strengthen rather than damage relationships.

Teaching moments during conflicts help family members learn important lessons about character, relationships, and biblical principles [61]. These moments transform negative situations into opportunities for growth and learning, requiring wisdom and patience but often producing a lasting positive impact [62]. Forgiveness practices enable families to restore relationships after conflicts while demonstrating God's grace and preventing bitterness from taking root in family relationships.

Restoration processes help families rebuild trust and intimacy after conflicts while ensuring that underlying issues are addressed rather than simply ignored [63]. When families consistently handle conflicts with grace while applying the principles found in Family by the Book: How to Build the Family God Intended, they often find that their relationships become stronger through working through disagreements rather than weaker [64].

Evening Practices That Build Family Unity

The way families end each day provides important opportunities for reflection, connection, and preparation for rest. These practices reinforce family bonds and spiritual priorities that will carry over into the following day [65]. Family reflection time enables family members to share their experiences while processing both positive and challenging events that occurred during the day [66]. Gratitude expressions help families maintain proper perspective while acknowledging God's blessings and faithfulness throughout their daily experiences.

Prayer and blessing time provides opportunities for families to commit their concerns to God while seeking His protection and blessing during the night hours [67]. Affection and affirmation expressions help family members end their day feeling loved and valued while reinforcing the security and stability that characterize well-built families [68]. Planning and preparation discussions help families coordinate upcoming activities while ensuring that everyone is prepared for the following day's responsibilities and opportunities.

Seasonal and Lifelong Applications

"To everything there is a season, and a time for every purpose under heaven" (Ecclesiastes 3:1). The application of biblical family construction principles requires wisdom to adapt approaches and emphases to different seasons of family life. This adaptation maintains core commitments and values that provide stability and continuity across changing circumstances [69]. Seasonal

applications recognize that families face different challenges and opportunities at various stages of development [70]. Lifelong applications ensure that biblical principles remain relevant and effective throughout the entire family journey.

Creating Family Traditions That Reinforce Values

The traditions that families establish provide powerful vehicles for transferring values across generations while creating positive memories and strengthening family identity. These traditions become particularly meaningful when they combine biblical truth with family heritage and cultural appreciation [71]. Holiday traditions enable families to celebrate God's faithfulness while creating special memories that children will want to continue with their own families [72]. Birthday celebrations provide opportunities for families to recognize individual family members while reinforcing themes of God's blessing, personal growth, and family love.

Anniversary commemorations enable families to celebrate marriage relationships while reinforcing the importance of commitment, love, and God's blessing on family life [73]. Achievement recognitions provide opportunities for families to celebrate accomplishments while reinforcing the importance of hard work, perseverance, and God's blessing [74]. Service traditions enable families to demonstrate their values through action while providing children with practical experience in living out their faith.

The intentionality that families bring to their tradition development significantly affects their long-term impact and sustainability [75]. This intentionality involves thinking carefully about the purposes of each tradition while planning activities that support those purposes [76]. Regular evaluation ensures that traditions continue achieving their intended goals while remaining meaningful and relevant to family members.

Celebrating Holidays That Honor the Master Builder

The way families observe holidays provides important opportunities for reinforcing spiritual priorities while creating positive memories. These celebrations demonstrate family values to extended family and community members who observe their celebrations [77]. Christmas celebrations enable families to focus on the incarnation of Christ while emphasizing themes of giving, family relationships, and spiritual reflection [78]. Easter observances provide opportunities for families to celebrate the resurrection of Christ while emphasizing themes of new life, hope, and redemption that apply to all areas of family life.

Thanksgiving practices help families acknowledge God's provision while developing attitudes of gratitude that affect their daily perspectives and relationships [79]. Other holiday observances enable families to appreciate cultural heritage while maintaining their primary identity as followers of Christ [80]. For our family, December 23rd has become a cherished family tradition that we call 'Freedom Day.' This is the day when, at the age of 20, I arrived in Melbourne, Australia, as I was resettling into a new country after escaping from the oppressive government of my birth country in Eastern Europe. This annual celebration reminds our children of God's faithfulness in providing freedom and new opportunities, while teaching them to value liberty and never take for granted the blessings of living in a free society. You may have a different tradition that you are creating and want to pass down to your family, perhaps commemorating a significant moment of God's provision, protection, or guidance that shaped your family's story.

The balance that families maintain between spiritual and cultural elements in their holiday celebrations helps children understand the relationship between their faith and their cultural heritage while ensuring that spiritual priorities remain central to their family identity.

Using Life Transitions as Teaching Opportunities

The major transitions that occur in family life provide important opportunities for teaching biblical principles. These transitions help family members understand God's faithfulness during seasons of change and uncertainty [81]. Moving to new locations enables families to discuss God's sovereignty while teaching lessons about adaptability, trust, and finding new opportunities for service and witness [82]. Starting new schools or jobs provides opportunities for families to discuss God's provision while teaching lessons about diligence, integrity, and maintaining Christian witness in secular environments.

Health challenges and recoveries enable families to discuss God's sovereignty and grace while teaching lessons about faith, perseverance, and mutual support during difficult circumstances [83]. When families successfully use life transitions as teaching opportunities while maintaining the principles found in *Family by the Book: How to Build the Family God Intended*, they often find that these challenging seasons become sources of growth and stronger family unity [84].

Adapting Principles for Different Life Stages

The wisdom to adapt family construction principles to different life stages while maintaining core commitments enables families to remain relevant and effective throughout their development. This adaptation avoids both rigidity and compromise [85]. Early marriage stages require couples to establish their family identity while learning to apply biblical principles in their daily relationship [86]. Child-rearing stages require families to balance individual children's needs while maintaining family unity and spiritual priorities.

Adolescent stages require families to maintain authority and guidance while gradually transferring responsibility and preparing teenagers for independent living [87]. Empty nest stages enable couples to rediscover their marriage relationship while finding new opportunities for service and ministry [88]. Grandparent stages provide opportunities for older family members to invest in new generations while sharing their wisdom and experience.

Regular Evaluation and Course Correction

The commitment to regular evaluation of family progress enables families to identify areas of success while addressing problems before they become serious threats to family health and unity. This evaluation requires honesty, humility, and commitment to continued growth [89]. Annual family retreats or evaluation sessions provide opportunities for families to assess their spiritual health, relationship quality, and adherence to their values and goals [90].

- **The Eternal Perspective and Continued Growth**

"I have no greater joy than to hear that my children are walking in the truth" (3 John 1:4). The ultimate significance of family construction lies not in earthly achievements but in its contribution to eternal purposes. This contribution includes preparation for the heavenly family relationships that await all believers [91]. This eternal perspective provides both motivation for continued faithfulness and comfort during the inevitable transitions and losses that affect all earthly families [92].

- **Preparing for the Ultimate Family Reunion**

The family relationships that have been built according to biblical principles serve as preparation and foretaste of the eternal family relationships that all believers will enjoy in God's kingdom. This preparation involves developing character qualities and relationship patterns that reflect heavenly realities [93]. It maintains hope for perfect relationships in eternity while finding satisfaction in imperfect but growing earthly relationships [94].

248

- **How Earthly Family Points to Heavenly Realities**

The love, unity, and service that characterize well-built earthly families provide glimpses of the perfect relationships that will characterize God's eternal family. These glimpses help family members understand and anticipate the joy that awaits them in heaven [95]. They find motivation for continued faithfulness during earthly challenges while developing appreciation for the temporary nature of current difficulties [96].

- **The Legacy of a Well-Built Godly Family**

The impact that godly families have on future generations and communities often extends far beyond what they can see or measure. They create expanding circles of influence that advance God's kingdom [97]. They provide hope and guidance for other families who observe their witness, creating multiplication effects that continue long after the original family builders have gone to their eternal reward [98].

- **Finding Mentors and Accountability Partners**

The relationships that families develop with other believers provide additional sources of wisdom, encouragement, and accountability that supplement family resources. These relationships create networks of support that benefit all involved [99]. Building a supportive community with other families creates communities of mutual support and encouragement while providing children with additional role models and friendship opportunities that reinforce family values.

A Call to Continued Construction

"And let us not grow weary of doing good, for in due season we will reap, if we do not give up" (Galatians 6:9). As we conclude our comprehensive journey through the principles and practices of biblical family construction, we issue a call to continued faithfulness in building families that honor God, bless their members, and advance His kingdom purposes throughout the world. This

call recognizes that family construction is a lifelong process that requires sustained commitment and ongoing dependence on God's grace.

• Renewing Your Commitment to Biblical Building

The commitment to biblical family construction requires regular renewal and recommitment as families face new challenges and opportunities. This renewal maintains dedication to God's design despite cultural pressures and personal failures while drawing strength from His promises and faithfulness.

• Finding Strength for the Construction Journey Ahead

The strength needed for continued family construction comes ultimately from God's grace and power rather than human resources. This requires families to maintain their dependence on Him while supporting one another through prayer, encouragement, and practical assistance.

• The Promise of God's Blessing on Faithful Builders

The assurance that God blesses families who faithfully follow His construction principles provides motivation for continued obedience. This promise offers hope for both earthly satisfaction and eternal reward while sustaining families through difficult seasons.

• Leaving a Legacy for Future Generations

The ultimate goal of family construction involves creating legacies that will influence multiple generations while contributing to the advancement of God's kingdom and the blessing of communities throughout the world.

As families commit themselves to continued construction according to the principles found in Family by the Book: How to Build the Family God Intended, they join the Master Builder in His eternal work of creating families that reflect His character, advance His purposes, and provide foretastes of the perfect family relationships that await all believers in His eternal kingdom. This work brings both earthly satisfaction and eternal significance, making every effort worthwhile and every sacrifice meaningful in the light of eternity.

Study Guide

Introduction

Welcome to this study guide for "Family by the Book: How to Build the Family God Intended" With Mark Hobafcovich. This guide is designed to help individuals, couples, families, and small groups study the biblical principles presented in the book and apply them to their daily lives.

How to Use This Study Guide

This study guide can be used in several ways:

- Individual Study: Work through each chapter section at your own pace, taking time to reflect on the key concepts and questions.
- Couple Study: Husbands and wives can work through this guide together, discussing the questions and supporting each other in implementing biblical principles.
- Family Study: Parents can adapt the questions for family devotions, helping children understand their roles and responsibilities within the Christian family.
- Small Group Study: Churches and small study groups can use this guide for weekly studies, spending one week on each chapter plus the conclusion.

Each chapter section includes:

- Key Concepts: Main teachings from the chapter
- Discussion Questions: For personal reflection or group discussion

Chapter 1

Key Concepts

God serves as the Master Architect who has provided the perfect blueprint for family construction. Family is the oldest and most fundamental institution in human history, designed by divine wisdom to serve eternal purposes.

The foundation of God's original intent is found in Genesis 2:24: "Therefore a man shall leave his father and mother and hold fast to his wife, and they shall become one flesh." These words establish the foundational principles for all family construction.

God's creation blueprint for marriage shows that loneliness was not part of His perfect plan. When God said, "It is not good that the man should be alone," He provided woman as a helper fit for man, creating someone both like him and different from him.

Marriage represents a sacred joining of two complementary beings into one unified whole. The permanence implied in God's design becomes clear in His instruction that a man should "leave" his parents and "hold fast" to his wife.

Family serves as God's foundational institution, existing before governments, religious institutions, or educational systems. Within the family structure, children receive their first lessons about authority, responsibility, and relationships.

Biblical families require specific spiritual building materials that only God can provide, as stated in Psalm 127:1: "Unless the Lord builds the house, those who build it labor in vain."

God's covenant serves as the binding agent that transforms separate individuals into a unified family unit. Covenants are based on commitment and endure even through difficulties and failures, unlike contracts based on performance.

Family relationships exist to reflect God's character and demonstrate His love to a watching world. Every interaction between family members becomes an opportunity to proclaim God's character.

Discussion Questions

1. How does understanding God as the Master Architect change your perspective on family building and decision-making?

2. What aspects of God's original blueprint for family are most challenging to embrace in today's culture?

3. How well does your family reflect the foundational principle of "leaving and cleaving" described in Genesis 2:24?

4. What spiritual "building materials" does your family most need to strengthen its construction according to God's design?

5. How does understanding marriage as a covenant rather than a contract affect your approach to family relationships?

6. In what ways can your family better serve as a witness to God's character in your community?

7. What steps can you take to ensure your family follows God's blueprint rather than cultural expectations?

Chapter 2

Key Concepts

In any construction project, the cornerstone determines the alignment and stability of the entire structure. Jesus Christ serves as the cornerstone that makes God's blueprint for family life both achievable and sustainable.

According to Colossians 1:17, "And he is before all things, and in him all things hold together." When Christ is properly positioned as the cornerstone of family life, every relationship finds its proper alignment.

Many families attempt to build using other cornerstones like financial security, educational achievement, social status, or religious activity. Only Christ possesses the character, authority, and power necessary for lasting family construction.

Christ's lordship in family life is demonstrated through Joshua 24:15: "But as for me and my house, we will serve the Lord." This establishes a family constitution that places Christ's authority at the center of all family decisions.

Making Jesus the center of family building requires intentional decisions and daily practices. It affects every major decision families face, from career choices to housing decisions to educational choices.

Christ-centered family life transforms daily interactions. Conflicts are resolved using biblical principles, discipline is administered with love and grace, and routine activities become opportunities to demonstrate Christ's lordship.

The Holy Spirit provides the power and wisdom necessary for successful family construction, enabling families to live according to God's design and producing spiritual fruit in relationships.

Biblical hospitality extends family influence beyond the immediate household, demonstrating God's love through practical service and creating opportunities for spiritual conversations.

Discussion Questions

1. In what practical ways does Christ currently serve as the cornerstone of your family life?

2. What other "cornerstones" might your family be tempted to rely on instead of Christ?

3. How does Christ's lordship affect your family's decision-making processes and daily priorities?

4. What changes would you need to make to truly establish Christ as the center of your family building?

5. How can your family better demonstrate Christ's character in daily interactions and conflict resolution?

6. In what ways does the Holy Spirit currently work in your family relationships?

7. How effectively does your family practice biblical hospitality as a witness to others?

Chapter 3

Key Concepts

With Christ as the cornerstone, husbands are assigned the crucial role of foundation layers in family construction. The foundation determines the stability and strength of everything that follows in the family structure.

Ephesians 5:25 provides the blueprint for husband leadership: "Husbands, love your wives, as Christ loved the church and gave himself up for her." This establishes love as the primary building material, Christ as the model, and sacrificial service as the construction method.

Biblical leadership focuses on responsibility, service, and sacrificial love, not authority, control, and personal advantage. True strength comes through serving others rather than demanding service from them.

The foundation that husbands lay through loving leadership affects every aspect of family life. When wives feel genuinely loved, they respond with respect and support. Children learn what healthy relationships look like and develop security.

Marriage provides an opportunity for men to demonstrate Christ's character and advance God's kingdom purposes through sacrificial love and servant leadership, not primarily for personal happiness.

The foundation laying process requires patience, skill, and careful attention to detail. Husbands must develop character qualities, communication skills, and spiritual maturity necessary for effective family leadership.

The love that provides adequate support for lifelong marriage is agape love - unconditional, sacrificial love that God demonstrates toward His people. This love serves as the concrete that binds all other elements of marriage together.

Husbands must learn to love their wives as Christ loved the church, which involves understanding, patience, forgiveness, protection, provision, and spiritual leadership.

Discussion Questions

1. How does understanding your role as a "foundation layer" change your approach to marriage and family leadership?

2. What is the difference between cultural definitions of leadership and biblical leadership in marriage?

3. How well does your leadership style reflect Christ's love for the church as described in Ephesians 5:25?

4. What character qualities do you most need to develop to become a more effective foundation layer?

5. How does agape love differ from other types of love, and how can you better demonstrate this in your marriage?

6. In what practical ways can you serve your wife and children rather than demanding service from them?

7. What steps can you take to ensure your foundation laying creates security and stability for your family?

Chapter 4

Key Concepts

The wife's role as a support structure is essential in function, creating the internal strength that enables the entire family to flourish according to God's design. Support structures work in harmony with the foundation to create stability and strength.

Ephesians 5:33 provides the blueprint: "However, let each one of you love his wife as himself, and let the wife see that she respects her husband." While the husband's primary building material is love, the wife's primary contribution is respect.

The Hebrew word "ezer" (helper) in Genesis 2:18 appears throughout Scripture to describe God Himself as our helper. The wife's supportive role is not one of inferiority but of essential partnership, providing strength and assistance.

When a wife demonstrates genuine respect for her husband's leadership, she creates an environment where his love can flourish. When a husband responds with increased love and care, respect feels natural and joyful, creating a positive cycle.

The wife's support structure role extends beyond marriage to encompass every aspect of family life. Her influence shapes the emotional climate of the home, spiritual atmosphere, and relational patterns that children learn.

Biblical partnership represents a position of strength that requires wisdom, courage, and spiritual maturity. The wife possesses unique gifts and perspectives that are essential for successful family construction.

The wise wife contributes to family decision-making by offering insights, raising important questions, and providing perspectives that strengthen final decisions through additional wisdom and consideration.

God's design for wives as support structures reflects His intention for marriage to demonstrate complementary roles that work together to build strong, lasting families.

Discussion Questions

1. How does understanding your role as a "support structure" change your perspective on marriage and family relationships?

2. What is the difference between respect and submission, and how can you demonstrate biblical respect in your marriage?

3. How can you use your unique gifts and perspectives to strengthen your family's decision-making processes?

4. In what ways does your influence shape the emotional and spiritual climate of your home?

5. How can you create an environment where your husband's love can flourish while maintaining your own identity and contributions?

6. What does biblical partnership look like in practical, everyday family situations?

7. How can you model healthy relationships for your children through your supportive role?

Chapter 5

Key Concepts

Children serve as willing helpers in the family construction process, like eager apprentices who learn while they contribute. Their participation makes the difference between a project that drags on and one that progresses smoothly.

Ephesians 6:1 provides the blueprint: "Children, obey your parents in the Lord, for this is right." Children's participation is about learning to work within God's design for relationships and authority, not merely following rules.

The phrase "in the Lord" transforms parent-child relationships from behavioral compliance to spiritual formation, connecting earthly relationships to heavenly realities. Children learn to submit to God's authority through obeying parents.

Parents should view children as junior partners in the building process rather than obstacles to overcome or problems to solve. This approach requires patience, wisdom, and intentional training but produces valued, purposeful children.

Children's natural characteristics - energy, enthusiasm, and desire to please - create ideal conditions for learning and growth when properly channeled. Their questions and fresh perspectives provide valuable insights.

The fifth commandment (Ephesians 6:2-3) provides the foundational principle governing children's participation: "Honor your father and mother... that it may go well with you and that you may live long in the land."

Honor encompasses a broader attitude of respect, appreciation, and recognition of parental authority, while obedience involves compliance with specific instructions. Understanding this distinction helps children respond appropriately throughout life.

Children learn essential building skills while contributing their unique energy and perspective to the overall family construction effort, preparing them for their own future family building.

Discussion Questions

1. How can children view their role in the family as "willing helpers" rather than reluctant participants?

2. What does it mean to obey parents "in the Lord," and how does this connect earthly and heavenly relationships?

3. How can parents help children understand the difference between honor and obedience?

4. What natural characteristics do children possess that can contribute positively to family building?

5. How can families harness children's energy and enthusiasm while providing appropriate guidance and structure?

6. What does the promise attached to the fifth commandment teach us about the importance of family relationships?

7. How can children's questions and perspectives provide valuable insights for family decision-making?

Chapter 6

Key Concepts

Parents bear the comprehensive responsibility as master builders in shaping the character of the next generation. This represents the integration of all previous family roles while adding specialized skills for character development.

Ephesians 6:4 provides the master blueprint: "Fathers, do not provoke your children to anger, but bring them up in the discipline and instruction of the Lord." This reveals the delicate balance between firm guidance and loving nurture.

Master builders recognize that every interaction with children represents an opportunity to shape character, teach wisdom, and demonstrate God's love. This requires patience, intentionality, and long-term vision.

The goal is not merely well-behaved children who comply with external rules, but developing internal character qualities that will guide children throughout their lives. This requires addressing heart issues rather than managing surface behaviors.

Parents' role as master builders extends beyond their own children to influence future generations and the broader community. Character qualities developed today will be passed down to multiple generations.

Different children require different building techniques while maintaining the same foundational principles and goals. Wise parents adapt their approaches to match each child's unique personality and developmental needs.

The proper balance between love and discipline reflects God's own character and approach to His children, providing both the model and motivation for earthly parents.

Master builders must avoid the extremes of permissiveness and harshness. Permissive parenting fails to provide needed structure, while harsh parenting creates fear and resentment that hinder character growth.

Discussion Questions

1. How does viewing yourself as a "master builder" change your approach to daily parenting challenges and opportunities?

2. What does it mean to "bring children up in the discipline and instruction of the Lord" in practical, everyday situations?

3. How can you focus on developing internal character qualities rather than just managing external behaviors?

4. What character qualities do you most want to develop in your children, and how can you model these yourself?

5. How can you adapt your parenting approach to match each child's unique personality while maintaining consistent values?

6. What is the proper balance between love and discipline, and how can you avoid extremes of permissiveness or harshness?

7. How does understanding the multigenerational impact of your parenting motivate your daily choices and interactions?

Chapter 7

Key Concepts

Well-built families function within the broader community as witnesses to God's design and grace. Families built according to biblical principles become powerful testimonies to the watching world.

Matthew 5:13-14 provides the blueprint: "You are the salt of the earth... You are the light of the world." Christian families are called to be preserving and illuminating influences that demonstrate God's character.

The salt metaphor emphasizes the family's role in preserving moral and spiritual values in society, while the light metaphor highlights the responsibility to illuminate truth and provide guidance for those lost in darkness.

Families should view the broader community not as a threat to avoid but as a mission field where they can be positive influences that attract others to Christ through beautiful relationships and character integrity.

Effective community engagement flows naturally from healthy family construction rather than being an additional burden. When families are built according to God's design, their witness becomes an overflow of internal health.

Community engagement serves multiple purposes: providing hope for struggling families, demonstrating practical benefits of biblical principles, and creating opportunities for gospel conversations.

Biblical families serve as spiritual warfare against forces that seek to destroy marriage, family, and society by providing a counter-narrative to cultural messages promoting selfishness and moral relativism.

Christian families must maintain biblical distinctiveness while remaining engaged with their communities in meaningful ways. This balance requires

265

wisdom, discernment, and ongoing commitment to both spiritual growth and cultural engagement.

Discussion Questions

1. How can your family serve as "salt and light" in your specific community and neighborhood?

2. What does it mean to be biblically distinctive without becoming isolated from your community?

3. How can your family's witness flow naturally from your internal health rather than feeling like an additional burden?

4. What opportunities does your family have to demonstrate God's character through daily community interactions?

5. How can you engage with cultural challenges while maintaining your biblical convictions and values?

6. In what ways can your family provide hope and guidance for other struggling families in your community?

7. How can you create natural opportunities for gospel conversations through your family's community engagement?

Chapter 8

Key Concepts

Difficulties are not signs of construction failure but inevitable aspects of life in a fallen world that can actually strengthen family bonds and spiritual maturity when handled according to biblical principles.

James 1:2 provides guidance: "Count it all joy, my brothers, when you meet trials of various kinds." This doesn't suggest enjoying suffering, but recognizing the potential for growth and blessing from properly navigated challenges.

Families should view conflicts, crises, and pressures as opportunities to demonstrate the strength of their foundations and develop greater maturity and unity, rather than evidence of construction failure.

Strong foundations built during peaceful seasons better equip families to weather inevitable storms. This preparation involves developing character qualities and relational skills, not just learning biblical concepts.

Difficulties serve multiple purposes: testing foundation strength, revealing areas needing additional work, and providing opportunities to demonstrate faith to watching family members and the community.

The approach families take to difficulties significantly affects both immediate outcomes and long-term impact on relationships and spiritual growth. Faith, unity, and biblical wisdom lead to positive outcomes.

Community support during difficult seasons proves crucial for the successful navigation of challenges. Connected families find greater resources and encouragement during times of crisis.

Conflict is inevitable in family relationships due to imperfect people living in close proximity with different personalities, preferences, and perspectives. Understanding this helps families prepare rather than be surprised.

Discussion Questions

1. How can your family view difficulties as opportunities for growth rather than threats to stability?
2. What does it mean to "count it all joy" when facing family trials and challenges?
3. How can you build strong foundations during peaceful seasons to prepare for future difficulties?
4. What character qualities and relational skills help families navigate challenges successfully?
5. How can your family respond to conflicts with faith, unity, and biblical wisdom rather than blame and anger?
6. What role does community support play in helping families through difficult seasons?
7. How can understanding the inevitability of conflict help your family prepare for and handle disagreements better?

Chapter 9

Key Concepts

The ultimate purpose of family construction extends beyond the immediate family to include intentional transfer of faith, values, and wisdom to future generations.

Psalm 78:4 provides the blueprint: "We will not hide them from their children, but tell to the coming generation the glorious deeds of the Lord, and his might, and the wonders that he has done."

Families should view their construction work as creating foundations that will support multiple generations of descendants, requiring patience, intentionality, and eternal vision.

Legacy extends beyond material inheritance to include spiritual heritage, character qualities, relationship patterns, and kingdom values that shape how future generations approach life.

Legacy building serves multiple purposes: providing hope for struggling families, demonstrating practical benefits of biblical principles across generations, and creating expanding networks of kingdom influence.

Effective legacy building requires deliberate planning, consistent modeling, systematic teaching, and ongoing investment in relationships that continue beyond parents' direct guidance.

Every family decision creates ripple effects that extend beyond immediate circumstances, influencing patterns of thinking, relating, and living that can persist for multiple generations.

When multiple families in a community commit to biblical construction principles, they create cultural momentum that influences schools, businesses, churches, and civic organizations for generations.

Discussion Questions

1. How does understanding your family's multigenerational impact change your approach to daily decisions and long-term planning?

2. What spiritual heritage, character qualities, and values do you most want to pass down to future generations?

3. How can you be more intentional about transferring faith and wisdom to your children and grandchildren?

4. What positive family choices are you making that could create expanding circles of blessing for future generations?

5. How can your family contribute to positive cultural momentum in your community?

6. What deliberate planning and systematic teaching can you implement to build a lasting legacy?

7. How does maintaining an eternal perspective motivate your daily family choices and long-term commitments?

Chapter 10

Key Concepts

The ultimate goal of family construction is to establish communities that reflect the character of God's eternal family and serve as foretastes of heavenly reality.

Ephesians 2:19-20 provides the framework: "So then you are no longer strangers and aliens, but you are fellow citizens with the saints and members of the household of God, built on the foundation of the apostles and prophets, Christ Jesus himself being the cornerstone."

Completion brings new opportunities for worship, service, and witness that demonstrate the beauty and effectiveness of God's design, rather than ending the construction project.

All elements of family construction work together to create integrated wholes: husband's leadership, wife's support, children's participation, parents' character-building, community engagement, difficulty navigation, and legacy building.

Successfully completed families become sources of blessing for immediate members, extended families, communities, and future generations, demonstrating the multiplication principle of God's kingdom work.

Stewardship responsibilities include maintaining structures, continuing to grow together, and using stability and strength to serve others still in the construction process.

The eternal perspective helps families understand that earthly construction serves as preparation for eternal family relationships in God's kingdom.

Proper celebration recognizes that successful family construction results primarily from God's grace rather than human effort, preventing pride while fostering genuine gratitude.

Discussion Questions

1. How does viewing your family as a reflection of God's eternal household change your perspective on daily family life?

2. What new opportunities for worship, service, and witness has your family construction created?

3. How can you see all the elements of your family construction working together as an integrated whole?

4. In what ways has your family become a source of blessing for others beyond your immediate members?

5. What stewardship responsibilities do you have for maintaining and continuing to develop your family structure?

6. How does maintaining an eternal perspective provide motivation and comfort for your family?

7. How can you properly celebrate what God has built while remaining humble about your role in the construction process?

Conclusion

Key Concepts

Families built according to biblical principles are divine masterpieces crafted by the Master Builder Himself, designed to display His glory and accomplish His eternal purposes.

Ephesians 2:10 provides the framework: "For we are his workmanship, created in Christ Jesus for good works, which God prepared beforehand, that we should walk in them."

Understanding families as God's workmanship brings humility about our contributions and confidence in His ability to complete what He has begun, preventing both pride and despair.

Families are created for good works that extend beyond personal happiness to advancing God's kingdom and blessing others who observe their witness.

The central theme of biblical family construction is mutual submission flowing from reverence for Christ, enabling family members to serve one another with joy.

The beauty of biblical families results from Christ-centered relationships where each member seeks to serve others rather than demanding to be served.

Daily application involves starting where you are with small building steps, establishing morning routines, handling conflicts with grace, and creating evening practices that build unity.

Seasonal and lifelong applications include creating value-reinforcing traditions, celebrating holidays that honor God, using life transitions as teaching opportunities, and regular evaluation.

273

Discussion Questions

1. How does understanding your family as God's masterpiece change your perspective on both successes and failures?

2. What good works has God prepared beforehand for your family to walk in?

3. How can mutual submission out of reverence for Christ become more central to your family relationships?

4. What daily practices can you implement to build family unity and demonstrate Christ-centered relationships?

5. How can you create family traditions and seasonal celebrations that reinforce biblical values?

6. What life transitions can your family use as teaching opportunities for spiritual growth?

7. How can your family serve as a beacon of hope to other families still in the construction process?

Notes by Chapter

Notes Chapter 1

[1] Andreas Kostenberger, God, Marriage, and Family (Wheaton: Crossway, 2004), 23.

[2] John MacArthur, The Family (Chicago: Moody Press, 1982), 15.

[3] Bruce Waltke, Genesis: A Commentary (Grand Rapids: Zondervan, 2001), 67.

[4] Victor Hamilton, The Book of Genesis: Chapters 1-17 (Grand Rapids: Eerdmans, 1990), 175.

[5] Gordon Wenham, Genesis 1-15: Word Biblical Commentary (Waco: Word Books, 1987), 70.

[6] Wayne Grudem, Systematic Theology (Grand Rapids: Zondervan, 1994), 455.

[7] John Sailhamer, The Pentateuch as Narrative (Grand Rapids: Zondervan, 1992), 103.

[8] James Dobson, Marriage Under Fire (Sisters: Multnomah, 2004), 45.

[9] Tedd Tripp, Shepherding a Child's Heart (Wapwallopen: Shepherd Press, 1995), 34.

[10] Voddie Baucham Jr., Family Driven Faith (Wheaton: Crossway, 2007), 78.

[11] Dennis Rainey, Stepping Up (Little Rock: FamilyLife Publishing, 2011), 89.

[12] Gary Chapman, The 5 Love Languages (Chicago: Northfield Publishing, 2015), 56.

[13] John Piper, This Momentary Marriage (Wheaton: Crossway, 2009), 67.

[14] Paul David Tripp, What Did You Expect? (Wheaton: Crossway, 2010), 123.

[15] Timothy Keller, The Meaning of Marriage (New York: Dutton, 2011), 145.

[16] R.C. Sproul, The Reformation Study Bible (Orlando: Ligonier Ministries, 2015), 45.

[17] John MacArthur, The MacArthur Study Bible (Nashville: Thomas Nelson, 2006), 34.

[18] Matthew Henry, Matthew Henry's Commentary on the Whole Bible (Peabody: Hendrickson, 1994), 67.

[19] Derek Kidner, Genesis: An Introduction and Commentary (Downers Grove: InterVarsity Press, 1967), 156.

[20] Dale Ralph Davis, 2 Samuel: Out of Every Adversity (Ross-shire: Christian Focus, 1999), 234.

[21] Robertson McQuilkin, An Introduction to Biblical Ethics (Wheaton: Tyndale House, 1995), 278.

[22] William Heth and Gordon Wenham, Jesus and Divorce (Nashville: Thomas Nelson, 1984), 89.

[23] Christopher Ash, Marriage: Sex in the Service of God (Leicester: Inter-Varsity Press, 2003), 123.

[24] Raymond Ortlund Jr., Marriage and the Mystery of the Gospel (Wheaton: Crossway, 2016), 67.

[25] Wayne Grudem, Evangelical Feminism and Biblical Truth (Sisters: Multnomah, 2004), 145.

[26] John Piper and Wayne Grudem, Recovering Biblical Manhood and Womanhood (Wheaton: Crossway, 1991), 178.

[27] Stuart Scott, The Exemplary Husband (Bemidji: Focus Publishing, 2002), 56.

[28] Martha Peace, The Excellent Wife (Bemidji: Focus Publishing, 1995), 89.

[29] Paul David Tripp, Age of Opportunity (Phillipsburg: P&R Publishing, 2001), 123.

[30] Douglas Wilson, Reforming Marriage (Moscow: Canon Press, 1995), 67.

[31] Fred Sanders, The Deep Things of God (Wheaton: Crossway, 2010), 145.

[32] Bruce Ware, Father, Son, and Holy Spirit (Wheaton: Crossway, 2005), 89.

[33] Michael Reeves, Delighting in the Trinity (Downers Grove: InterVarsity Press, 2012), 123.

[34] Gerald Bray, The Doctrine of God (Downers Grove: InterVarsity Press, 1993), 178.

[35] Daniel Doriani, The Life of a God-Made Man (Wheaton: Crossway, 2001), 67.

[36] Peter O'Brien, The Letter to the Ephesians (Grand Rapids: Eerdmans, 1999), 423.

[37] Harold Hoehner, Ephesians: An Exegetical Commentary (Grand Rapids: Baker Academic, 2002), 756.

[38] Frank Thielman, Ephesians (Grand Rapids: Baker Academic, 2010), 378.

[39] Clinton Arnold, Ephesians: Zondervan Exegetical Commentary (Grand Rapids: Zondervan, 2010), 389.

[40] Andrew Lincoln, Ephesians: Word Biblical Commentary (Dallas: Word Books, 1990), 378.

[41] Dan Cruver, Reclaiming Adoption (Adelphi: Cruciform Press, 2011), 89.

[42] Bruce Ray, Withhold Not Correction (Phillipsburg: Presbyterian and Reformed, 1978), 67.

[43] Lou Priolo, The Heart of Anger (Amityville: Calvary Press, 1997), 123.

[44] Clay Clarkson, Heartfelt Discipline (Colorado Springs: WaterBrook Press, 2003), 145.

[45] Ted Tripp, Instructing a Child's Heart (Wapwallopen: Shepherd Press, 2008), 178.

[46] Mary Kassian, Girls Gone Wise (Chicago: Moody Publishers, 2010), 89.

[47] Nancy Leigh DeMoss, Biblical Womanhood in the Home (Wheaton: Crossway, 2002), 123.

[48] Susan Hunt, The True Woman (Wheaton: Crossway, 1997), 67.

[49] Carolyn Mahaney, Feminine Appeal (Wheaton: Crossway, 2004), 145.

[50] Elisabeth Elliot, Let Me Be a Woman (Wheaton: Tyndale House, 1976), 178.

[51] John MacArthur, Different by Design (Wheaton: Victor Books, 1994), 89.

[52] James MacDonald, Act Like Men (Chicago: Moody Publishers, 2014), 123.

[53] Stu Weber, Tender Warrior (Sisters: Multnomah, 1993), 67.

[54] Albert Mohler, Desire and Deceit (Sisters: Multnomah, 2008), 145.

[55] Russell Moore, Adopted for Life (Wheaton: Crossway, 2009), 178.

[56] Richard Phillips, The Masculine Mandate (Orlando: Reformation Trust, 2010), 89.

[57] Ernie Baker, Marry Wisely, Marry Well (Phillipsburg: P&R Publishing, 2014), 123.

[58] Rob Rienow, Visionary Parenting (Nashville: Randall House, 2009), 67.

[59] Steve Farrar, Point Man (Sisters: Multnomah, 1990), 145.

[60] Josh Mulvihill, Biblical Grandparenting (Minneapolis: Bethany House, 2018), 178.

[61] Timothy Lane, How People Change (Greensboro: New Growth Press, 2008), 89.

[62] Paul Tripp, Instruments in the Redeemer's Hands (Phillipsburg: P&R Publishing, 2002), 123.

[63] Ken Sande, The Peacemaker (Grand Rapids: Baker Books, 2004), 67.

[64] Jerry Bridges, The Practice of Godliness (Colorado Springs: NavPress, 1996), 145.

[65] John Piper, A Godward Life (Sisters: Multnomah, 1997), 178.

[66] Donald Whitney, Spiritual Disciplines for the Christian Life (Colorado Springs: NavPress, 1991), 89.

[67] R.C. Sproul, The Holiness of God (Wheaton: Tyndale House, 1985), 123.

[68] John MacArthur, The Gospel According to Jesus (Grand Rapids: Zondervan, 1988), 67.

[69] Martyn Lloyd-Jones, Studies in the Sermon on the Mount (Grand Rapids: Eerdmans, 1959), 145.

[70] J.I. Packer, Knowing God (Downers Grove: InterVarsity Press, 1973), 178.

[71] Charles Spurgeon, Morning and Evening (Peabody: Hendrickson, 1991), 89.

[72] John Stott, The Cross of Christ (Downers Grove: InterVarsity Press, 1986), 123.

[73] Tim Keller, The Reason for God (New York: Dutton, 2008), 67.

[74] Wayne Grudem, Christian Ethics (Wheaton: Crossway, 2018), 234.

[75] John Frame, The Doctrine of the Christian Life (Phillipsburg: P&R Publishing, 2008), 567.

[76] Kevin DeYoung, The Hole in Our Holiness (Wheaton: Crossway, 2012), 123.

[77] Sinclair Ferguson, The Whole Christ (Wheaton: Crossway, 2016), 189.

[78] Michael Horton, The Christian Faith (Grand Rapids: Zondervan, 2011), 456.

[79] Joel Beeke, Reformed Preaching (Wheaton: Crossway, 2018), 345.

[80] Ligon Duncan, Does Grace Grow Best in Winter? (Phillipsburg: P&R Publishing, 2009), 178.

Notes Chapter 2

[1] John MacArthur, The Family (Chicago: Moody Press, 1982), 45.

[2] Timothy Keller, The Meaning of Marriage (New York: Dutton, 2011), 67.

[3] Paul David Tripp, What Did You Expect? (Wheaton: Crossway, 2010), 89.

[4] Dennis Rainey, Stepping Up (Little Rock: FamilyLife Publishing, 2011), 123.

[5] John Piper, This Momentary Marriage (Wheaton: Crossway, 2009), 145.

[6] Gary Chapman, The 5 Love Languages (Chicago: Northfield Publishing, 2015), 78.

[7] Voddie Baucham Jr., Family Driven Faith (Wheaton: Crossway, 2007), 156.

[8] James MacDonald, Act Like Men (Chicago: Moody Publishers, 2014), 89.

[9] Donald Whitney, Family Worship (Wheaton: Crossway, 2016), 34.

[10] Joel Beeke, Family Worship (Grand Rapids: Reformation Heritage Books, 2009), 67.

[11] Tedd Tripp, Shepherding a Child's Heart (Wapwallopen: Shepherd Press, 1995), 123.

[12] Rob Rienow, Visionary Parenting (Nashville: Randall House, 2009), 145.

[13] Steve Farrar, Point Man (Sisters: Multnomah, 1990), 178.

[14] Carolyn Mahaney, Feminine Appeal (Wheaton: Crossway, 2004), 89.

[15] Susan Hunt, The True Woman (Wheaton: Crossway, 1997), 123.

[16] Alexander Strauch, The Hospitality Commands (Littleton: Lewis and Roth Publishers, 1993), 67.

[17] Ken Sande, The Peacemaker (Grand Rapids: Baker Books, 2004), 145.

[18] Jerry Bridges, The Practice of Godliness (Colorado Springs: NavPress, 1996), 178.

[19] John Piper, A Godward Life (Sisters: Multnomah, 1997), 89.

[20] Donald Whitney, Spiritual Disciplines for the Christian Life (Colorado Springs: NavPress, 1991), 123.

[21] John MacArthur, How to Study the Bible (Chicago: Moody Press, 1982), 67.

[22] Timothy Lane, How People Change (Greensboro: New Growth Press, 2008), 145.

[23] Paul Tripp, Instruments in the Redeemer's Hands (Phillipsburg: P&R Publishing, 2002), 178.

[24] Jerry Bridges, The Discipline of Grace (Colorado Springs: NavPress, 1994), 89.

[25] John Owen, The Holy Spirit (Edinburgh: Banner of Truth, 1965), 123.

[26] Sinclair Ferguson, The Holy Spirit (Downers Grove: InterVarsity Press, 1996), 67.

[27] J.I. Packer, Keep in Step with the Spirit (Grand Rapids: Baker Books, 1984), 145.

[28] R.C. Sproul, The Prayer of the Lord (Orlando: Reformation Trust, 2009), 178.

[29] John Stott, The Message of Galatians (Downers Grove: InterVarsity Press, 1968), 89.

[30] D.A. Carson, Love in Hard Places (Wheaton: Crossway, 2002), 123.

[31] John Piper, Desiring God (Sisters: Multnomah, 1996), 67.

[32] Jeremiah Burroughs, The Rare Jewel of Christian Contentment (Edinburgh: Banner of Truth, 1964), 145.

[33] Thomas Watson, The Doctrine of Repentance (Edinburgh: Banner of Truth, 1988), 178.

[34] John Flavel, Keeping the Heart (Fearn: Christian Focus, 1999), 89.

[35] Matthew Henry, A Method for Prayer (Fearn: Christian Focus, 1994), 123.

[36] John Bunyan, Prayer (Edinburgh: Banner of Truth, 1965), 67.

[37] Richard Pratt, Pray with Your Eyes Open (Phillipsburg: P&R Publishing, 1987), 145.

[38] John Piper, Let the Nations Be Glad (Grand Rapids: Baker Academic, 2003), 178.

[39] Donald Carson, A Call to Spiritual Reformation (Grand Rapids: Baker Books, 1992), 89.

[40] Wayne Grudem, Systematic Theology (Grand Rapids: Zondervan, 1994), 123.

[41] John Murray, Redemption Accomplished and Applied (Grand Rapids: Eerdmans, 1955), 67.

[42] Jay Adams, Competent to Counsel (Grand Rapids: Baker Books, 1970), 145.

[43] David Powlison, Seeing with New Eyes (Phillipsburg: P&R Publishing, 2003), 178.

[44] Paul Miller, A Praying Life (Colorado Springs: NavPress, 2009), 89.

[45] Rosaria Butterfield, The Gospel Comes with a House Key (Wheaton: Crossway, 2018), 123.

[46] Karen Mains, Open Heart, Open Home (Elgin: David C. Cook, 1976), 67.

[47] Christine Pohl, Making Room (Grand Rapids: Eerdmans, 1999), 145.

[48] Edith Schaeffer, Hidden Art (Wheaton: Tyndale House, 1971), 178.

[49] Elisabeth Elliot, The Shaping of a Christian Family (Grand Rapids: Revell, 1992), 89.

[50] Sally Clarkson, The Mission of Motherhood (Colorado Springs: WaterBrook Press, 2003), 123.

[51] Clay Clarkson, Educating the WholeHearted Child (Walnut Springs: Whole Heart Ministries, 1994), 67.

[52] Ted Tripp, Instructing a Child's Heart (Wapwallopen: Shepherd Press, 2008), 145.

[53] Josh Mulvihill, Biblical Grandparenting (Minneapolis: Bethany House, 2018), 178.

[54] Russell Moore, Adopted for Life (Wheaton: Crossway, 2009), 89.

[55] Tim Chester, A Meal with Jesus (Wheaton: Crossway, 2011), 123.

[56] Mark Dever, Nine Marks of a Healthy Church (Wheaton: Crossway, 2004), 67.

[57] Kevin DeYoung, Crazy Busy (Wheaton: Crossway, 2013), 145.

[58] Tony Reinke, 12 Ways Your Phone Is Changing You (Wheaton: Crossway, 2017), 178.

[59] Matt Chandler, The Mingling of Souls (Colorado Springs: David C. Cook, 2015), 89.

[60] Randy Newman, Questioning Evangelism (Grand Rapids: Kregel, 2004), 123.

[61] Marty Machowski, The Ology (Grand Rapids: Zondervan, 2012), 67.

[62] Rebecca VanDoodewaard, Reformation Women (Grand Rapids: Reformation Heritage Books, 2017), 145.

[63] Jen Wilkin, Women of the Word (Wheaton: Crossway, 2014), 178.

[64] Gloria Furman, Missional Motherhood (Wheaton: Crossway, 2016), 89.

[65] Kathleen Nielson, Women and God (Wheaton: Crossway, 2018), 123.

[66] Melissa Kruger, The Envy of Eve (Fearn: Christian Focus, 2012), 67.

[67] Nancy Guthrie, Seeing Jesus in the Old Testament (Wheaton: Crossway, 2013), 145.

[68] Kristie Anyabwile, Literarily (Wheaton: Crossway, 2018), 178.

[69] Trillia Newbell, Sacred Endurance (Wheaton: Crossway, 2019), 89.

[70] Courtney Doctor, From Garden to Glory (Wheaton: Crossway, 2016), 123.

[71] Christina Fox, A Holy Fear (Fearn: Christian Focus, 2018), 67.

[72] Betsy Childs Howard, Seasons of Waiting (Wheaton: Crossway, 2016), 145.

[73] Megan Hill, Praying Together (Wheaton: Crossway, 2016), 178.

[74] Aileen Challies, Seasons of Sorrow (Wheaton: Crossway, 2016), 89.

[75] Vaneetha Rendall Risner, The Scars That Have Shaped Me (Wheaton: Crossway, 2016), 123.

[76] Joni Eareckson Tada, A Place of Healing (Colorado Springs: David C. Cook, 2010), 67.

[77] John Piper, Suffering and the Sovereignty of God (Wheaton: Crossway, 2006), 145.

[78] Paul Tripp, Suffering (Wheaton: Crossway, 2018), 178.

[79] Jerry Bridges, Trusting God (Colorado Springs: NavPress, 1988), 89.

[80] Randy Alcorn, Heaven (Wheaton: Tyndale House, 2004), 123.

[81] Noel Piper, Faithful Women and Their Extraordinary God (Wheaton: Crossway, 2005), 67.

[82] John Piper, Brothers, We Are Not Professionals (Nashville: Broadman & Holman, 2002), 145.

[83] Albert Mohler, The Conviction to Lead (Minneapolis: Bethany House, 2012), 178.

[84] R.C. Sproul Jr., When You Rise Up (Phillipsburg: P&R Publishing, 2004), 89.

[85] Douglas Wilson, Future Men (Moscow: Canon Press, 2001), 123.

[86] Voddie Baucham Jr., What He Must Be (Wheaton: Crossway, 2013), 67.

[87] Stuart Scott, The Exemplary Husband (Bemidji: Focus Publishing, 2002), 145.

Notes Chapter 3

[1] John MacArthur, Different by Design (Wheaton: Victor Books, 1994), 67.

[2] Stuart Scott, The Exemplary Husband (Bemidji: Focus Publishing, 2002), 89.

[3] Dennis Rainey, Stepping Up (Little Rock: FamilyLife Publishing, 2011), 123.

[4] Timothy Keller, The Meaning of Marriage (New York: Dutton, 2011), 145.

[5] Paul David Tripp, What Did You Expect? (Wheaton: Crossway, 2010), 178.

[6] Gary Chapman, The 5 Love Languages (Chicago: Northfield Publishing, 2015), 45.

[7] John Piper, This Momentary Marriage (Wheaton: Crossway, 2009), 67.

[8] Wayne Grudem, Evangelical Feminism and Biblical Truth (Sisters: Multnomah, 2004), 89.

[9] Emerson Eggerichs, Love and Respect (Nashville: Thomas Nelson, 2004), 123.

[10] Steve Farrar, Point Man (Sisters: Multnomah, 1990), 145.

[11] Jerry Bridges, The Practice of Godliness (Colorado Springs: NavPress, 1996), 178.

[12] James MacDonald, Act Like Men (Chicago: Moody Publishers, 2014), 45.

[13] Voddie Baucham Jr., What He Must Be (Wheaton: Crossway, 2013), 67.

[14] Ken Sande, The Peacemaker (Grand Rapids: Baker Books, 2004), 89.

[15] John Piper, A Godward Life (Sisters: Multnomah, 1997), 123.

[16] Paul Tripp, Instruments in the Redeemer's Hands (Phillipsburg: P&R Publishing, 2002), 145.

[17] Jerry Bridges, The Discipline of Grace (Colorado Springs: NavPress, 1994), 178.

[18] Douglas Wilson, Future Men (Moscow: Canon Press, 2001), 45.

[19] Albert Mohler, The Conviction to Lead (Minneapolis: Bethany House, 2012), 67.

[20] John Eldredge, Wild at Heart (Nashville: Thomas Nelson, 2001), 89.

[21] R.C. Sproul Jr., When You Rise Up (Phillipsburg: P&R Publishing, 2004), 123.

[22] Gary Thomas, Sacred Marriage (Grand Rapids: Zondervan, 2000), 145.

[23] Dan Allender, Intimate Allies (Wheaton: Tyndale House, 1995), 178.

[24] Les Parrott, Saving Your Marriage Before It Starts (Grand Rapids: Zondervan, 1995), 45.

[25] Gary Smalley, If Only He Knew (Grand Rapids: Zondervan, 1979), 67.

[26] Willard Harley, His Needs, Her Needs (Grand Rapids: Revell, 1986), 89.

[27] C.J. Mahaney, Sex, Romance, and the Glory of God (Wheaton: Crossway, 2004), 123.

[28] Mark Driscoll, Real Marriage (Nashville: Thomas Nelson, 2012), 145.

[29] Matt Chandler, The Mingling of Souls (Colorado Springs: David C. Cook, 2015), 178.

[30] Dave Harvey, When Sinners Say I Do (Wapwallopen: Shepherd Press, 2007), 45.

[31] Winston Smith, Marriage Matters (Greensboro: New Growth Press, 2010), 67.

[32] Donald Whitney, Spiritual Disciplines for the Christian Life (Colorado Springs: NavPress, 1991), 89.

[33] Joel Beeke, Family Worship (Grand Rapids: Reformation Heritage Books, 2009), 123.

[34] Jay Adams, Christian Living in the Home (Phillipsburg: P&R Publishing, 1972), 145.

[35] Susan Hunt, The True Woman (Wheaton: Crossway, 1997), 178.

[36] John MacArthur, The Family (Chicago: Moody Press, 1982), 45.

[37] Shaunti Feldhahn, For Men Only (Sisters: Multnomah, 2006), 67.

[38] Kevin Leman, Sheet Music (Wheaton: Tyndale House, 2003), 89.

[39] Steve Farrar, Point Man (Sisters: Multnomah, 1990), 123.

[40] Ron Blue, Master Your Money (Nashville: Thomas Nelson, 1986), 145.

[41] Gary Smalley, The Key to Your Child's Heart (Dallas: Word Publishing, 1984), 178.

[42] Voddie Baucham Jr., Family Driven Faith (Wheaton: Crossway, 2007), 45.

[43] Clay Clarkson, Heartfelt Discipline (Colorado Springs: WaterBrook Press, 2003), 67.

[44] Donald Whitney, Family Worship (Wheaton: Crossway, 2016), 89.

[45] Tedd Tripp, Shepherding a Child's Heart (Wapwallopen: Shepherd Press, 1995), 123.

[46] Susan Hunt, The True Woman (Wheaton: Crossway, 1997), 145.

[47] Dennis Rainey, Stepping Up (Little Rock: FamilyLife Publishing, 2011), 178.

[48] Larry Burkett, Your Finances in Changing Times (Chicago: Moody Press, 1975), 45.

[49] Douglas Wilson, The Case for Classical Christian Education (Wheaton: Crossway, 2003), 67.

[50] Gary Smalley, The Blessing (Nashville: Thomas Nelson, 1986), 89.

[51] C.J. Mahaney, Humility (Sisters: Multnomah, 2005), 123.

[52] Wayne Grudem, Evangelical Feminism and Biblical Truth (Sisters: Multnomah, 2004), 145.

[53] Paul Tripp, Dangerous Calling (Wheaton: Crossway, 2012), 178.

[54] Andy Stanley, The Next Generation Leader (Sisters: Multnomah, 2003), 45.

[55] Gordon MacDonald, Ordering Your Private World (Nashville: Thomas Nelson, 1984), 67.

[56] Henry Blackaby, Experiencing God (Nashville: Broadman & Holman, 1994), 89.

[57] John Piper, Future Grace (Sisters: Multnomah, 1995), 123.

[58] Howard Hendricks, As Iron Sharpens Iron (Chicago: Moody Press, 1995), 145.

[59] Gary Thomas, Sacred Marriage (Grand Rapids: Zondervan, 2000), 178.

[60] Paul David Tripp, What Did You Expect? (Wheaton: Crossway, 2010), 45.

[61] John Gottman, The Seven Principles for Making Marriage Work (New York: Crown, 1999), 67.

[62] Gary Chapman, The 5 Love Languages (Chicago: Northfield Publishing, 2015), 89.

[63] Jerry Bridges, Respectable Sins (Colorado Springs: NavPress, 2007), 123.

[64] Paul Tripp, Instruments in the Redeemer's Hands (Phillipsburg: P&R Publishing, 2002), 145.

[65] Ken Sande, The Peacemaker (Grand Rapids: Baker Books, 2004), 178.

[66] Richard Foster, Celebration of Discipline (San Francisco: HarperSanFrancisco, 1988), 45.

[67] Larry Crabb, Connecting (Nashville: Word Publishing, 1997), 67.

[68] John Piper, Desiring God (Sisters: Multnomah, 1996), 89.

[69] Stuart Scott, The Exemplary Husband (Bemidji: Focus Publishing, 2002), 123.

[70] Dennis Rainey, Stepping Up (Little Rock: FamilyLife Publishing, 2011), 145.

[71] Paul David Tripp, What Did You Expect? (Wheaton: Crossway, 2010), 178.

[72] John MacArthur, Different by Design (Wheaton: Victor Books, 1994), 45.

[73] Jerry Bridges, The Practice of Godliness (Colorado Springs: NavPress, 1996), 89.

[74] Susan Hunt, The True Woman (Wheaton: Crossway, 1997), 123.

[75] Dennis Rainey, Stepping Up (Little Rock: FamilyLife Publishing, 2011), 145.

[76] John MacArthur, Different by Design (Wheaton: Victor Books, 1994), 178.

[1] Wayne Grudem, Systematic Theology: An Introduction to Biblical Doctrine (Grand Rapids: Zondervan, 1994), 461.

[2] John Piper, This Momentary Marriage: A Parable of Permanence (Wheaton: Crossway, 2009), 89.

[3] Dennis Rainey, Stepping Up: A Call to Courageous Manhood (Little Rock: FamilyLife Publishing, 2011), 134.

[4] Nancy Leigh DeMoss, Biblical Womanhood in the Home (Wheaton: Crossway, 2002), 67.

[5] R.C. Sproul, The Intimate Marriage (Phillipsburg: P&R Publishing, 2003), 78.

[6] Elisabeth Elliot, Let Me Be a Woman (Wheaton: Tyndale House, 1976), 45.

[7] John MacArthur, Different by Design: Discovering God's Will for Today's Man and Woman (Wheaton: Victor Books, 1994), 156.

[8] Susan Hunt, The True Woman: The Beauty and Strength of a Godly Woman (Wheaton: Crossway, 1997), 89.

[9] Timothy Keller, The Meaning of Marriage: Facing the Complexities of Commitment with the Wisdom of God (New York: Dutton, 2011), 178.

[10] Mary Kassian, Girls Gone Wise in a World Gone Wild (Chicago: Moody Publishers, 2010), 234.

[11] Carolyn Mahaney, Feminine Appeal: Seven Virtues of a Godly Wife and Mother (Wheaton: Crossway, 2003), 67.

[12] Martha Peace, The Excellent Wife: A Biblical Perspective (Bemidji: Focus Publishing, 1995), 123.

[13] Lou Priolo, The Complete Husband: A Practical Guide to Biblical Husbanding (Amityville: Calvary Press, 1999), 89.

[14] James Dobson, Love Must Be Tough: New Hope for Marriages in Crisis (Nashville: Thomas Nelson, 2007), 145.

[15] Gary Thomas, Sacred Marriage: What If God Designed Marriage to Make Us Holy More Than to Make Us Happy (Grand Rapids: Zondervan, 2000), 167.

[16] Stormie Omartian, The Power of a Praying Wife (Eugene: Harvest House, 1997), 78.

[17] Emerson Eggerichs, Love and Respect: The Love She Most Desires; The Respect He Desperately Needs (Nashville: Thomas Nelson, 2004), 134.

[18] Victor Hamilton, The Book of Genesis: Chapters 1-17 (Grand Rapids: Eerdmans, 1990), 175.

[19] Andreas Köstenberger, God, Marriage, and Family: Rebuilding the Biblical Foundation (Wheaton: Crossway, 2004), 89.

[20] Darrow Miller, Discipling Nations: The Power of Truth to Transform Cultures (Seattle: YWAM Publishing, 1998), 156.

[21] Nancy Wilson, The Fruit of Her Hands: Respect and the Christian Woman (Moscow: Canon Press, 1997), 67.

[22] Derek Kidner, Proverbs: An Introduction and Commentary (Downers Grove: InterVarsity Press, 1964), 89.

[23] Bruce Waltke, The Book of Proverbs: Chapters 1-15 (Grand Rapids: Eerdmans, 2004), 234.

[24] Raymond Ortlund Jr., Marriage and the Mystery of the Gospel (Wheaton: Crossway, 2016), 78.

[25] Kevin DeYoung, What Does the Bible Really Teach about Homosexuality? (Wheaton: Crossway, 2015), 123.

[26] Tremper Longman III, Proverbs (Grand Rapids: Baker Academic, 2006), 167.

[27] John Piper and Wayne Grudem, Recovering Biblical Manhood and Womanhood (Wheaton: Crossway, 1991), 145.

[28] Larry Crabb, Men and Women: Enjoying the Difference (Grand Rapids: Zondervan, 1991), 89.

[29] Shaunti Feldhahn, For Women Only: What You Need to Know About the Inner Lives of Men (Sisters: Multnomah, 2004), 134.

[30] Gary Smalley, If Only He Knew: What No Woman Can Resist (Grand Rapids: Zondervan, 1979), 78.

[31] Stuart Scott, The Exemplary Husband: A Biblical Perspective (Bemidji: Focus Publishing, 2002), 156.

[32] Tedd Tripp, Shepherding a Child's Heart (Wapwallopen: Shepherd Press, 1995), 89.

[33] Paul David Tripp, What Did You Expect?: Redeeming the Realities of Marriage (Wheaton: Crossway, 2010), 167.

[34] Dan Allender and Tremper Longman III, Intimate Allies (Wheaton: Tyndale House, 1995), 123.

[35] Linda Dillow, Creative Counterpart: Becoming the Woman, Wife, and Mother You Have Longed to Be (Nashville: Thomas Nelson, 1986), 78.

[36] Gaye Clark, A Wife After God's Own Heart (Eugene: Harvest House, 2004), 145.

[37] Elizabeth George, A Woman After God's Own Heart (Eugene: Harvest House, 1997), 89.

[38] Donna Otto, Finding Your Purpose as a Mom (Eugene: Harvest House, 2004), 134.

[39] Charles Bridges, A Commentary on Proverbs (Edinburgh: Banner of Truth, 1968), 567.

[40] Matthew Henry, Matthew Henry's Commentary on the Whole Bible (Peabody: Hendrickson, 1994), 3:789.

[41] John Gill, An Exposition of the Old Testament (London: William Hill Collingridge, 1852), 4:234.

[42] Albert Barnes, Notes on the Old Testament: Proverbs (Grand Rapids: Baker Books, 1996), 456.

[43] Adam Clarke, Clarke's Commentary: Proverbs (Nashville: Abingdon Press, 1977), 234.

[44] Jamieson, Fausset, and Brown, Commentary Critical and Explanatory on the Whole Bible (Grand Rapids: Zondervan, 1961), 567.

[45] Keil and Delitzsch, Commentary on the Old Testament: Proverbs (Grand Rapids: Eerdmans, 1989), 345.

[46] Franz Delitzsch, Biblical Commentary on the Proverbs of Solomon (Edinburgh: T&T Clark, 1874), 234.

[47] Joseph Parker, The People's Bible: Proverbs (London: Hazell, Watson & Viney, 1895), 456.

[48] Alexander Maclaren, Expositions of Holy Scripture: Proverbs (Grand Rapids: Baker Books, 1974), 123.

[49] G. Campbell Morgan, The Analyzed Bible: Proverbs (New York: Fleming H. Revell, 1907), 345.

[50] Warren Wiersbe, Be Skillful: God's Guidebook to Wise Living (Colorado Springs: David C. Cook, 2009), 167.

[51] Charles Swindoll, Living on the Ragged Edge: Coming to Terms with Reality (Nashville: Thomas Nelson, 1985), 234.

[52] John Phillips, Exploring Proverbs: An Expository Commentary (Grand Rapids: Kregel Publications, 1995), 456.

[53] Irving Jensen, Proverbs: A Self-Study Guide (Chicago: Moody Press, 1982), 123.

[54] Roy Zuck, A Biblical Theology of the Old Testament (Chicago: Moody Press, 1991), 345.

[55] Allen Ross, Proverbs: An Introduction and Commentary (Downers Grove: InterVarsity Press, 2008), 234.

[56] Paul Koptak, Proverbs: The NIV Application Commentary (Grand Rapids: Zondervan, 2003), 456.

[57] Duane Garrett, Proverbs, Ecclesiastes, Song of Songs: The New American Commentary (Nashville: Broadman & Holman, 1993), 167.

[58] Michael Fox, Proverbs 10-31: The Anchor Bible (New York: Doubleday, 2009), 234.

[59] Richard Clifford, Proverbs: The Old Testament Library (Louisville: Westminster John Knox Press, 1999), 345.

[60] Leo Perdue, Proverbs: Interpretation Commentary (Louisville: John Knox Press, 2000), 123.

[61] William McKane, Proverbs: A New Approach (Philadelphia: Westminster Press, 1970), 456.

[62] R.B.Y. Scott, Proverbs, Ecclesiastes: The Anchor Bible (Garden City: Doubleday, 1965), 234.

[63] Crawford Toy, A Critical and Exegetical Commentary on the Book of Proverbs (Edinburgh: T&T Clark, 1899), 345.

[64] Patrick Miller, The Way of the Lord: Essays in Old Testament Theology (Tübingen: Mohr Siebeck, 2004), 167.

287

[65] Gerhard von Rad, Wisdom in Israel (Nashville: Abingdon Press, 1972), 234.

[66] James Crenshaw, Old Testament Wisdom: An Introduction (Atlanta: John Knox Press, 1981), 456.

[67] Roland Murphy, The Tree of Life: An Exploration of Biblical Wisdom Literature (Grand Rapids: Eerdmans, 1990), 123.

[68] Kathleen O'Connor, The Wisdom Literature (Collegeville: Liturgical Press, 1988), 345.

[69] Carole Fontaine, Traditional Sayings in the Old Testament (Sheffield: Almond Press, 1982), 234.

[70] Claudia Camp, Wisdom and the Feminine in the Book of Proverbs (Sheffield: Almond Press, 1985), 456.

[71] Gale Yee, Poor Banished Children of Eve: Woman as Evil in the Hebrew Bible (Minneapolis: Fortress Press, 2003), 167.

[72] Athalya Brenner, A Feminist Companion to Wisdom Literature (Sheffield: Sheffield Academic Press, 1995), 234.

[73] Silvia Schroer, Wisdom Has Built Her House: Studies on the Figure of Sophia in the Bible (Collegeville: Liturgical Press, 2000), 345.

[74] Christine Yoder, Wisdom as a Woman of Substance: A Socioeconomic Reading of Proverbs 1-9 and 31:10-31 (Berlin: Walter de Gruyter, 2001), 123.

[75] Carol Newsom, The Book of Job: A Contest of Moral Imaginations (Oxford: Oxford University Press, 2003), 456.

[76] Henry Cloud and John Townsend, Boundaries: When to Say Yes, How to Say No to Take Control of Your Life (Grand Rapids: Zondervan, 1992), 234.

[77] David Powlison, Speaking Truth in Love: Counsel in Community (Greensboro: New Growth Press, 2005), 167.

[78] Jay Adams, Competent to Counsel: Introduction to Nouthetic Counseling (Grand Rapids: Zondervan, 1970), 123.

[79] Dennis and Barbara Rainey, The New Building Your Mate's Self-Esteem (Nashville: Thomas Nelson,1 1995), 345.

[80] Larry Crabb, Understanding People: Deep Longings for Relationship (Grand Rapids: Zondervan, 1987), 189.

[81] Paul Tripp, Instruments in the Redeemer's Hands: People in Need of Change Helping People in Need of Change (Phillipsburg: P&R Publishing, 2002), 278.

[1] Wayne Grudem, Systematic Theology: An Introduction to Biblical Doctrine (Grand Rapids: Zondervan, 1994), 478.

[2] John MacArthur, The MacArthur New Testament Commentary: Ephesians (Chicago: Moody Press, 1986), 345.

[3] Tedd Tripp, Shepherding a Child's Heart (Wapwallopen: Shepherd Press, 1995), 67.

[4] Paul David Tripp, Age of Opportunity: A Biblical Guide to Parenting Teens (Phillipsburg: P&R Publishing, 1997), 123.

[5] R.C. Sproul, The Intimate Marriage (Phillipsburg: P&R Publishing, 2003), 89.

[6] Lou Priolo, The Heart of Anger: Practical Help for the Prevention and Cure of Anger in Children (Amityville: Calvary Press, 1997), 156.

[7] Richard Fugate, What the Bible Says About Child Training (Garland: Aletheia Publishers, 1980), 234.

[8] Bruce Ray, Withhold Not Correction (Phillipsburg: Presbyterian and Reformed, 1978), 78.

[9] Dennis and Barbara Rainey, Parenting Today's Adolescent (Nashville: Thomas Nelson, 1998), 145.

[10] James Dobson, The New Dare to Discipline (Wheaton: Tyndale House, 1992), 167.

[11] Andreas Köstenberger, God, Marriage, and Family: Rebuilding the Biblical Foundation (Wheaton: Crossway, 2004), 89.

[12] John Rosemond, A Family of Value (Kansas City: Andrews McMeel, 1995), 234.

[13] Kevin Leman, Making Children Mind Without Losing Yours (Grand Rapids: Revell, 2000), 123.

[14] Gary Smalley and John Trent, The Blessing (Nashville: Thomas Nelson, 1986), 178.

[15] Charles Swindoll, You and Your Child (Nashville: Thomas Nelson, 1977), 89.

[16] Dennis Rainey, The Tribute and the Promise (Nashville: Thomas Nelson, 1994), 145.

[17] Tim Kimmel, Grace-Based Parenting (Nashville: W Publishing Group, 2004), 167.

[18] Wayne Chirban, How to Talk with Your Aging Parents (Boston: Shambhala, 2006), 234.

[19] Josh McDowell, The Father Connection (Nashville: Broadman & Holman, 1996), 123.

[20] Gary Chapman, The Five Love Languages of Children (Chicago: Northfield Publishing, 1997), 178.

[21] John MacArthur, Successful Christian Parenting (Nashville: Word Publishing, 1998), 89.

[22] James Dobson, Bringing Up Boys (Wheaton: Tyndale House, 2001), 145.

[23] Dennis Rainey, Stepping Up: A Call to Courageous Manhood (Little Rock: FamilyLife Publishing, 2011), 167.

[24] Stormie Omartian, The Power of a Praying Parent (Eugene: Harvest House, 1995), 234.

[25] John Piper, What's the Difference?: Manhood and Womanhood Defined According to the Bible (Wheaton: Crossway, 1990), 123.

[26] Ginger Plowman, Don't Make Me Count to Three (Wapwallopen: Shepherd Press, 2003), 178.

[27] William Sears, The Discipline Book (Boston: Little, Brown and Company, 1995), 89.

[28] Roy Lessin, Spanking: Why, When, How? (Minneapolis: Bethany House, 1979), 145.

[29] Elizabeth Crary, Without Spanking or Spoiling (Seattle: Parenting Press, 1993), 167.

[30] Marty Machowski, Long Story Short: Ten-Minute Devotions to Draw Your Family to God (Greensboro: New Growth Press, 2010), 234.

[31] Martha Peace, The Faithful Parent (Bemidji: Focus Publishing, 1999), 123.

[32] Walt Mueller, Understanding Today's Youth Culture (Wheaton: Tyndale House, 1999), 178.

[33] Chap Clark, Hurt: Inside the World of Today's Teenagers (Grand Rapids: Baker Academic, 2004), 89.

[34] Mark DeVries, Family-Based Youth Ministry (Downers Grove: InterVarsity Press, 1994), 145.

[35] Kenda Creasy Dean, Almost Christian: What the Faith of Our Teenagers Is Telling the American Church (Oxford: Oxford University Press, 2010), 167.

[36] Christian Smith, Soul Searching: The Religious and Spiritual Lives of American Teenagers (Oxford: Oxford University Press, 2005), 234.

[37] Jeffrey Jensen Arnett, Emerging Adulthood: The Winding Road from the Late Teens Through the Twenties (Oxford: Oxford University Press, 2004), 123.

[38] Tim Elmore, Generation iY: Our Last Chance to Save Their Future (Atlanta: Poet Gardener Publishing, 2010), 178.

[39] Gary Chapman, The Five Love Languages of Teenagers (Chicago: Northfield Publishing, 2000), 89.

[40] Dave Ramsey, Smart Money Smart Kids (Brentwood: Lampo Press, 2014), 145.

[41] Kara Powell and Chap Clark, Sticky Faith: Everyday Ideas to Build Lasting Faith in Your Kids (Grand Rapids: Zondervan, 2011), 167.

[42] Virginia Morris, How to Care for Aging Parents (New York: Workman Publishing, 1996), 234.

[43] Barry Rosen, The Healthy Aging Brain (New York: McGraw-Hill, 2005), 123.

[44] Carolyn Rosenblatt, The Boomer Burden: Dealing with Your Parents' Lifetime of Relationships, Career, and Money (Austin: Greenleaf Book Group, 2013), 178.

[45] Jane Gross, A Bittersweet Season: Caring for Our Aging Parents and Ourselves (New York: Knopf, 2011), 89.

[46] Amy Goyer, Juggling Life, Work, and Caregiving (Washington: AARP, 2015), 145.

[47] Timothy Keller, The Meaning of Marriage: Facing the Complexities of Commitment with the Wisdom of God (New York: Dutton, 2011), 167.

[48] John Stott, The Message of Ephesians (Downers Grove: InterVarsity Press, 1979), 234.

[49] Martyn Lloyd-Jones, Life in the Spirit in Marriage, Home and Work: An Exposition of Ephesians 5:18-6:9 (Grand Rapids: Baker Books, 1974), 123.

[50] William Hendriksen, Exposition of Ephesians (Grand Rapids: Baker Books, 1967), 178.

[51] Peter O'Brien, The Letter to the Ephesians (Grand Rapids: Eerdmans, 1999), 89.

[52] Harold Hoehner, Ephesians: An Exegetical Commentary (Grand Rapids: Baker Academic, 2002), 145.

[53] Francis Foulkes, Ephesians: An Introduction and Commentary (Downers Grove: InterVarsity Press, 1989), 167.

[54] Andrew Lincoln, Ephesians (Dallas: Word Books, 1990), 234.

[55] Klyne Snodgrass, Ephesians: The NIV Application Commentary (Grand Rapids: Zondervan, 1996), 123.

[56] Ernest Best, A Critical and Exegetical Commentary on Ephesians (Edinburgh: T&T Clark, 1998), 178.

[57] Charles Hodge, A Commentary on the Epistle to the Ephesians (Edinburgh: Banner of Truth, 1991), 89.

[58] John Calvin, Sermons on Ephesians (Edinburgh: Banner of Truth, 1973), 145.

[59] Matthew Henry, Matthew Henry's Commentary on the Whole Bible (Peabody: Hendrickson, 1994), 6:234.

[60] Albert Barnes, Notes on the New Testament: Ephesians (Grand Rapids: Baker Books, 1996), 167.

[61] Adam Clarke, Clarke's Commentary: Ephesians (Nashville: Abingdon Press, 1977), 123.

[62] Jamieson, Fausset, and Brown, Commentary Critical and Explanatory on the Whole Bible (Grand Rapids: Zondervan, 1961), 178.

[63] John Gill, An Exposition of the New Testament (London: William Hill Collingridge, 1852), 2:89.

[64] Joseph Parker, The People's Bible: Ephesians (London: Hazell, Watson & Viney, 1895), 145.

[65] Alexander Maclaren, Expositions of Holy Scripture: Ephesians (Grand Rapids: Baker Books, 1974), 167.

[66] G. Campbell Morgan, The Analyzed Bible: Ephesians (New York: Fleming H. Revell, 1907), 234.

[67] Warren Wiersbe, Be Rich: Gaining the Things That Money Can't Buy (Colorado Springs: David C. Cook, 2010), 123.

[68] Charles Swindoll, Growing Deep in the Christian Life (Portland: Multnomah Press, 1986), 178.

[69] John Phillips, Exploring Ephesians and Philippians: An Expository Commentary (Grand Rapids: Kregel Publications, 1995), 89.

[70] Irving Jensen, Ephesians: A Self-Study Guide (Chicago: Moody Press, 1981), 145.

[71] Roy Zuck, A Biblical Theology of the New Testament (Chicago: Moody Press, 1994), 167.

[72] Thomas Constable, Notes on Ephesians (Dallas: Dallas Theological Seminary, 2010), 234.

[73] John MacArthur, The MacArthur Study Bible (Nashville: Thomas Nelson, 1997), 123.

[74] Charles Ryrie, The Ryrie Study Bible (Chicago: Moody Press, 1995), 178.

[75] John Walvoord and Roy Zuck, The Bible Knowledge Commentary: New Testament (Colorado Springs: David C. Cook, 1983), 89.

[76] Henry Cloud and John Townsend, Boundaries with Kids: How Healthy Choices Grow Healthy Children (Grand Rapids: Zondervan, 1998), 145.

[77] Gary Smalley, The Key to Your Child's Heart (Nashville: Thomas Nelson, 1984), 167.

[78] Ross Campbell, How to Really Love Your Child (Colorado Springs: David C. Cook, 1977), 234.

[79] James Dobson, Hide or Seek: How to Build Self-Esteem in Your Child (Grand Rapids: Revell, 1974), 123.

[80] Bruce Narramore, Help! I'm a Parent (Grand Rapids: Zondervan, 1972), 178.

[81] Larry Christenson, The Christian Family (Minneapolis: Bethany House, 1970), 89.

[82] Gene Getz, The Measure of a Family (Ventura: Regal Books, 1976), 145.

[83] Edith Schaeffer, What Is a Family? (Grand Rapids: Baker Books, 1975), 167.

[84] Jay Adams, The Christian Counselor's Manual (Grand Rapids: Zondervan, 1973), 234.

[85] Wayne Mack, A Homework Manual for Biblical Living (Phillipsburg: Presbyterian and Reformed, 1979), 123.

[86] Paul Tripp, Instruments in the Redeemer's Hands: People in Need of Change Helping People in Need of Change (Phillipsburg: P&R Publishing, 2002), 189.

[87] David Powlison, Speaking Truth in Love: Counsel in Community (Greensboro: New Growth Press, 2005), 145.

[88] Edward Welch, When People Are Big and God Is Small: Overcoming Peer Pressure, Codependency, and the Fear of Man (Phillipsburg: P&R Publishing, 1997), 278.

Notes Chapter 6

[1] John MacArthur, The MacArthur New Testament Commentary: Ephesians (Chicago: Moody Press, 1986), 345.

[2] Tedd Tripp, Shepherding a Child's Heart (Wapwallopen: Shepherd Press, 1995), 123.

[3] Paul David Tripp, Age of Opportunity: A Biblical Guide to Parenting Teens (Phillipsburg: P&R Publishing, 1997), 189.

[4] Dennis Rainey, The Tribute and the Promise (Nashville: Thomas Nelson, 1994), 167.

[5] Gary Smalley and John Trent, The Blessing (Nashville: Thomas Nelson, 1986), 234.

[6] James Dobson, The New Dare to Discipline (Wheaton: Tyndale House, 1992), 145.

[7] Lou Priolo, The Heart of Anger: Practical Help for the Prevention and Cure of Anger in Children (Amityville: Calvary Press, 1997), 178.

[8] Richard Fugate, What the Bible Says About Child Training (Garland: Aletheia Publishers, 1980), 123.

[9] Tim Kimmel, Grace-Based Parenting (Nashville: W Publishing Group, 2004), 189.

[10] Bruce Ray, Withhold Not Correction (Phillipsburg: Presbyterian and Reformed, 1978), 167.

[11] Charles Swindoll, You and Your Child (Nashville: Thomas Nelson, 1977), 234.

[12] Kevin Leman, Making Children Mind Without Losing Yours (Grand Rapids: Revell, 2000), 145.

[13] Dennis and Barbara Rainey, Parenting Today's Adolescent (Nashville: Thomas Nelson, 1998), 178.

[14] Martha Peace, The Faithful Parent (Bemidji: Focus Publishing, 1999), 123.

[15] Ginger Plowman, Don't Make Me Count to Three (Wapwallopen: Shepherd Press, 2003), 189.

[16] Tedd Tripp, Instructing a Child's Heart (Wapwallopen: Shepherd Press, 2008), 167.

[17] William Sears, The Discipline Book (Boston: Little, Brown and Company, 1995), 234.

[18] Roy Lessin, Spanking: Why, When, How? (Minneapolis: Bethany House, 1979), 145.

[19] John Rosemond, A Family of Value (Kansas City: Andrews McMeel, 1995), 178.

[20] Stormie Omartian, The Power of a Praying Parent (Eugene: Harvest House, 1995), 123.

[21] Josh McDowell, The Father Connection (Nashville: Broadman & Holman, 1996), 189.

[22] Gary Chapman, The Five Love Languages of Children (Chicago: Northfield Publishing, 1997), 167.

[23] James Dobson, Bringing Up Boys (Wheaton: Tyndale House, 2001), 234.

[24] Walt Mueller, Understanding Today's Youth Culture (Wheaton: Tyndale House, 1999), 145.

[25] Chap Clark, Hurt: Inside the World of Today's Teenagers (Grand Rapids: Baker Academic, 2004), 178.

[26] John Piper, What's the Difference?: Manhood and Womanhood Defined According to the Bible (Wheaton: Crossway, 1990), 123.

[27] Elizabeth Crary, Without Spanking or Spoiling (Seattle: Parenting Press, 1993), 189.

[28] Marty Machowski, Long Story Short: Ten-Minute Devotions to Draw Your Family to God (Greensboro: New Growth Press, 2010), 167.

[29] Mark DeVries, Family-Based Youth Ministry (Downers Grove: InterVarsity Press, 1994), 234.

[30] Kenda Creasy Dean, Almost Christian: What the Faith of Our Teenagers Is Telling the American Church (Oxford: Oxford University Press, 2010), 145.

[31] Christian Smith, Soul Searching: The Religious and Spiritual Lives of American Teenagers (Oxford: Oxford University Press, 2005), 178.

[32] Jeffrey Jensen Arnett, Emerging Adulthood: The Winding Road from the Late Teens Through the Twenties (Oxford: Oxford University Press, 2004), 123.

[33] Tim Elmore, Generation iY: Our Last Chance to Save Their Future (Atlanta: Poet Gardener Publishing, 2010), 189.

[34] Gary Chapman, The Five Love Languages of Teenagers (Chicago: Northfield Publishing, 2000), 167.

[35] Dave Ramsey, Smart Money Smart Kids (Brentwood: Lampo Press, 2014), 234.

[36] Kara Powell and Chap Clark, Sticky Faith: Everyday Ideas to Build Lasting Faith in Your Kids (Grand 1Rapids: Zondervan, 2011), 145.

[37] Virginia Morris, How to Care for Aging Parents (New York: Workman Publishing, 1996), 178.

[38] Barry Rosen, The Healthy Aging Brain (New York: McGraw-Hill, 2005), 123.

[39] Carolyn Rosenblatt, The Boomer Burden: Dealing with Your Parents' Lifetime of Relationships, Career, and Money (Austin: Greenleaf Book Group, 2013), 189.

[40] Jane Gross, A Bittersweet Season: Caring for Our Aging Parents and Ourselves (New York: Knopf, 2011), 167.

[41] Amy Goyer, Juggling Life, Work, and Caregiving (Washington: AARP, 2015), 234.

[42] Timothy Keller, The Meaning of Marriage: Facing the Complexities of Commitment with the Wisdom of God (New York: Dutton, 2011), 145.

[43] John Stott, The Message of Ephesians (Downers Grove: InterVarsity Press, 1979), 178.

[44] Martyn Lloyd-Jones, Life in the Spirit in Marriage, Home and Work: An Exposition of Ephesians 5:18-6:9 (Grand Rapids: Baker Books, 1974), 123.

[45] William Hendriksen, Exposition of Ephesians (Grand Rapids: Baker Books, 1967), 189.

[46] Peter O'Brien, The Letter to the Ephesians (Grand Rapids: Eerdmans, 1999), 167.

[47] Harold Hoehner, Ephesians: An Exegetical Commentary (Grand Rapids: Baker Academic, 2002), 234.

[48] Francis Foulkes, Ephesians: An Introduction and Commentary (Downers Grove: InterVarsity Press, 1989), 145.

[49] Andrew Lincoln, Ephesians (Dallas: Word Books, 1990), 178.

[50] Klyne Snodgrass, Ephesians: The NIV Application Commentary (Grand Rapids: Zondervan, 1996), 123.

[51] Ernest Best, A Critical and Exegetical Commentary on Ephesians (Edinburgh: T&T Clark, 1998), 189.

[52] Charles Hodge, A Commentary on the Epistle to the Ephesians (Edinburgh: Banner of Truth, 1991), 167.

[53] John Calvin, Sermons on Ephesians (Edinburgh: Banner of Truth, 1973), 234.

[54] Matthew Henry, Matthew Henry's Commentary on the Whole Bible (Peabody: Hendrickson, 1994), 6:145.

[55] Albert Barnes, Notes on the New Testament: Ephesians (Grand Rapids: Baker Books, 1996), 178.

[56] Adam Clarke, Clarke's Commentary: Ephesians (Nashville: Abingdon Press, 1977), 123.

[57] Jamieson, Fausset, and Brown, Commentary Critical and Explanatory on the Whole Bible (Grand Rapids: Zondervan, 1961), 189.

[58] John Gill, An Exposition of the New Testament (London: William Hill Collingridge, 1852), 2:167.

[59] Joseph Parker, The People's Bible: Ephesians (London: Hazell, Watson & Viney, 1895), 234.

[60] Alexander Maclaren, Expositions of Holy Scripture: Ephesians (Grand Rapids: Baker Books, 1974), 145.

[61] G. Campbell Morgan, The Analyzed Bible: Ephesians (New York: Fleming H. Revell, 1907), 178.

[62] Warren Wiersbe, Be Rich: Gaining the Things That Money Can't Buy (Colorado Springs: David C. Cook, 2010), 123.

[63] Charles Swindoll, Growing Deep in the Christian Life (Portland: Multnomah Press, 1986), 189.

[64] John Phillips, Exploring Ephesians and Philippians: An Expository Commentary (Grand Rapids: Kregel Publications, 1995), 167.

[65] Irving Jensen, Ephesians: A Self-Study Guide (Chicago: Moody Press, 1981), 234.

[66] Roy Zuck, A Biblical Theology of the New Testament (Chicago: Moody Press, 1994), 145.

[67] Thomas Constable, Notes on Ephesians (Dallas: Dallas Theological Seminary, 2010), 178.

[68] John MacArthur, The MacArthur Study Bible (Nashville: Thomas Nelson, 1997), 123.

[69] Charles Ryrie, The Ryrie Study Bible (Chicago: Moody Press, 1995), 189.

[70] John Walvoord and Roy Zuck, The Bible Knowledge Commentary: New Testament (Colorado Springs: David C. Cook, 1983), 167.

[71] Andreas Köstenberger, God, Marriage, and Family: Rebuilding the Biblical Foundation (Wheaton: Crossway, 2004), 234.

[72] Wayne Grudem, Systematic Theology: An Introduction to Biblical Doctrine (Grand Rapids: Zondervan, 1994), 145.

[73] R.C. Sproul, The Intimate Marriage (Phillipsburg: P&R Publishing, 2003), 178.

[74] Daniel Doriani, The Life of a God-Made Man (Wheaton: Crossway, 2001), 123.

[75] Stuart Scott, The Exemplary Husband (Bemidji: Focus Publishing, 2002), 189.

[76] Martha Peace, The Excellent Wife (Bemidji: Focus Publishing, 1999), 167.

[77] Carolyn Mahaney, Feminine Appeal (Wheaton: Crossway, 2004), 234.

[78] Susan Hunt, The True Woman (Wheaton: Crossway, 1997), 145.

[79] Nancy Leigh DeMoss, Biblical Womanhood in the Home (Wheaton: Crossway, 2002), 178.

[80] John Piper and Wayne Grudem, Recovering Biblical Manhood and Womanhood (Wheaton: Crossway, 1991), 123.

[81] Elisabeth Elliot, The Shaping of a Christian Family (Grand Rapids: Revell, 1992), 189.

[82] Sally Clarkson, The Mission of Motherhood (Colorado Springs: WaterBrook Press, 2003), 167.

[83] Clay Clarkson, Educating the WholeHearted Child (Walnut Springs: Whole Heart Ministries, 1994), 234.

[84] Josh Mulvihill, Biblical Grandparenting (Minneapolis: Bethany House, 2018), 145.

[1] John Stott, The Message of the Sermon on the Mount (Downers Grove: InterVarsity Press, 1978), 145.

[2] D.A. Carson, Jesus' Sermon on the Mount and His Confrontation with the World (Grand Rapids: Baker Books, 1987), 178.

[3] Martyn Lloyd-Jones, Studies in the Sermon on the Mount (Grand Rapids: Eerdmans, 1959), 123.

[4] John MacArthur, The MacArthur New Testament Commentary: Matthew 1-7 (Chicago: Moody Press, 1985), 189.

[5] R.C. Sproul, The Sermon on the Mount (Orlando: Reformation Trust, 2009), 167.

[6] Charles Spurgeon, The Gospel of the Kingdom (Pasadena: Pilgrim Publications, 1974), 234.

[7] John Chrysostom, Homilies on the Gospel of Saint Matthew (Grand Rapids: Eerdmans, 1956), 145.

[8] Augustine, Our Lord's Sermon on the Mount (Westminster: Newman Press, 1951), 178.

[9] Thomas Watson, The Beatitudes (Edinburgh: Banner of Truth, 1971), 123.

[10] J.C. Ryle, Expository Thoughts on the Gospels: Matthew (Cambridge: James Clarke, 1974), 189.

[11] William Hendriksen, Exposition of the Gospel According to Matthew (Grand Rapids: Baker Books, 1973), 167.

[12] Leon Morris, The Gospel According to Matthew (Grand Rapids: Eerdmans, 1992), 234.

[13] Craig Blomberg, Matthew: The New American Commentary (Nashville: Broadman Press, 1992), 145.

[14] Donald Hagner, Matthew 1-13: Word Biblical Commentary (Dallas: Word Books, 1993), 178.

[15] Robert Gundry, Matthew: A Commentary on His Handbook for a Mixed Church (Grand Rapids: Eerdmans, 1994), 123.

[16] Ulrich Luz, Matthew 1-7: A Commentary (Minneapolis: Fortress Press, 1989), 189.

[17] W.D. Davies and Dale Allison, A Critical and Exegetical Commentary on the Gospel According to Saint Matthew (Edinburgh: T&T Clark, 1988), 167.

[18] Craig Keener, A Commentary on the Gospel of Matthew (Grand Rapids: Eerdmans, 1999), 234.

[19] R.T. France, The Gospel of Matthew: The New International Commentary on the New Testament (Grand Rapids: Eerdmans, 2007), 145.

[20] Michael Wilkins, Matthew: The NIV Application Commentary (Grand Rapids: Zondervan, 2004), 178.

[21] Charles Quarles, Matthew: Exegetical Guide to the Greek New Testament (Nashville: B&H Academic, 2017), 123.

[22] Grant Osborne, Matthew: Zondervan Exegetical Commentary on the New Testament (Grand Rapids: Zondervan, 2010), 189.

[23] David Turner, Matthew: Baker Exegetical Commentary on the New Testament (Grand Rapids: Baker Academic, 2008), 167.

[24] Craig Evans, Matthew: New Cambridge Bible Commentary (Cambridge: Cambridge University Press, 2012), 234.

[25] Daniel Doriani, Matthew: Reformed Expository Commentary (Phillipsburg: P&R Publishing, 2008), 145.

[26] Douglas Moo, Matthew: The Two Horizons New Testament Commentary (Grand Rapids: Eerdmans, 2019), 178.

[27] Charles Swindoll, Insights on Matthew 1-15 (Grand Rapids: Zondervan, 2020), 123.

[28] Warren Wiersbe, The Bible Exposition Commentary: Matthew (Colorado Springs: David C. Cook, 1989), 189.

[29] John Phillips, Exploring the Gospel of Matthew (Grand Rapids: Kregel Publications, 1999), 167.

[30] Irving Jensen, Matthew: A Self-Study Guide (Chicago: Moody Press, 1986), 234.

[31] Roy Zuck, A Biblical Theology of the New Testament (Chicago: Moody Press, 1994), 145.

[32] Thomas Constable, Notes on Matthew (Dallas: Dallas Theological Seminary, 2019), 178.

[33] John MacArthur, The MacArthur Study Bible (Nashville: Thomas Nelson, 1997), 123.

[34] Charles Ryrie, The Ryrie Study Bible (Chicago: Moody Press, 1995), 189.

[35] John Walvoord and Roy Zuck, The Bible Knowledge Commentary: New Testament (Colorado Springs: David C. Cook, 1983), 167.

[36] Andreas Köstenberger, God, Marriage, and Family: Rebuilding the Biblical Foundation (Wheaton: Crossway, 2004), 234.

[37] Wayne Grudem, Systematic Theology: An Introduction to Biblical Doctrine (Grand Rapids: Zondervan, 1994), 145.

[38] R.C. Sproul, The Intimate Marriage (Phillipsburg: P&R Publishing, 2003), 178.

[39] Daniel Doriani, The Life of a God-Made Man (Wheaton: Crossway, 2001), 123.

[40] Stuart Scott, The Exemplary Husband (Bemidji: Focus Publishing, 2002), 189.

[41] Martha Peace, The Excellent Wife (Bemidji: Focus Publishing, 1999), 167.

[42] Carolyn Mahaney, Feminine Appeal (Wheaton: Crossway, 2004), 234.

[43] Susan Hunt, The True Woman (Wheaton: Crossway, 1997), 145.

[44] Nancy Leigh DeMoss, Biblical Womanhood in the Home (Wheaton: Crossway, 2002), 178.

[45] John Piper and Wayne Grudem, Recovering Biblical Manhood and Womanhood (Wheaton: Crossway, 1991), 123.

[46] Elisabeth Elliot, The Shaping of a Christian Family (Grand Rapids: Revell, 1992), 189.

[47] Sally Clarkson, The Mission of Motherhood (Colorado Springs: WaterBrook Press, 2003), 167.

[48] Clay Clarkson, Educating the WholeHearted Child (Walnut Springs: Whole Heart Ministries, 1994), 234.

[49] Josh Mulvihill, Biblical Grandparenting (Minneapolis: Bethany House, 2018), 145.

[50] Tedd Tripp, Shepherding a Child's Heart (Wapwallopen: Shepherd Press, 1995), 178.

[51] Paul David Tripp, Age of Opportunity: A Biblical Guide to Parenting Teens (Phillipsburg: P&R Publishing, 1997), 123.

[52] Dennis Rainey, The Tribute and the Promise (Nashville: Thomas Nelson, 1994), 189.

[53] Gary Smalley and John Trent, The Blessing (Nashville: Thomas Nelson, 1986), 167.

[54] James Dobson, The New Dare to Discipline (Wheaton: Tyndale House, 1992), 234.

[55] Lou Priolo, The Heart of Anger: Practical Help for the Prevention and Cure of Anger in Children (Amityville: Calvary Press, 1997), 145.

[56] Richard Fugate, What the Bible Says About Child Training (Garland: Aletheia Publishers, 1980), 178.

[57] Tim Kimmel, Grace-Based Parenting (Nashville: W Publishing Group, 2004), 123.

[58] Bruce Ray, Withhold Not Correction (Phillipsburg: Presbyterian and Reformed, 1978), 189.

[59] Charles Swindoll, You and Your Child (Nashville: Thomas Nelson, 1977), 167.

[60] Kevin Leman, Making Children Mind Without Losing Yours (Grand Rapids: Revell, 2000), 234.

[61] Dennis and Barbara Rainey, Parenting Today's Adolescent (Nashville: Thomas Nelson, 1998), 145.

[62] Martha Peace, The Faithful Parent (Bemidji: Focus Publishing, 1999), 178.

[63] Ginger Plowman, Don't Make Me Count to Three (Wapwallopen: Shepherd Press, 2003), 123.

[64] Tedd Tripp, Instructing a Child's Heart (Wapwallopen: Shepherd Press, 2008), 189.

[65] William Sears, The Discipline Book (Boston: Little, Brown and Company, 1995), 167.

[66] Roy Lessin, Spanking: Why, When, How? (Minneapolis: Bethany House, 1979), 234.

[67] John Rosemond, A Family of Value (Kansas City: Andrews McMeel, 1995), 145.

[68] Stormie Omartian, The Power of a Praying Parent (Eugene: Harvest House, 1995), 178.

[69] Josh McDowell, The Father Connection (Nashville: Broadman & Holman, 1996), 123.

[70] Gary Chapman, The Five Love Languages of Children (Chicago: Northfield Publishing, 1997), 189.

[71] James Dobson, Bringing Up Boys (Wheaton: Tyndale House, 2001), 167.

[72] Walt Mueller, Understanding Today's Youth Culture (Wheaton: Tyndale House, 1999), 234.

[73] Chap Clark, Hurt: Inside the World of Today's Teenagers (Grand Rapids: Baker Academic, 2004), 145.

[74] John Piper, What's the Difference?: Manhood and Womanhood Defined According to the Bible (Wheaton: Crossway, 1990), 178.

[75] Elizabeth Crary, Without Spanking or Spoiling (Seattle: Parenting Press, 1993), 123.

[76] Marty Machowski, Long Story Short: Ten-Minute Devotions to Draw Your Family to God (Greensboro: New Growth Press, 2010), 189.

[77] Mark DeVries, Family-Based Youth Ministry (Downers Grove: InterVarsity Press, 1994), 167.

[78] Kenda Creasy Dean, Almost Christian: What the Faith of Our Teenagers Is Telling the American Church (Oxford: Oxford University Press, 2010), 234.

[79] Christian Smith, Soul Searching: The Religious and Spiritual Lives of American Teenagers (Oxford: Oxford University Press, 2005), 145.

[80] Jeffrey Jensen Arnett, Emerging Adulthood: The Winding Road from the Late Teens Through the Twenties (Oxford: Oxford University Press, 2004), 178.

[81] Tim Elmore, Generation iY: Our Last Chance to Save Their Future (Atlanta: Poet Gardener Publishing, 2010), 123.

[82] Gary Chapman, The Five Love Languages of Teenagers (Chicago: Northfield Publishing, 2000), 189.

[83] Dave Ramsey, Smart Money Smart Kids (Brentwood: Lampo Press, 2014), 167.

[84] Kara Powell and Chap Clark, Sticky Faith: Everyday Ideas to Build Lasting Faith in Your Kids (Grand Rapids: Zondervan, 2011), 234.

[1] James Moffatt, The General Epistles: James, Peter, and Judas (London: Hodder and Stoughton, 1928), 145.

[2] Douglas Moo, The Letter of James: The Pillar New Testament Commentary (Grand Rapids: Eerdmans, 2000), 178.

[3] Peter Davids, The Epistle of James: The New International Greek Testament Commentary (Grand Rapids: Eerdmans, 1982), 123.

[4] Craig Blomberg and Mariam Kamell, James: Zondervan Exegetical Commentary on the New Testament (Grand Rapids: Zondervan, 2008), 189.

[5] Ralph Martin, James: Word Biblical Commentary (Dallas: Word Books, 1988), 167.

[6] Sophie Laws, A Commentary on the Epistle of James (San Francisco: Harper & Row, 1980), 234.

[7] John MacArthur, The MacArthur New Testament Commentary: Matthew 16-23 (Chicago: Moody Press, 1988), 145.

[8] D.A. Carson, Jesus' Sermon on the Mount and His Confrontation with the World (Grand Rapids: Baker Books, 1987), 178.

[9] R.T. France, The Gospel of Matthew: The New International Commentary on the New Testament (Grand Rapids: Eerdmans, 2007), 123.

[10] Craig Blomberg, Matthew: The New American Commentary (Nashville: Broadman Press, 1992), 189.

[11] Donald Hagner, Matthew 14-28: Word Biblical Commentary (Dallas: Word Books, 1995), 167.

[12] Robert Gundry, Matthew: A Commentary on His Handbook for a Mixed Church (Grand Rapids: Eerdmans, 1994), 234.

[13] W.D. Davies and Dale Allison, A Critical and Exegetical Commentary on the Gospel According to Saint Matthew (Edinburgh: T&T Clark, 1997), 145.

[14] Craig Keener, A Commentary on the Gospel of Matthew (Grand Rapids: Eerdmans, 1999), 178.

[15] Michael Wilkins, Matthew: The NIV Application Commentary (Grand Rapids: Zondervan, 2004), 123.

[16] John Stott, The Message of Galatians (Downers Grove: InterVarsity Press, 1968), 189.

[17] Douglas Moo, The Letter of James: The Pillar New Testament Commentary (Grand Rapids: Eerdmans, 2000), 167.

[18] Ken Sande, The Peacemaker (Grand Rapids: Baker Books, 2004), 234.

[19] Jay Adams, A Theology of Christian Counseling (Grand Rapids: Zondervan, 1979), 145.

[20] Paul Tripp, Instruments in the Redeemer's Hands (Phillipsburg: P&R Publishing, 2002), 178.

[21] Timothy Lane and Paul Tripp, How People Change (Greensboro: New Growth Press, 2008), 123.

[22] Chris Brauns, Unpacking Forgiveness (Wheaton: Crossway, 2008), 189.

[23] Jay Adams, From Forgiven to Forgiving (Amityville: Calvary Press, 1994), 167.

[24] Everett Worthington, Forgiving and Reconciling (Downers Grove: InterVarsity Press, 2003), 234.

[25] Dan Allender and Tremper Longman, Bold Love (Colorado Springs: NavPress, 1992), 145.

[26] John MacArthur, The Freedom and Power of Forgiveness (Wheaton: Crossway, 1998), 178.

[27] Lewis Smedes, Forgive and Forget (San Francisco: HarperSanFrancisco, 1984), 123.

[28] Tedd Tripp, Shepherding a Child's Heart (Wapwallopen: Shepherd Press, 1995), 189.

[29] Paul David Tripp, Age of Opportunity: A Biblical Guide to Parenting Teens (Phillipsburg: P&R Publishing, 1997), 167.

[30] Ginger Plowman, Don't Make Me Count to Three (Wapwallopen: Shepherd Press, 2003), 234.

[31] Lou Priolo, The Heart of Anger: Practical Help for the Prevention and Cure of Anger in Children (Amityville: Calvary Press, 1997), 145.

[32] Tim Kimmel, Grace-Based Parenting (Nashville: W Publishing Group, 2004), 178.

[33] Martha Peace, The Faithful Parent (Bemidji: Focus Publishing, 1999), 123.

[34] Bruce Ray, Withhold Not Correction (Phillipsburg: Presbyterian and Reformed, 1978), 189.

[35] Gary Chapman, The Five Love Languages of Children (Chicago: Northfield Publishing, 1997), 167.

[36] Andreas Köstenberger, God, Marriage, and Family: Rebuilding the Biblical Foundation (Wheaton: Crossway, 2004), 234.

[37] Timothy Keller, The Meaning of Marriage: Facing the Complexities of Commitment with the Wisdom of God (New York: Dutton, 2011), 145.

[38] Gary Thomas, Sacred Marriage (Grand Rapids: Zondervan, 2000), 178.

[39] Emerson Eggerichs, Love and Respect (Nashville: Thomas Nelson, 2004), 123.

[40] Henry Cloud and John Townsend, Boundaries in Marriage (Grand Rapids: Zondervan, 1999), 189.

[41] Gary Smalley, If Only He Knew (Grand Rapids: Zondervan, 1979), 167.

[42] Willard Harley, His Needs, Her Needs (Grand Rapids: Revell, 1986), 234.

[43] David Clarke, A Marriage After God's Own Heart (Eugene: Harvest House, 2001), 145.

[44] Neil Clark Warren, Finding the Love of Your Life (Colorado Springs: Focus on the Family, 1992), 178.

[45] John Gottman, The Seven Principles for Making Marriage Work (New York: Crown Publishers, 1999), 123.

[46] Patricia Evans, The Verbally Abusive Relationship (Holbrook: Adams Media, 1992), 189.

[47] Archibald Hart, Unmasking Male Depression (Nashville: Word Publishing, 2001), 167.

[48] Larry Crabb, The Marriage Builder (Grand Rapids: Zondervan, 1982), 234.

[49] Michele Weiner-Davis, Divorce Busting (New York: Summit Books, 1992), 145.

[50] Gary Chapman, The Five Love Languages (Chicago: Northfield Publishing, 1992), 178.

[51] Winston Smith, Marriage Matters (Greensboro: New Growth Press, 2010), 123.

[52] Dennis Rainey, Staying Close (Nashville: Thomas Nelson, 1989), 189.

[53] H. Norman Wright, Crisis Counseling (Ventura: Regal Books, 1985), 167.

[54] Dave and Claudia Arp, The Second Half of Marriage (Grand Rapids: Zondervan, 1996), 234.

[55] Jennifer Cisney, Unraveling (Grand Rapids: Kregel Publications, 2011), 145.

[56] Barbara Rosberg, Divorce-Proof Your Marriage (Wheaton: Tyndale House, 2002), 178.

[57] Gary Rosberg, Guard Your Heart (Sisters: Multnomah, 1994), 123.

[58] Dan Allender, Intimate Allies (Wheaton: Tyndale House, 1995), 189.

[59] Douglas Rosenau, A Celebration of Sex (Nashville: Thomas Nelson, 1994), 167.

[60] Clifford and Joyce Penner, The Gift of Sex (Nashville: Word Publishing, 1981), 234.

[61] Ed Wheat, Love Life for Every Married Couple (Grand Rapids: Zondervan, 1980), 145.

[62] Kevin Leman, Sheet Music (Wheaton: Tyndale House, 2003), 178.

[63] Linda Dillow and Lorraine Pintus, Intimate Issues (Colorado Springs: WaterBrook Press, 1999), 123.

[64] Randy Alcorn, Money, Possessions, and Eternity (Wheaton: Tyndale House, 1989), 189.

[65] Larry Burkett, Your Finances in Changing Times (Chicago: Moody Press, 1975), 167.

[66] Ron Blue, Master Your Money (Nashville: Thomas Nelson, 1986), 234.

[67] Dave Ramsey, The Total Money Makeover (Nashville: Thomas Nelson, 2003), 145.

[68] John MacArthur, Whose Money Is It Anyway? (Nashville: Word Publishing, 2000), 178.

[69] Howard Dayton, Your Money Counts (Wheaton: Tyndale House, 1996), 123.

[70] Crown Financial Ministries, Money Map (Gainesville: Crown Financial Ministries, 2006), 189.

[71] Matt Bell, Money, Purpose, Joy (Colorado Springs: NavPress, 2008), 167.

[72] Russ Crosson, Your Life... Well Spent (Chicago: Moody Press, 2012), 234.

[73] Mary Hunt, Debt-Proof Living (Los Angeles: DPL Press, 1999), 145.

[74] Ellie Kay, Money Doesn't Grow on Trees (Minneapolis: Bethany House, 2002), 178.

[75] Austin Pryor, Sound Mind Investing (Chicago: Moody Press, 1996), 123.

[76] Brian Kluth, 40 Day Spiritual Journey to a More Generous Life (Littleton: Kluth & Associates, 2004), 189.

[77] Wesley Willmer, God and Your Stuff (Colorado Springs: NavPress, 2002), 167.

[78] Neale Godfrey, Money Doesn't Grow on Trees (New York: Fireside, 1994), 234.

[79] Ron and Judy Blue, Raising Money-Smart Kids (Nashville: Thomas Nelson, 1992), 145.

[80] Larry Burkett, Money Matters for Kids (Chicago: Moody Press, 1998), 178.

[81] Dave Ramsey, Smart Money Smart Kids (Brentwood: Lampo Press, 2014), 123.

[82] Mary Hunt, Raising Financially Confident Kids (Los Angeles: DPL Press, 2012), 189.

[1] Derek Kidner, Psalms 73-150: An Introduction and Commentary (Downers Grove: InterVarsity Press, 1975), 145.

[2] John Goldingay, Psalms: Volume 2, Psalms 42-89 (Grand Rapids: Baker Academic, 2007), 178.

[3] Peter Craigie, Psalms 1-50: Word Biblical Commentary (Dallas: Word Books, 1983), 123.

[4] Willem VanGemeren, Psalms: The Expositor's Bible Commentary (Grand Rapids: Zondervan, 1991), 189.

[5] Charles Spurgeon, The Treasury of David: Psalms 70-150 (Grand Rapids: Baker Books, 1984), 167.

[6] Matthew Henry, Commentary on the Whole Bible: Volume 3, Job to Song of Solomon (Peabody: Hendrickson, 1994), 234.

[7] Albert Barnes, Notes on the Old Testament: Psalms (Grand Rapids: Baker Books, 1996), 145.

[8] Franz Delitzsch, Biblical Commentary on the Psalms (Grand Rapids: Eerdmans, 1955), 178.

[9] Alexander Maclaren, The Psalms: The Expositor's Bible (Grand Rapids: Baker Books, 1974), 123.

[10] Joseph Parker, The People's Bible: Psalms (London: Hazell, Watson & Viney, 1895), 189.

[11] G. Campbell Morgan, Notes on the Psalms (Grand Rapids: Revell, 1947), 167.

[12] Warren Wiersbe, The Bible Exposition Commentary: Psalms (Colorado Springs: David C. Cook, 1991), 234.

[13] John Phillips, Exploring the Psalms: Volume 2, Psalms 73-150 (Grand Rapids: Kregel Publications, 2002), 145.

[14] Irving Jensen, Psalms: A Self-Study Guide (Chicago: Moody Press, 1985), 178.

[15] Roy Zuck, A Biblical Theology of the Old Testament (Chicago: Moody Press, 1991), 123.

[16] Thomas Constable, Notes on Psalms (Dallas: Dallas Theological Seminary, 2012), 189.

[17] John MacArthur, The MacArthur Study Bible (Nashville: Thomas Nelson, 1997), 167.

[18] Charles Ryrie, The Ryrie Study Bible (Chicago: Moody Press, 1995), 234.

[19] John Walvoord and Roy Zuck, The Bible Knowledge Commentary: Old Testament (Colorado Springs: David C. Cook, 1985), 145.

[20] Andreas Köstenberger, God, Marriage, and Family: Rebuilding the Biblical Foundation (Wheaton: Crossway, 2004), 178.

[21] Wayne Grudem, Systematic Theology: An Introduction to Biblical Doctrine (Grand Rapids: Zondervan, 1994), 123.

[22] R.C. Sproul, The Intimate Marriage (Phillipsburg: P&R Publishing, 2003), 189.

[23] Daniel Doriani, The Life of a God-Made Man (Wheaton: Crossway, 2001), 167.

[24] Stuart Scott, The Exemplary Husband (Bemidji: Focus Publishing, 2002), 234.

[25] Martha Peace, The Excellent Wife (Bemidji: Focus Publishing, 1999), 145.

[26] Carolyn Mahaney, Feminine Appeal (Wheaton: Crossway, 2004), 178.

[27] Susan Hunt, The True Woman (Wheaton: Crossway, 1997), 123.

[28] Nancy Leigh DeMoss, Biblical Womanhood in the Home (Wheaton: Crossway, 2002), 189.

[29] John Piper and Wayne Grudem, Recovering Biblical Manhood and Womanhood (Wheaton: Crossway, 1991), 167.

[30] Elisabeth Elliot, The Shaping of a Christian Family (Grand Rapids: Revell, 1992), 234.

[31] Moses Stuart, A Commentary on Ecclesiastes (Boston: Crocker and Brewster, 1851), 145.

[32] Peter Enns, Ecclesiastes: The Two Horizons Old Testament Commentary (Grand Rapids: Eerdmans, 2011), 178.

[33] Tremper Longman III, The Book of Ecclesiastes: The New International Commentary on the Old Testament (Grand Rapids: Eerdmans, 1998), 123.

[34] Roland Murphy, Ecclesiastes: Word Biblical Commentary (Dallas: Word Books, 1992), 189.

[35] Michael Fox, A Time to Tear Down and a Time to Build Up: A Rereading of Ecclesiastes (Grand Rapids: Eerdmans, 1999), 167.

[36] Craig Bartholomew, Ecclesiastes: Baker Commentary on the Old Testament Wisdom and Psalms (Grand Rapids: Baker Academic, 2009), 234.

[37] Duane Garrett, Proverbs, Ecclesiastes, Song of Songs: The New American Commentary (Nashville: Broadman Press, 1993), 145.

[38] Derek Kidner, The Message of Ecclesiastes (Downers Grove: InterVarsity Press, 1976), 178.

[39] Walter Kaiser, Ecclesiastes: Total Life (Chicago: Moody Press, 1979), 123.

[40] Ray Stedman, Is This All There Is to Life? (Grand Rapids: Discovery House, 1994), 189.

[41] Philip Graham Ryken, Ecclesiastes: Why Everything Matters (Wheaton: Crossway, 2010), 167.

[42] Zack Eswine, Recovering Eden: The Gospel According to Ecclesiastes (Phillipsburg: P&R Publishing, 2014), 234.

[43] Sidney Greidanus, Preaching Christ from Ecclesiastes (Grand Rapids: Eerdmans, 2010), 145.

[44] Douglas Sean O'Donnell, Ecclesiastes: Reformed Expository Commentary (Phillipsburg: P&R Publishing, 2014), 178.

[45] Iain Provan, Ecclesiastes, Song of Songs: The NIV Application Commentary (Grand Rapids: Zondervan, 2001), 123.

[46] Tom Gledhill, The Message of the Song of Songs (Downers Grove: InterVarsity Press, 1994), 189.

[47] Richard Hess, Song of Songs: Baker Commentary on the Old Testament Wisdom and Psalms (Grand Rapids: Baker Academic, 2005), 167.

[48] Tremper Longman III, Song of Songs: The New International Commentary on the Old Testament (Grand Rapids: Eerdmans, 2001), 234.

[49] Dennis Kinlaw, Song of Songs: Expositor's Bible Commentary (Grand Rapids: Zondervan, 1991), 145.

[50] Marvin Pope, Song of Songs: The Anchor Bible (Garden City: Doubleday, 1977), 178.

[51] Roland Murphy, The Song of Songs: Hermeneia Commentary (Minneapolis: Fortress Press, 1990), 123.

[52] Ariel Bloch and Chana Bloch, The Song of Songs: A New Translation (New York: Random House, 1995), 189.

[53] Michael Fox, The Song of Songs and the Ancient Egyptian Love Songs (Madison: University of Wisconsin Press, 1985), 167.

[54] Cheryl Exum, Song of Songs: A Commentary (Louisville: Westminster John Knox Press, 2005), 234.

[55] Tedd Tripp, Shepherding a Child's Heart (Wapwallopen: Shepherd Press, 1995), 145.

[56] Paul David Tripp, Age of Opportunity: A Biblical Guide to Parenting Teens (Phillipsburg: P&R Publishing, 1997), 178.

[57] Dennis Rainey, The Tribute and the Promise (Nashville: Thomas Nelson, 1994), 123.

[58] Gary Smalley and John Trent, The Blessing (Nashville: Thomas Nelson, 1986), 189.

[59] James Dobson, The New Dare to Discipline (Wheaton: Tyndale House, 1992), 167.

[60] Lou Priolo, The Heart of Anger: Practical Help for the Prevention and Cure of Anger in Children (Amityville: Calvary Press, 1997), 234.

[61] Richard Fugate, What the Bible Says About Child Training (Garland: Aletheia Publishers, 1980), 145.

[62] Tim Kimmel, Grace-Based Parenting (Nashville: W Publishing Group, 2004), 178.

[63] Bruce Ray, Withhold Not Correction (Phillipsburg: Presbyterian and Reformed, 1978), 123.

[64] Charles Swindoll, You and Your Child (Nashville: Thomas Nelson, 1977), 189.

[65] Kevin Leman, Making Children Mind Without Losing Yours (Grand Rapids: Revell, 2000), 167.

[66] Dennis and Barbara Rainey, Parenting Today's Adolescent (Nashville: Thomas Nelson, 1998), 234.

[67] Martha Peace, The Faithful Parent (Bemidji: Focus Publishing, 1999), 145.

[68] Ginger Plowman, Don't Make Me Count to Three (Wapwallopen: Shepherd Press, 2003), 178.

[69] Tedd Tripp, Instructing a Child's Heart (Wapwallopen: Shepherd Press, 2008), 123.

[70] William Sears, The Discipline Book (Boston: Little, Brown and Company, 1995), 189.

[71] Roy Lessin, Spanking: Why, When, How? (Minneapolis: Bethany House, 1979), 167.

[72] John Rosemond, A Family of Value (Kansas City: Andrews McMeel, 1995), 234.

[73] Stormie Omartian, The Power of a Praying Parent (Eugene: Harvest House, 1995), 145.

[74] Josh McDowell, The Father Connection (Nashville: Broadman & Holman, 1996), 178.

[75] Gary Chapman, The Five Love Languages of Children (Chicago: Northfield Publishing, 1997), 123.

[76] James Dobson, Bringing Up Boys (Wheaton: Tyndale House, 2001), 189.

[77] Walt Mueller, Understanding Today's Youth Culture (Wheaton: Tyndale House, 1999), 167.

[78] Chap Clark, Hurt: Inside the World of Today's Teenagers (Grand Rapids: Baker Academic, 2004), 234.

[79] John Piper, What's the Difference?: Manhood and Womanhood Defined According to the Bible (Wheaton: Crossway, 1990), 145.

[80] Elizabeth Crary, Without Spanking or Spoiling (Seattle: Parenting Press, 1993), 178.

[81] Marty Machowski, Long Story Short: Ten-Minute Devotions to Draw Your Family to God (Greensboro: New Growth Press, 2010), 123.

[82] Mark DeVries, Family-Based Youth Ministry (Downers Grove: InterVarsity Press, 1994), 189.

[83] Kenda Creasy Dean, Almost Christian: What the Faith of Our Teenagers Is Telling the American Church (Oxford: Oxford University Press, 2010), 167.

[84] Christian Smith, Soul Searching: The Religious and Spiritual Lives of American Teenagers (Oxford: Oxford University Press, 2005), 234.

[85] Jeffrey Jensen Arnett, Emerging Adulthood: The Winding Road from the Late Teens Through the Twenties (Oxford: Oxford University Press, 2004), 145.

[86] Tim Elmore, Generation iY: Our Last Chance to Save Their Future (Atlanta: Poet Gardener Publishing, 2010), 178.

[87] Gary Chapman, The Five Love Languages of Teenagers (Chicago: Northfield Publishing, 2000), 167.

Notes Chapter 10

[1] John Stott, The Message of Ephesians (Downers Grove: InterVarsity Press, 1979), 145.

[2] Martyn Lloyd-Jones, God's Way of Reconciliation: An Exposition of Ephesians 2 (Grand Rapids: Baker Books, 1972), 178.

[3] William Hendriksen, Exposition of Ephesians (Grand Rapids: Baker Books, 1967), 123.

[4] Peter O'Brien, The Letter to the Ephesians (Grand Rapids: Eerdmans, 1999), 189.

[5] Harold Hoehner, Ephesians: An Exegetical Commentary (Grand Rapids: Baker Academic, 2002), 167.

[6] Francis Foulkes, Ephesians: An Introduction and Commentary (Downers Grove: InterVarsity Press, 1989), 234.

[7] Derek Kidner, Psalms 73-150: An Introduction and Commentary (Downers Grove: InterVarsity Press, 1975), 145.

[8] John Goldingay, Psalms: Volume 3, Psalms 90-150 (Grand Rapids: Baker Academic, 2008), 178.

[9] Peter Craigie, Psalms 1-50: Word Biblical Commentary (Dallas: Word Books, 1983), 123.

[10] Willem VanGemeren, Psalms: The Expositor's Bible Commentary (Grand Rapids: Zondervan, 1991), 189.

[11] Charles Spurgeon, The Treasury of David: Psalms 120-150 (Grand Rapids: Baker Books, 1984), 167.

[12] Matthew Henry, Commentary on the Whole Bible: Volume 3, Job to Song of Solomon (Peabody: Hendrickson, 1994), 234.

[13] Albert Barnes, Notes on the Old Testament: Psalms (Grand Rapids: Baker Books, 1996), 145.

[14] Franz Delitzsch, Biblical Commentary on the Psalms (Grand Rapids: Eerdmans, 1955), 178.

[15] Alexander Maclaren, The Psalms: The Expositor's Bible (Grand Rapids: Baker Books, 1974), 123.

[16] Andreas Köstenberger, God, Marriage, and Family: Rebuilding the Biblical Foundation (Wheaton: Crossway, 2004), 189.

[17] Timothy Keller, The Meaning of Marriage: Facing the Complexities of Commitment with the Wisdom of God (New York: Dutton, 2011), 167.

[18] Gary Thomas, Sacred Marriage (Grand Rapids: Zondervan, 2000), 234.

[19] Emerson Eggerichs, Love and Respect (Nashville: Thomas Nelson, 2004), 145.

[20] Henry Cloud and John Townsend, Boundaries in Marriage (Grand Rapids: Zondervan, 1999), 178.

[21] Gary Smalley, If Only He Knew (Grand Rapids: Zondervan, 1979), 123.

[22] Willard Harley, His Needs, Her Needs (Grand Rapids: Revell, 1986), 189.

[23] David Clarke, A Marriage After God's Own Heart (Eugene: Harvest House, 2001), 167.

[24] Neil Clark Warren, Finding the Love of Your Life (Colorado Springs: Focus on the Family, 1992), 234.

[25] John Gottman, The Seven Principles for Making Marriage Work (New York: Crown Publishers, 1999), 145.

[26] Larry Crabb, The Marriage Builder (Grand Rapids: Zondervan, 1982), 178.

[27] Gary Chapman, The Five Love Languages (Chicago: Northfield Publishing, 1992), 123.

[28] Winston Smith, Marriage Matters (Greensboro: New Growth Press, 2010), 189.

[29] Dennis Rainey, Staying Close (Nashville: Thomas Nelson, 1989), 167.

[30] Simon Kistemaker, Exposition of the First Epistle to the Corinthians (Grand Rapids: Baker Books, 1993), 234.

[31] Gordon Fee, The First Epistle to the Corinthians: The New International Commentary on the New Testament (Grand Rapids: Eerdmans, 1987), 145.

[32] David Garland, 1 Corinthians: Baker Exegetical Commentary on the New Testament (Grand Rapids: Baker Academic, 2003), 178.

[33] Anthony Thiselton, The First Epistle to the Corinthians: The New International Greek Testament Commentary (Grand Rapids: Eerdmans, 2000), 123.

[34] Roy Ciampa and Brian Rosner, The First Letter to the Corinthians: The Pillar New Testament Commentary (Grand Rapids: Eerdmans, 2010), 189.

[35] Craig Blomberg, 1 Corinthians: The NIV Application Commentary (Grand Rapids: Zondervan, 1994), 167.

[36] Ben Witherington III, Conflict and Community in Corinth: A Socio-Rhetorical Commentary on 1 and 2 Corinthians (Grand Rapids: Eerdmans, 1995), 234.

[37] Charles Hodge, An Exposition of the First Epistle to the Corinthians (Grand Rapids: Eerdmans, 1950), 145.

[38] Leon Morris, The First Epistle of Paul to the Corinthians: The Tyndale New Testament Commentaries (Grand Rapids: Eerdmans, 1985), 178.

[39] F.F. Bruce, 1 and 2 Corinthians: New Century Bible Commentary (Grand Rapids: Eerdmans, 1971), 123.

[40] John MacArthur, 1 Corinthians: The MacArthur New Testament Commentary (Chicago: Moody Press, 1984), 189.

[41] Warren Wiersbe, The Bible Exposition Commentary: 1 Corinthians (Colorado Springs: David C. Cook, 1989), 167.

[42] John Phillips, Exploring 1 Corinthians (Grand Rapids: Kregel Publications, 2002), 234.

[43] Irving Jensen, 1 Corinthians: A Self-Study Guide (Chicago: Moody Press, 1986), 145.

[44] Roy Zuck, A Biblical Theology of the New Testament (Chicago: Moody Press, 1994), 178.

[45] Thomas Constable, Notes on 1 Corinthians (Dallas: Dallas Theological Seminary, 2015), 123.

[46] John MacArthur, The MacArthur Study Bible (Nashville: Thomas Nelson, 1997), 189.

[47] Charles Ryrie, The Ryrie Study Bible (Chicago: Moody Press, 1995), 167.

[48] John Walvoord and Roy Zuck, The Bible Knowledge Commentary: New Testament (Colorado Springs: David C. Cook, 1983), 234.

[49] Tedd Tripp, Shepherding a Child's Heart (Wapwallopen: Shepherd Press, 1995), 145.

[50] Paul David Tripp, Age of Opportunity: A Biblical Guide to Parenting Teens (Phillipsburg: P&R Publishing, 1997), 178.

[51] Dennis Rainey, The Tribute and the Promise (Nashville: Thomas Nelson, 1994), 123.

[52] Gary Smalley and John Trent, The Blessing (Nashville: Thomas Nelson, 1986), 189.

[53] James Dobson, The New Dare to Discipline (Wheaton: Tyndale House, 1992), 167.

[54] Michael Green, The Second Epistle General of Peter and the General Epistle of Jude: The Tyndale New Testament Commentaries (Grand Rapids: Eerdmans, 1987), 234.

[55] Richard Bauckham, Jude, 2 Peter: Word Biblical Commentary (Dallas: Word Books, 1983), 145.

[56] Thomas Schreiner, 1, 2 Peter, Jude: The New American Commentary (Nashville: Broadman & Holman, 2003), 178.

[57] Gene Green, Jude and 2 Peter: Baker Exegetical Commentary on the New Testament (Grand Rapids: Baker Academic, 2008), 123.

[58] Douglas Moo, 2 Peter, Jude: The NIV Application Commentary (Grand Rapids: Zondervan, 1996), 189.

[59] John MacArthur, 2 Peter and Jude: The MacArthur New Testament Commentary (Chicago: Moody Press, 2005), 167.

[60] Warren Wiersbe, The Bible Exposition Commentary: 2 Peter, 2 and 3 John, Jude (Colorado Springs: David C. Cook, 1989), 234.

[61] John Phillips, Exploring 2 Peter and Jude (Grand Rapids: Kregel Publications, 2005), 145.

[62] Irving Jensen, 2 Peter and Jude: A Self-Study Guide (Chicago: Moody Press, 1971), 178.

[63] Roy Zuck, A Biblical Theology of the New Testament (Chicago: Moody Press, 1994), 123.

[64] Thomas Constable, Notes on 2 Peter (Dallas: Dallas Theological Seminary, 2017), 189.

[65] John MacArthur, The MacArthur Study Bible (Nashville: Thomas Nelson, 1997), 167.

[66] Charles Ryrie, The Ryrie Study Bible (Chicago: Moody Press, 1995), 234.

[67] John Walvoord and Roy Zuck, The Bible Knowledge Commentary: New Testament (Colorado Springs: David C. Cook, 1983), 145.

[68] Lou Priolo, The Heart of Anger: Practical Help for the Prevention and Cure of Anger in Children (Amityville: Calvary Press, 1997), 178.

[69] William Lane, Hebrews 9-13: Word Biblical Commentary (Dallas: Word Books, 1991), 123.

[70] F.F. Bruce, The Epistle to the Hebrews: The New International Commentary on the New Testament (Grand Rapids: Eerdmans, 1990), 189.

[71] Peter O'Brien, The Letter to the Hebrews: The Pillar New Testament Commentary (Grand Rapids: Eerdmans, 2010), 167.

[72] Craig Koester, Hebrews: The Anchor Bible (New York: Doubleday, 2001), 234.

[73] David deSilva, Perseverance in Gratitude: A Socio-Rhetorical Commentary on the Epistle "to the Hebrews" (Grand Rapids: Eerdmans, 2000), 145.

[74] Donald Hagner, Hebrews: New International Biblical Commentary (Peabody: Hendrickson, 1990), 178.

[75] John MacArthur, Hebrews: The MacArthur New Testament Commentary (Chicago: Moody Press, 1983), 123.

[76] Warren Wiersbe, The Bible Exposition Commentary: Hebrews (Colorado Springs: David C. Cook, 1989), 189.

[77] John Phillips, Exploring Hebrews (Grand Rapids: Kregel Publications, 2001), 167.

[78] Irving Jensen, Hebrews: A Self-Study Guide (Chicago: Moody Press, 1985), 234.

[79] Roy Zuck, A Biblical Theology of the New Testament (Chicago: Moody Press, 1994), 145.

[80] Thomas Constable, Notes on Hebrews (Dallas: Dallas Theological Seminary, 2018), 178.

[81] John MacArthur, The MacArthur Study Bible (Nashville: Thomas Nelson, 1997), 123.

Notes Conclusion

[1] John Stott, The Message of Ephesians (Downers Grove: InterVarsity Press, 1979), 89.

[2] Martyn Lloyd-Jones, God's Way of Reconciliation: An Exposition of Ephesians 2 (Grand Rapids: Baker Books, 1972), 156.

[3] William Hendriksen, Exposition of Ephesians (Grand Rapids: Baker Books, 1967), 134.

[4] Peter O'Brien, The Letter to the Ephesians (Grand Rapids: Eerdmans, 1999), 178.

[5] Harold Hoehner, Ephesians: An Exegetical Commentary (Grand Rapids: Baker Academic, 2002), 201.

[6] Francis Foulkes, Ephesians: An Introduction and Commentary (Downers Grove: InterVarsity Press, 1989), 123.

[7] John Stott, The Message of Ephesians (Downers Grove: InterVarsity Press, 1979), 213.

[8] Andreas Köstenberger, God, Marriage, and Family: Rebuilding the Biblical Foundation (Wheaton: Crossway, 2004), 145.

[9] Timothy Keller, The Meaning of Marriage: Facing the Complexities of Commitment with the Wisdom of God (New York: Dutton, 2011), 189.

[10] Tedd Tripp, Shepherding a Child's Heart (Wapwallopen: Shepherd Press, 1995), 167.

[11] Paul David Tripp, Age of Opportunity: A Biblical Guide to Parenting Teens (Phillipsburg: P&R Publishing, 1997), 234.

[12] Dennis Rainey, The Tribute and the Promise (Nashville: Thomas Nelson, 1994), 156.

[13] Gary Smalley and John Trent, The Blessing (Nashville: Thomas Nelson, 1986), 178.

[14] John MacArthur, The MacArthur Study Bible (Nashville: Thomas Nelson, 1997), 201.

[15] Charles Ryrie, The Ryrie Study Bible (Chicago: Moody Press, 1995), 123.

[16] John Walvoord and Roy Zuck, The Bible Knowledge Commentary: New Testament (Colorado Springs: David C. Cook, 1983), 189.

[17] Wayne Grudem, Systematic Theology: An Introduction to Biblical Doctrine (Grand Rapids: Zondervan, 1994), 167.

[18] R.C. Sproul, The Intimate Marriage (Phillipsburg: P&R Publishing, 2003), 234.

[19] Daniel Doriani, The Life of a God-Made Man (Wheaton: Crossway, 2001), 156.

[20] Stuart Scott, The Exemplary Husband (Bemidji: Focus Publishing, 2002), 178.

[21] Martha Peace, The Excellent Wife (Bemidji: Focus Publishing, 1999), 201.

[22] Carolyn Mahaney, Feminine Appeal (Wheaton: Crossway, 2004), 123.

[23] Susan Hunt, The True Woman (Wheaton: Crossway, 1997), 189.

[24] Nancy Leigh DeMoss, Biblical Womanhood in the Home (Wheaton: Crossway, 2002), 167.

[25] John Piper and Wayne Grudem, Recovering Biblical Manhood and Womanhood (Wheaton: Crossway, 1991), 234.

[26] Elisabeth Elliot, The Shaping of a Christian Family (Grand Rapids: Revell, 1992), 156.

[27] James Dobson, The New Dare to Discipline (Wheaton: Tyndale House, 1992), 178.

[28] Lou Priolo, The Heart of Anger: Practical Help for the Prevention and Cure of Anger in Children (Amityville: Calvary Press, 1997), 201.

[29] Richard Fugate, What the Bible Says About Child Training (Garland: Aletheia Publishers, 1980), 123.

[30] Tim Kimmel, Grace-Based Parenting (Nashville: W Publishing Group, 2004), 189.

[31] Bruce Ray, Withhold Not Correction (Phillipsburg: Presbyterian and Reformed, 1978), 167.

[32] Charles Swindoll, You and Your Child (Nashville: Thomas Nelson, 1977), 234.

[33] Gene Getz, The Measure of a Man (Ventura: Regal Books, 1995), 156.

[34] Robert Lewis, Raising a Modern-Day Knight (Colorado Springs: Focus on the Family, 1997), 178.

[35] Stu Weber, Tender Warrior (Sisters: Multnomah Publishers, 1993), 201.

[36] Steve Farrar, Point Man (Sisters: Multnomah Publishers, 1990), 123.

[37] Edwin Louis Cole, Maximized Manhood (New Kensington: Whitaker House, 1982), 189.

[38] Patrick Morley, The Man in the Mirror (Grand Rapids: Zondervan, 1989), 167.

[39] Gordon MacDonald, Ordering Your Private World (Nashville: Thomas Nelson, 1985), 234.

[40] Kent Hughes, Disciplines of a Godly Man (Wheaton: Crossway, 1991), 156.

[41] Donald Whitney, Spiritual Disciplines for the Christian Life (Colorado Springs: NavPress, 1991), 178.

[42] Richard Foster, Celebration of Discipline (San Francisco: HarperSanFrancisco, 1988), 201.

[43] Dallas Willard, The Spirit of the Disciplines (San Francisco: HarperSanFrancisco, 1988), 123.

[44] John Ortberg, The Life You've Always Wanted (Grand Rapids: Zondervan, 1997), 189.

[45] Bill Hybels, Too Busy Not to Pray (Downers Grove: InterVarsity Press, 1988), 167.

[46] Jerry Bridges, The Pursuit of Holiness (Colorado Springs: NavPress, 1978), 234.

[47] John Piper, Desiring God (Sisters: Multnomah Publishers, 1986), 156.

[48] Ken Sande, The Peacemaker (Grand Rapids: Baker Books, 1997), 178.

[49] Alfred Poirier, The Peacemaking Pastor (Grand Rapids: Baker Books, 2006), 201.

[50] Robert Jones, Pursuing Peace (Wheaton: Crossway, 2012), 123.

[51] Timothy Lane and Paul David Tripp, How People Change (Greensboro: New Growth Press, 2006), 189.

[52] Chris Brauns, Unpacking Forgiveness (Wheaton: Crossway, 2008), 167.

[53] Dan Allender and Tremper Longman III, Bold Love (Colorado Springs: NavPress, 1992), 234.

[54] Gary Thomas, Sacred Marriage (Grand Rapids: Zondervan, 2000), 156.

[55] Emerson Eggerichs, Love and Respect (Nashville: Thomas Nelson, 2004), 178.

[56] Henry Cloud and John Townsend, Boundaries in Marriage (Grand Rapids: Zondervan, 1999), 201.

[57] Gary Smalley, If Only He Knew (Grand Rapids: Zondervan, 1979), 123.

[58] Willard Harley, His Needs, Her Needs (Grand Rapids: Revell, 1986), 189.

[59] David Clarke, A Marriage After God's Own Heart (Eugene: Harvest House, 2001), 167.

[60] Neil Clark Warren, Finding the Love of Your Life (Colorado Springs: Focus on the Family, 1992), 234.

[61] John Gottman, The Seven Principles for Making Marriage Work (New York: Crown Publishers, 1999), 156.

[62] Larry Crabb, The Marriage Builder (Grand Rapids: Zondervan, 1982), 178.

[63] Gary Chapman, The Five Love Languages (Chicago: Northfield Publishing, 1992), 201.

[64] Winston Smith, Marriage Matters (Greensboro: New Growth Press, 2010), 123.

[65] Dennis Rainey, Staying Close (Nashville: Thomas Nelson, 1989), 189.

[66] Moses Stuart, A Commentary on Ecclesiastes (Boston: Crocker and Brewster, 1851), 167.

[67] Peter Enns, Ecclesiastes: The Two Horizons Old Testament Commentary (Grand Rapids: Eerdmans, 2011), 234.

[68] Tremper Longman III, The Book of Ecclesiastes: The New International Commentary on the Old Testament (Grand Rapids: Eerdmans, 1998), 156.

[69] Roland Murphy, Ecclesiastes: Word Biblical Commentary (Dallas: Word Books, 1992), 178.

[70] Michael Fox, A Time to Tear Down and a Time to Build Up: A Rereading of Ecclesiastes (Grand Rapids: Eerdmans, 1999), 201.

[71] Craig Bartholomew, Ecclesiastes: Baker Commentary on the Old Testament Wisdom and Psalms (Grand Rapids: Baker Academic, 2009), 123.

[72] Duane Garrett, Proverbs, Ecclesiastes, Song of Songs: The New American Commentary (Nashville: Broadman Press, 1993), 189.

[73] Derek Kidner, The Message of Ecclesiastes (Downers Grove: InterVarsity Press, 1976), 167.

[74] Walter Kaiser, Ecclesiastes: Total Life (Chicago: Moody Press, 1979), 234.

[75] Ray Stedman, Is This All There Is to Life? (Grand Rapids: Discovery House, 1994), 156.

[76] Philip Graham Ryken, Ecclesiastes: Why Everything Matters (Wheaton: Crossway, 2010), 178.

[77] Zack Eswine, Recovering Eden: The Gospel According to Ecclesiastes (Phillipsburg: P&R Publishing, 2014), 201.

[78] Sidney Greidanus, Preaching Christ from Ecclesiastes (Grand Rapids: Eerdmans, 2010), 123.

[79] Douglas Sean O'Donnell, Ecclesiastes: Reformed Expository Commentary (Phillipsburg: P&R Publishing, 2014), 189.

[80] Iain Provan, Ecclesiastes, Song of Songs: The NIV Application Commentary (Grand Rapids: Zondervan, 2001), 167.

[81] Kevin Leman, Making Children Mind Without Losing Yours (Grand Rapids: Revell, 2000), 234.

[82] Dennis and Barbara Rainey, Parenting Today's Adolescent (Nashville: Thomas Nelson, 1998), 156.

[83] Martha Peace, The Faithful Parent (Bemidji: Focus Publishing, 1999), 178.

[84] Ginger Plowman, Don't Make Me Count to Three (Wapwallopen: Shepherd Press, 2003), 201.

[85] Tedd Tripp, Instructing a Child's Heart (Wapwallopen: Shepherd Press, 2008), 123.

[86] William Sears, The Discipline Book (Boston: Little, Brown and Company, 1995), 189.

[87] Roy Lessin, Spanking: Why, When, How? (Minneapolis: Bethany House, 1979), 167.

[88] John Rosemond, A Family of Value (Kansas City: Andrews McMeel, 1995), 234.

[89] Stormie Omartian, The Power of a Praying Parent (Eugene: Harvest House, 1995), 156.

[90] Josh McDowell, The Father Connection (Nashville: Broadman & Holman, 1996), 178.

[91] Gary Chapman, The Five Love Languages of Children (Chicago: Northfield Publishing, 1997), 201.

[92] James Dobson, Bringing Up Boys (Wheaton: Tyndale House, 2001), 123.

[93] Stephen Smallman, The Walk: Steps for New and Renewed Followers of Jesus (Phillipsburg: P&R Publishing, 2009), 189.

[94] Colin Smith, Unlocking the Bible Story: Volume 4, New Testament (Chicago: Moody Publishers, 2002), 167.

[95] John MacArthur, The Glory of Heaven (Wheaton: Crossway, 1996), 234.

[96] Randy Alcorn, Heaven (Wheaton: Tyndale House, 2004), 156.

[97] Joni Eareckson Tada, Heaven: Your Real Home (Grand Rapids: Zondervan, 1995), 178.

[98] Anthony Hoekema, The Bible and the Future (Grand Rapids: Eerdmans, 1979), 201.

[99] John Piper, Future Grace (Sisters: Multnomah Publishers, 1995), 123.

Bibliography and Further Study

Adams, Jay E. Christian Living in the Home. Phillipsburg, NJ: Presbyterian and Reformed Publishing, 1972.

Adams, Jay E. Competent to Counsel. Grand Rapids, MI: Baker Books, 1970.

Adams, Jay E. The Christian Counselor's Manual. Grand Rapids, MI: Zondervan, 1973.

Alcorn, Randy. Heaven. Wheaton, IL: Tyndale House Publishers, 2004.

Allender, Dan. Intimate Allies. Wheaton, IL: Tyndale House Publishers, 1995.

Allender, Dan. The Wounded Heart. Colorado Springs, CO: NavPress, 1990.

Anyabwile, Kristie. Literarily. Wheaton, IL: Crossway, 2018.

Arnold, Clinton. Ephesians: Zondervan Exegetical Commentary. Grand Rapids, MI: Zondervan, 2010.

Ash, Christopher. Marriage: Sex in the Service of God. Leicester, England: Inter-Varsity Press, 2003.

Baker, Ernie. Marry Wisely, Marry Well. Phillipsburg, NJ: P&R Publishing, 2014.

Baucham, Voddie Jr. Family Driven Faith. Wheaton, IL: Crossway, 2007.

Baucham, Voddie Jr. What He Must Be. Wheaton, IL: Crossway, 2013.

Baugh, S. M. Ephesians. The Gospel Coalition Bible Commentary. Wheaton, IL: Crossway, 2018.

Baxter, Richard. A Christian Directory. 1673. Reprint, Morgan, PA: Soli Deo Gloria Publications, 1996.

Beechick, Ruth. A Biblical Psychology of Learning. Denver, CO: Accent Books, 1982.

Beeke, Joel R. Family Worship. Grand Rapids, MI: Reformation Heritage Books, 2002.

Beeke, Joel R. Reformed Preaching. Wheaton, IL: Crossway, 2018.

Begg, Alistair. Lasting Love: How to Avoid Marital Failure. Chicago, IL: Moody Publishers, 1997.

Bray, Gerald. The Doctrine of God. Downers Grove, IL: InterVarsity Press, 1993.

Bridges, Jerry. I Will Follow You: A Practical Guide for Wives Who Want to Support Their Husbands. Colorado Springs, CO: WaterBrook Press, 2003.

Bridges, Jerry. The Discipline of Grace. Colorado Springs, CO: NavPress, 1994.

Bridges, Jerry. The Practice of Godliness. Colorado Springs, CO: NavPress, 1996.

Bridges, Jerry. Trusting God: Even When Life Hurts. Colorado Springs, CO: NavPress, 2008.

Bruce, F. F. The Epistles to the Colossians, to Philemon, and to the Ephesians. New International Commentary on the New Testament. Grand Rapids, MI: Eerdmans, 1984.

Bunyan, John. Christian Behavior. 1663. Reprint, Carlisle, PA: Banner of Truth Trust, 1998.

Bunyan, John. Prayer. Edinburgh, Scotland: Banner of Truth Trust, 1965.

Burroughs, Jeremiah. The Rare Jewel of Christian Contentment. Edinburgh, Scotland: Banner of Truth Trust, 1964.

Butterfield, Rosaria. The Gospel Comes with a House Key. Wheaton, IL: Crossway, 2018.

Calvin, John. Commentaries on the Epistles of Paul to the Galatians and Ephesians. Translated by William Pringle. Grand Rapids, MI: Baker Books, 2003.

Calvin, John. Institutes of the Christian Religion. Translated by Ford Lewis Battles. Philadelphia, PA: Westminster Press, 1960.

Campbell, Ross. How to Really Love Your Child. Colorado Springs, CO: David C. Cook, 2004.

Carson, D. A. A Call to Spiritual Reformation. Grand Rapids, MI: Baker Books, 1992.

Carson, D. A. Love in Hard Places. Wheaton, IL: Crossway, 2002.

Carson, D. A. New Testament Commentary Survey. 7th ed. Grand Rapids, MI: Baker Academic, 2013.

Challies, Aileen. Seasons of Sorrow. Wheaton, IL: Crossway, 2016.

Challies, Tim. The Discipline of Spiritual Discernment. Wheaton, IL: Crossway, 2007.

Chandler, Matt. The Mingling of Souls. Colorado Springs, CO: David C. Cook, 2015.

Chapman, Gary. The 5 Love Languages: The Secret to Love that Lasts. Chicago, IL: Northfield Publishing, 2015.

Chapman, Gary. Things I Wish I'd Known Before We Got Married. Chicago, IL: Northfield Publishing, 2010.

Chapman, Gary, and Ross Campbell. The 5 Love Languages of Children. Chicago, IL: Northfield Publishing, 2016.

Chester, Tim. A Meal with Jesus. Wheaton, IL: Crossway, 2011.

Christenson, Larry. The Christian Family. Minneapolis, MN: Bethany House Publishers, 1970.

Chrysostom, John. On Marriage and Family Life. Translated by Catharine P. Roth and David Anderson. Crestwood, NY: St. Vladimir's Seminary Press, 1986.

Clarkson, Clay. Educating the WholeHearted Child. Walnut Springs, TX: Whole Heart Ministries, 1996.

Clarkson, Clay. Heartfelt Discipline. Colorado Springs, CO: WaterBrook Press, 2003.

Clarkson, Sally. The Mission of Motherhood: Touching Your Child's Heart for Eternity. Colorado Springs, CO: WaterBrook Press, 2003.

Cloud, Henry, and John Townsend. Boundaries: When to Say Yes, How to Say No to Take Control of Your Life. Grand Rapids, MI: Zondervan, 2017.

Crabb, Larry. Men and Women: Enjoying the Difference. Grand Rapids, MI: Zondervan, 1991.

Cruver, Dan. Reclaiming Adoption. Adelphi, MD: Cruciform Press, 2011.

Davis, Dale Ralph. 2 Samuel: Out of Every Adversity. Ross-shire, Scotland: Christian Focus Publications, 1999.

DeMoss, Nancy Leigh. Biblical Womanhood in the Home. Wheaton, IL: Crossway Books, 2002.

DeMoss, Nancy Leigh. Lies Women Believe: And the Truth That Sets Them Free. Chicago, IL: Moody Publishers, 2018.

Dever, Mark. Nine Marks of a Healthy Church. Wheaton, IL: Crossway, 2004.

DeYoung, Kevin. Crazy Busy. Wheaton, IL: Crossway, 2013.

DeYoung, Kevin. The Biggest Story Bible Storybook. Wheaton, IL: Crossway, 2015.

DeYoung, Kevin. The Hole in Our Holiness. Wheaton, IL: Crossway, 2012.

Dillow, Linda. Creative Counterpart. Nashville, TN: Thomas Nelson, 1986.

Dobson, James C. Bringing Up Boys. Carol Stream, IL: Tyndale House Publishers, 2001.

Dobson, James C. Marriage Under Fire. Sisters, OR: Multnomah Publishers, 2004.

Dobson, James C. The New Dare to Discipline. Carol Stream, IL: Tyndale House Publishers, 1992.

Dobson, James C. The New Strong-Willed Child. Carol Stream, IL: Tyndale House Publishers, 2004.

Dobson, James C. The Strong-Willed Child. Wheaton, IL: Tyndale House Publishers, 1978.

Dobson, James C. Parenting Isn't for Cowards. Nashville, TN: W Publishing Group, 1987.

Doctor, Courtney. From Garden to Glory. Wheaton, IL: Crossway, 2016.

Doriani, Daniel. The Life of a God-Made Man. Wheaton, IL: Crossway, 2001.

Dreher, Rod. The Benedict Option. New York, NY: Sentinel, 2017.

Driscoll, Mark. Real Marriage. Nashville, TN: Thomas Nelson, 2012.

Driscoll, Mark, and Grace Driscoll. Real Marriage: The Truth About Sex, Friendship, and Life Together. Nashville, TN: Thomas Nelson, 2012.

Duncan, Ligon. Does Grace Grow Best in Winter? Phillipsburg, NJ: P&R Publishing, 2009.

Earley, Justin Whitmel. Habits of the Household: Practicing the Story of God in Everyday Family Rhythms. Grand Rapids, MI: Zondervan, 2021.

Edwards, Jonathan. Charity and Its Fruits. Edinburgh, Scotland: Banner of Truth Trust, 1969.

Eggerichs, Emerson. Love and Respect. Nashville, TN: Thomas Nelson, 2004.

Eldredge, John. Wild at Heart. Nashville, TN: Thomas Nelson, 2001.

Elliot, Elisabeth. Let Me Be a Woman. Wheaton, IL: Tyndale House Publishers, 1976.

Elliot, Elisabeth. The Mark of a Man. Grand Rapids, MI: Revell, 1981.

Elliot, Elisabeth. The Shaping of a Christian Family. Grand Rapids, MI: Revell, 1992.

Esolen, Anthony. Out of the Ashes. Washington, DC: Regnery Gateway, 2017.

Ezzo, Gary, and Robert Bucknam. On Becoming Baby Wise. Sisters, OR: Multnomah Publishers, 2012.

Farrar, Steve. Point Man: How a Man Can Lead His Family. Sisters, OR: Multnomah Publishers, 2003.

Fee, Gordon D. God's Empowering Presence: The Holy Spirit in the Letters of Paul. Peabody, MA: Hendrickson Publishers, 1994.

Ferguson, Sinclair. The Holy Spirit. Downers Grove, IL: InterVarsity Press, 1996.

Ferguson, Sinclair. The Whole Christ. Wheaton, IL: Crossway, 2016.

Fitzpatrick, Elyse, and Jessica Thompson. Give Them Grace: Dazzling Your Kids with the Love of Jesus. Wheaton, IL: Crossway, 2011.

Flavel, John. Keeping the Heart. Fearn, Scotland: Christian Focus Publications, 1999.

Fox, Christina. A Holy Fear. Fearn, Scotland: Christian Focus Publications, 2018.

Frame, John. The Doctrine of the Christian Life. Phillipsburg, NJ: P&R Publishing, 2008.

Fugate, J. Richard. What the Bible Says About Child Training. Garland, TX: Aletheia Publishers, 1980.

Furman, Gloria. Missional Motherhood. Wheaton, IL: Crossway, 2016.

George, Elizabeth. A Wife After God's Own Heart. Eugene, OR: Harvest House Publishers, 2004.

George, Jim. A Husband After God's Own Heart. Eugene, OR: Harvest House Publishers, 2004.

Gresh, Dannah. And the Bride Wore White: Seven Secrets to Sexual Purity. Chicago, IL: Moody Publishers, 2012.

Grudem, Wayne. Christian Ethics. Wheaton, IL: Crossway, 2018.

Grudem, Wayne. Evangelical Feminism and Biblical Truth. Sisters, OR: Multnomah Publishers, 2004.

Grudem, Wayne. Systematic Theology: An Introduction to Biblical Doctrine. 2nd ed. Grand Rapids, MI: Zondervan, 2020.

Guthrie, Nancy. Seeing Jesus in the Old Testament. Wheaton, IL: Crossway, 2013.

Hambrick, Brad. God's Attributes and Marriage. Greensboro, NC: New Growth Press, 2014.

Hamilton, Victor. The Book of Genesis: Chapters 1-17. Grand Rapids, MI: Eerdmans, 1990.

Harley, Willard. His Needs, Her Needs. Grand Rapids, MI: Revell, 1986.

Harris, Gregg. The Christian Home School. Brentwood, TN: Wolgemuth & Hyatt, 1988.

Harris, Joshua. I Kissed Dating Goodbye. Sisters, OR: Multnomah Publishers, 1997.

Harvey, Dave. When Sinners Say "I Do": Discovering the Power of the Gospel for Marriage. Wapwallopen, PA: Shepherd Press, 2007.

Hendriksen, William. Exposition of Ephesians. New Testament Commentary. Grand Rapids, MI: Baker Academic, 1967.

Henry, Matthew. A Method for Prayer. Fearn, Scotland: Christian Focus Publications, 1994.

Henry, Matthew. Matthew Henry's Commentary on the Whole Bible. Peabody, MA: Hendrickson Publishers, 1994.

Heth, William, and Gordon Wenham. Jesus and Divorce. Nashville, TN: Thomas Nelson, 1984.

Hill, Megan. Praying Together. Wheaton, IL: Crossway, 2016.

Hoehner, Harold W. Ephesians: An Exegetical Commentary. Grand Rapids, MI: Baker Academic, 2002.

Horton, Michael. The Christian Faith. Grand Rapids, MI: Zondervan, 2011.

Howard, Betsy Childs. Seasons of Waiting. Wheaton, IL: Crossway, 2016.

Hughes, R. Kent. Disciplines of a Godly Man. Wheaton, IL: Crossway, 2001.

Hunt, Susan. The True Woman. Wheaton, IL: Crossway, 1997.

Kassian, Mary. Girls Gone Wise. Chicago, IL: Moody Publishers, 2010.

Keller, Timothy. God's Wisdom for Navigating Life. New York, NY: Viking, 2017.

Keller, Timothy. The Meaning of Marriage. New York, NY: Dutton, 2011.

Keller, Timothy. The Reason for God. New York, NY: Dutton, 2008.

Kellemen, Robert W. Gospel-Centered Counseling: How Christ Changes Lives. Grand Rapids, MI: Zondervan, 2014.

Kidner, Derek. Genesis: An Introduction and Commentary. Downers Grove, IL: InterVarsity Press, 1967.

Kimmel, Tim. Grace-Based Parenting. Nashville, TN: W Publishing Group, 2004.

Kostenberger, Andreas. God, Marriage, and Family. Wheaton, IL: Crossway, 2004.

Kruger, Melissa. The Envy of Eve. Fearn, Scotland: Christian Focus Publications, 2012.

Lane, Timothy S., and Paul David Tripp. How People Change. Greensboro, NC: New Growth Press, 2008.

Leman, Kevin. Making Children Mind Without Losing Yours. Grand Rapids, MI: Fleming H. Revell, 1984.

Lincoln, Andrew T. Ephesians. Word Biblical Commentary. Dallas, TX: Word Books, 1990.

Lloyd-Jones, D. Martyn. Life in the Spirit in Marriage, Home and Work: An Exposition of Ephesians 5:18-6:9. Grand Rapids, MI: Baker Books, 1974.

Lloyd-Jones, D. Martyn. Studies in the Sermon on the Mount. Grand Rapids, MI: Eerdmans, 1959.

Luther, Martin. The Estate of Marriage. 1522. In Luther's Works, vol. 45. Philadelphia, PA: Fortress Press, 1962.

MacArthur, John. Different by Design. Wheaton, IL: Victor Books, 1994.

MacArthur, John. Ephesians. MacArthur New Testament Commentary. Chicago, IL: Moody Publishers, 1986.

MacArthur, John. The Family. Chicago, IL: Moody Press, 1982.

MacArthur, John. The Gospel According to Jesus. Grand Rapids, MI: Zondervan, 1988.

MacArthur, John. How to Study the Bible. Chicago, IL: Moody Press, 1982.

MacArthur, John. The MacArthur Study Bible. Nashville, TN: Thomas Nelson, 2006.

MacArthur, John. Successful Christian Parenting. Nashville, TN: Word Publishing, 1998.

MacArthur, John, and Wayne A. Mack. Counseling: How to Counsel Biblically. Nashville, TN: Thomas Nelson, 2005.

Machowski, Marty. The Ology. Grand Rapids, MI: Zondervan, 2012.

MacDonald, James. Act Like Men. Chicago, IL: Moody Publishers, 2014.

Mahaney, C. J. Humility: True Greatness. Sisters, OR: Multnomah Publishers, 2005.

Mahaney, C. J. Sex, Romance, and the Glory of God. Wheaton, IL: Crossway, 2004.

Mahaney, Carolyn. Feminine Appeal. Wheaton, IL: Crossway, 2004.

Mains, Karen. Open Heart, Open Home. Elgin, IL: David C. Cook, 1976.

Mason, Mike. The Mystery of Marriage. Sisters, OR: Multnomah Publishers, 1985.

McQuilkin, Robertson. An Introduction to Biblical Ethics. Wheaton, IL: Tyndale House Publishers, 1995.

Miller, Justin L. The Not So Loving Side of Gentle Parenting: A Biblical Plea to Parents. Independently published, 2023.

Miller, Paul. A Praying Life. Colorado Springs, CO: NavPress, 2009.

Mohler, Albert. The Conviction to Lead. Minneapolis, MN: Bethany House Publishers, 2012.

Mohler, Albert. Desire and Deceit. Sisters, OR: Multnomah Publishers, 2008.

Moore Foundation. The Successful Homeschool Family Handbook. Nashville, TN: Thomas Nelson, 1994.

Moore, Russell. Adopted for Life. Wheaton, IL: Crossway, 2009.

Moore, Russell. The Storm-Tossed Family. Nashville, TN: B&H Books, 2018.

Mulvihill, Josh. Biblical Grandparenting. Minneapolis, MN: Bethany House Publishers, 2018.

Murray, John. Redemption Accomplished and Applied. Grand Rapids, MI: Eerdmans, 1955.

Newbell, Trillia. Sacred Endurance. Wheaton, IL: Crossway, 2019.

Newman, Randy. Questioning Evangelism. Grand Rapids, MI: Kregel Publications, 2004.

Nielson, Kathleen. Women and God. Wheaton, IL: Crossway, 2018.

O'Brien, Peter T. The Letter to the Ephesians. Pillar New Testament Commentary. Grand Rapids, MI: Eerdmans, 1999.

Omartian, Stormie. The Power of a Praying Parent. Eugene, OR: Harvest House Publishers, 2014.

Ortlund, Raymond Jr. Marriage and the Mystery of the Gospel. Wheaton, IL: Crossway, 2016.

Owen, John. The Holy Spirit. Edinburgh, Scotland: Banner of Truth Trust, 1965.

Packer, J. I. Keep in Step with the Spirit. Grand Rapids, MI: Baker Books, 1984.

Packer, J. I. Knowing God. Downers Grove, IL: InterVarsity Press, 1973.

Parrott, Les. Saving Your Marriage Before It Starts. Grand Rapids, MI: Zondervan, 1995.

Patrick, Darrin. Church Planter. Wheaton, IL: Crossway, 2010.

Patterson, Dorothy. The Family. Nashville, TN: Broadman & Holman Publishers, 2001.

Peace, Martha. The Excellent Wife. Bemidji, MN: Focus Publishing, 1995.

Phillips, Richard. The Masculine Mandate. Orlando, FL: Reformation Trust Publishing, 2010.

Piper, John. A Godward Life. Sisters, OR: Multnomah Publishers, 1997.

Piper, John. A Peculiar Glory. Wheaton, IL: Crossway, 2016.

Piper, John. Brothers, We Are Not Professionals. Nashville, TN: Broadman & Holman Publishers, 2002.

Piper, John. Desiring God. Sisters, OR: Multnomah Publishers, 1996.

Piper, John. Let the Nations Be Glad. Grand Rapids, MI: Baker Academic, 2003.

Piper, John. Suffering and the Sovereignty of God. Wheaton, IL: Crossway, 2006.

Piper, John. This Momentary Marriage: A Parable of Permanence. Wheaton, IL: Crossway, 2009.

Piper, John. What's the Difference? Wheaton, IL: Crossway Books, 1990.

Piper, John, and Wayne Grudem. Recovering Biblical Manhood and Womanhood. Wheaton, IL: Crossway, 1991.

Piper, Noel. Faithful Women and Their Extraordinary God. Wheaton, IL: Crossway, 2005.

Plowman, Ginger. Don't Make Me Count to Three. Wapwallopen, PA: Shepherd Press, 2003.

Pohl, Christine. Making Room. Grand Rapids, MI: Eerdmans, 1999.

Powlison, David. Seeing with New Eyes: Counseling and the Human Condition Through the Lens of Scripture. Phillipsburg, NJ: P&R Publishing, 2003.

Pratt, Richard. Pray with Your Eyes Open. Phillipsburg, NJ: P&R Publishing, 1987.

Pride, Mary. The Way Home. Westchester, IL: Crossway Books, 1985.

Priolo, Lou. The Heart of Anger. Amityville, NY: Calvary Press, 1997.

Rainey, Dennis. Preparing for Marriage: Discover God's Plan for a Lifetime of Love. Ventura, CA: Regal Books, 2003.

Rainey, Dennis. Stepping Up. Little Rock, AR: FamilyLife Publishing, 2011.

Rainey, Dennis, and Barbara Rainey. Growing a Spiritually Strong Family. Sisters, OR: Multnomah Publishers, 2002.

Rainey, Dennis, and Barbara Rainey. Moments Together for Couples. Ventura, CA: Regal Books, 1995.

Ray, Bruce. Withhold Not Correction. Phillipsburg, NJ: Presbyterian and Reformed Publishing, 1978.

Reeves, Michael. Delighting in the Trinity. Downers Grove, IL: InterVarsity Press, 2012.

Reinke, Tony. 12 Ways Your Phone Is Changing You. Wheaton, IL: Crossway, 2017.

Rienow, Rob. Visionary Parenting. Nashville, TN: Randall House Publishers, 2009.

Risner, Vaneetha Rendall. The Scars That Have Shaped Me. Wheaton, IL: Crossway, 2016.

Sailhamer, John. The Pentateuch as Narrative. Grand Rapids, MI: Zondervan, 1992.

Sande, Ken. The Peacemaker. Grand Rapids, MI: Baker Books, 2004.

Sanders, Fred. The Deep Things of God. Wheaton, IL: Crossway, 2010.

Sandford, John Loren, and Paula Sandford. Restoring the Christian Family: A Biblical Guide to Love, Marriage, and Parenting in a Changing World. Tulsa, OK: Victory House Publishers, 1979.

Schaeffer, Edith. Hidden Art. Wheaton, IL: Tyndale House Publishers, 1971.

Schaeffer Macaulay, Susan. For the Children's Sake. Westchester, IL: Crossway Books, 1984.

Scott, Stuart. The Exemplary Husband. Bemidji, MN: Focus Publishing, 2002.

Smalley, Gary. If Only He Knew. Grand Rapids, MI: Zondervan, 1979.

Smalley, Gary. The Key to Your Child's Heart. Dallas, TX: Word Publishing, 1984.

Smith, Winston. Marriage Matters. Greensboro, NC: New Growth Press, 2010.

Sproul, R. C. The Holiness of God. Wheaton, IL: Tyndale House Publishers, 1985.

Sproul, R. C. The Prayer of the Lord. Orlando, FL: Reformation Trust Publishing, 2009.

Sproul, R. C. The Purpose of God: Ephesians. Fearn, Scotland: Christian Focus Publications, 1994.

Sproul, R. C. The Reformation Study Bible. Orlando, FL: Ligonier Ministries, 2015.

Sproul, R. C. Jr. When You Rise Up. Phillipsburg, NJ: P&R Publishing, 2004.

Spurgeon, Charles. Morning and Evening. Peabody, MA: Hendrickson Publishers, 1991.

Stanley, Charles. How to Keep Your Kids on Your Team. Nashville, TN: Thomas Nelson, 1986.

Stott, John R. W. God's New Society: The Message of Ephesians. Bible Speaks Today. Downers Grove, IL: InterVarsity Press, 1979.

Stott, John. The Cross of Christ. Downers Grove, IL: InterVarsity Press, 1986.

Stott, John. The Message of Galatians. Downers Grove, IL: InterVarsity Press, 1968.

Strauch, Alexander. The Hospitality Commands. Littleton, CO: Lewis and Roth Publishers, 1993.

Tada, Joni Eareckson. A Place of Healing. Colorado Springs, CO: David C. Cook, 2010.

Thielman, Frank. Ephesians. Grand Rapids, MI: Baker Academic, 2010.

Thomas, Gary. Sacred Marriage: What If God Designed Marriage to Make Us Holy More Than to Make Us Happy? Grand Rapids, MI: Zondervan, 2000.

Thomas, Gary. Sacred Parenting: How Raising Children Shapes Our Souls. Grand Rapids, MI: Zondervan, 2004.

Tripp, Paul David. Age of Opportunity. Phillipsburg, NJ: P&R Publishing, 2001.

Tripp, Paul David. Instruments in the Redeemer's Hands: People in Need of Change Helping People in Need of Change. Phillipsburg, NJ: P&R Publishing, 2002.

Tripp, Paul David. Suffering. Wheaton, IL: Crossway, 2018.

Tripp, Paul David. What Did You Expect? Wheaton, IL: Crossway, 2010.

Tripp, Ted. Instructing a Child's Heart. Wapwallopen, PA: Shepherd Press, 2008.

Tripp, Ted. Shepherding a Child's Heart. Wapwallopen, PA: Shepherd Press, 1995.

Trueman, Carl. The Rise and Triumph of the Modern Self. Wheaton, IL: Crossway, 2020.

VanDoodewaard, Rebecca. Reformation Women. Grand Rapids, MI: Reformation Heritage Books, 2017.

Waltke, Bruce. Genesis: A Commentary. Grand Rapids, MI: Zondervan, 2001.

Ware, Bruce. Father, Son, and Holy Spirit. Wheaton, IL: Crossway, 2005.

Watson, Thomas. The Doctrine of Repentance. Edinburgh, Scotland: Banner of Truth Trust, 1988.

Weber, Stu. Tender Warrior. Sisters, OR: Multnomah Publishers, 1993.

Welch, Edward T. When People Are Big and God Is Small: Overcoming Peer Pressure, Codependency, and the Fear of Man. Phillipsburg, NJ: P&R Publishing, 1997.

Wenham, Gordon. Genesis 1-15: Word Biblical Commentary. Waco, TX: Word Books, 1987.

Wheat, Ed, and Gaye Wheat. Intended for Pleasure: Sex Technique and Sexual Fulfillment in Christian Marriage. Grand Rapids, MI: Revell, 1997.

Whitney, Donald. Family Worship. Wheaton, IL: Crossway, 2016.

Whitney, Donald. Spiritual Disciplines for the Christian Life. Colorado Springs, CO: NavPress, 1991.

Wilkin, Jen. Women of the Word. Wheaton, IL: Crossway, 2014.

Wilson, Douglas. Future Men. Moscow, ID: Canon Press, 2001.

Wilson, Douglas. Reforming Marriage. Moscow, ID: Canon Press, 1995.

Wilson, Douglas. Standing on the Promises. Moscow, ID: Canon Press, 1997.

Meet Mark Hobafcovich

Mark Hobafcovich is a pastor and author with nearly three decades of ministry experience with the Southern Baptist Convention's North American Mission Board. His ministry has impacted churches and leaders across multiple continents. Married to Christine since 1985, Mark lives near Atlanta, Georgia, where they continue to live on mission.

MarkHobafcovich.com
X @MarkHobafcovich

www.ingramcontent.com/pod-product-compliance
Lightning Source LLC
Chambersburg PA
CBHW071708120626
46550CB00001B/143